# English Teachers at Work

Ideas a
F

# English Teachers at Work

## Ideas and Strategies from Five Countries

EDITED BY

**STEPHEN TCHUDI**
*Michigan State University, United States*
and
**GARTH BOOMER**
*Commonwealth Schools Commission, Australia*
**MARY MAGUIRE**
*McGill University, Canada*
**J. W. PATRICK CREBER**
*University of Exeter, England*
**PAT D'ARCY**
*Wiltshire Schools, England*
**FRED JOHNSON**
*Papanui High School, New Zealand*
for
**The International Federation for the Teaching of English**

**BOYNTON/COOK** PUBLISHERS, INC.
UPPER MONTCLAIR, NEW JERSEY 07043

**Library of Congress Cataloging in Publication Data**

English teachers at work.

Bibliography: p.
1. English language—Study and teaching.
I. Tchudi, Stephen, 1942–    . II. International
Federation for the Teaching of English.
PE1065.E66    1986    428'.007'1    86–14706
ISBN 0-86709-165-7

For information address Boynton/Cook Publishers, Inc.,
52 Upper Montcalir Plaza, P.O. Box 860, Upper Montclair, NJ 07043

Printed in the United States of America

86  87  88  89  10  9  8  7  6  5  4  3  2  1

# Contributors

Peter Adams
Meningie Area School
Meningie, South Australia,
Australia

Steve Bicknell
South Marstan Primary School
Swindon, England

L. Jeanne Biddulph
Christchurch Teachers College
Christchurch, New Zealand

Jean Blunt
Summerhill School
Kingswinford, England

Garth Boomer
Commonwealth Schools
   Commission
Woden,
Australian Capital Territory,
Australia

Candy Carter
Truckee Junior High School
Truckee, California,
United States

Christine Chick
Acting Head,
Neston Primary School
Corsham, England

Lorraine Cockle
Calgary Board of Education
Calgary, Alberta, Canada

Richard E. Coles
Givans-Shaw School
Toronto, Ontario, Canada

J. W. Patrick Creber
School of Education,
University of Exeter
Exeter, England

Pat D'Arcy
English Supervisor
Wiltshire Schools
Malmesbury, England

Barney Devlin
Stirling College
Stirling, Queensland, Australia

Nancy Eddis
Kahnawake Survival School
Quebec, Canada

Rudi Engbrecht
Grant Park High School
Winnipeg, Manitoba, Canada

Jo-Anne Everingham
Triabunna District High School
Triabunna, Tasmania, Australia

Cora Five
Edgewood School
Scarsdale, New York,
United States

Andrew Folker
St. Michael's School
Melksham, England

Peter Forrestal
Waneroo High School
Waneroo, Western Australia,
Australia

Bernard Gadd
Hillary College
Otaua, New Zealand

Sharon Gladman
Alternative High School
Calgary, Alberta, Canada

Bruce Hammonds
Advisor for Art and Craft
Taranaki, New Zealand

John Heenan
Waihopi Primary School
Invercargill, New Zealand

Marian Hobbs
Hagley High School
Christchurch, New Zealand

Sue Irving
Worcester Middle School
Worcester, England

Meryl Jennings
Concordia College
South Australia, Australia

Fred Johnson
Papanui High School
Christchurch, New Zealand

Nancy J. Johnson
Michigan State University
East Lansing, Michigan,
United States

Charlotte Jones
St. Mary's College
Raleigh, North Carolina,
United States

James Lalley
Loyola Academy
Wilmette, Illinois, United States

Mary Maguire
McGill University
Montreal, Quebec, Canada

Mike Marshall
Ilfracombe School
Ilfracombe, England

Bill Mowat
Alternative High School
Calgary, Alberta, Canada

Debbie Myhill
Collompton School
Wiltshire, England

Shauna O'Connor
Woodridge State High School
Woodridge, Queensland, Australia

Lesley Pasquin
Christmas Park School
Beaconsfield, Quebec, Canada

Philip D. Pedersen
Wabannutoo Eyou School
Eastmain, James Bay, Quebec,
Canada

Noel Price
Tangaroa College
Auckland, New Zealand

Beverly Pyke
Kahnawake Survival School
Quebec, Canada

Malcolm Reed
Hackney Downs School
London, England

Janet Rickwood
Stirling College
Stirling, Queensland, Australia

Elaine Snowden
Turnagain Elementary School
Anchorage, Alaska, United States

Robert Squires
Oneonta High School
Oneonta, New York,
United States

Carol A. Stamm
St. George's Elementary School
Montreal, Quebec, Canada

Jonathan Swift
Stevenson High School
Livonia, Michigan, United States

Betty Swiggett
Hampton City Schools
Hampton, Virginia, United States

Jocelyn Tarrant
former teacher of English,
Geography, Social Studies
New Zealand

Stephen Tchudi
Michigan State University
East Lansing, Michigan,
United States

Helen Watson
Birkdale College High School
Birkdale, New Zealand

Trevor Williams
Taita College
Lower Hutt, New Zealand

# Preface

This book was conceived at an executive board meeting of the International Federation for the Teaching of English (IFTE), Montreal, Canada, in the spring of 1983. In casting about for projects for the Federation, board members had discussed possible research seminars, digests of professional publications, and projects on topics of interest in language learning theory. At one point in the deliberations, some of us realized that the true constituents of the IFTE—teachers in Australia, New Zealand, Canada, England, and the United States—were being left out of the plans. Shouldn't the IFTE be concerned with teaching practices as well as with theory and research? That question led to even more interesting ones: Just what *are* teachers of English in those five countries doing in their classrooms? Is there any consistency in English teaching methods around the globe? Is there reason to believe that the "new" English of the past two decades is finding a place in classrooms? What are the problems and frustrations experienced by teachers who implement contemporary theory in their schools? The executive board concluded that a book on nuts-and-bolts classroom practices, written for teachers by teachers, was in order—*English Teachers at Work: Ideas and Strategies from Five Countries.*

From that conception, it proved easier to give birth to a plan for developing the book than to produce the book itself. The plan was this: editors from the five member nations were selected; each editor was to identify ten teachers in his or her country who by reputation, visibility, or other criteria were deemed to be good, successful teachers in their schools and in their states or provinces; each teacher was to respond to his or her choices of questions from a list prepared by the editors. The questions, drafted and revised over a period of several months through international correspondence, were these, which led to the nine parts of this book.

1. *New Directions in Teaching English.* Please describe what seem to you the most exciting and interesting new directions in the teaching of English. What's new (without being faddish)? What practices are working out well in your classroom? In what directions do research and

pedagogy seem to be taking your teaching? What are your unanswered questions about teaching? What changes would you like to see in English teaching in your country over the next 10 years?

2. *The Teaching of Literature and Reading.* Describe what seem to you your best practices as a teacher of literature/reading. What theoretical principles underlie them? Describe specific approaches you take with: "nonreaders," literature discussions, structuring your reading/literature program. Is there a particular theory of literature or criticism that underlies your teaching? How is the literature curriculum organized in your school? Are there problems with censorship of reading materials? Describe how you teach a particular favorite literary work.

3. *The Teaching of Writing.* Describe one or two particularly successful strategies you use in teaching writing. Set your description in the context of national, local, parental, and student influences, and give some idea of the key issues in the teaching of writing as you see them in your stance both in theory and practice.

4. *Oral Language and Drama.* How do you "teach" oral language? Does your oral language program refer principally to public speaking or to informal speaking (or both)? Describe how you use drama in your classroom. What portion of the curriculum in English at your school is given over to oral English and drama?

5. *Language and Learning.* [These questions were aimed at what we traditionally think of as "language instruction," but they were to elicit general principles of language learning as well.] Describe how you believe language is best taught and learned. What are the theoretical principles which underlie your teaching? How do you deal with the question/issue/problem of nonstandard dialects in speech and writing? What is the current state of grammar instruction in your country?

6. *Multicultural Education.* [This topic included English as a second language (ESL).] Describe the multicultural/multiethnic mix of students in your classes. Is this typical of your country? How are nonnative speakers taught? Who teaches them? To what extent does your curriculum reflect multicultural/multiethnic literature and values?

7. *Classroom Management.* This very broad topic allows you to discuss the practical day-to-day routines of teaching. Possible topics include: individualizing instruction, book supplies, classroom sets of things, class size, organization of the curriculum, time allotments, discipline, integration of students, streaming, and tracking.

8. *The English Curriculum.* Who plans your curriculum? Who controls it? What is the mix of state-mandated versus teacher-created materials? Present samples of units and/or curricula that have been developed for your school. What sort of curriculum philosophy prevails in your country? What sorts of curriculum development processes and procedures are followed?

9. *Evaluation and Assessment.* Describe the external examination system (if any) in your country. Who is testing whom? For what purposes? What is the impact of external testing on your curriculum and your students? Also describe the procedures you use for classroom assessment and grading of students. How do these reflect your educational philosophy?

Writing those questions proved to be one of the easier tasks of the editors. Getting 50 teachers to write (over and above their classroom work) required considerable correspondence and cajoling. (In some cases, we learned that good teachers simply don't want to write about their work, not because they're reluctant to share, but because they're either modest about their achievements or are simply not certain why certain strategies lead to success.)

Eventually, however, the manuscripts came together, and, in November 1984, most of the editors assembled in East Lansing, Michigan, in conjunction with the seminar of the IFTE on "Language, Schooling and Society" to review the collection. At that time we made some attempts to regularize the collection in terms of length, content, and focus. We also chose to solicit additional manuscripts to fill perceived holes in the volume. The revised and additional manuscripts were sent to me in June 1985 for final editing, with actual publication planned to coincide with the next conference of the International Federation for the Teaching of English in Ottawa, Canada, in May 1986.

In writing this preface, I am resisting the temptation to write a commentary on the trends and patterns reflected in the manuscripts. In fact, the essays come from so many diverse sources that coherent analysis is not possible. I leave it to the reader to make connections and generalizations about English teaching in the five countries. I have, however, offered a few brief comments at the beginning of each of the nine parts, alerting the reader to what seem to me important or just plain interesting themes, issues, and topics which emerge.

I especially want to thank five men and women who served with me as editors on this project:

Garth Boomer; Commonwealth Schools Commission; Woden, Australian Capital Territory, Australia.

J. W. Patrick Creber; School of Education, University of Exeter; Exeter, England.

Pat D'Arcy; English Supervisor, Wiltshire Schools; Malmesbury, England.

Fred Johnson; Papanui High School; Christchurch, New Zealand.

Mary Maguire; McGill University; Montreal, Quebec, Canada.

The reader will hear their voices in the Introduction, where they set the stage for the remainder of the book by describing what they see as the significant issues and trends in their countries in the past two decades. I am grateful to them for their efforts, and through them to the people who did the real work of writing, the contributing *English Teachers at Work*.

Stephen Tchudi<br>
Michigan State University<br>
May 1986

# Contents

*Preface*

**Introduction: A Recent History of Teaching English
in Five Countries**                                    **1**

Australia  2
*Garth Boomer*

Canada  4
*Mary Maguire*

England  7
*J. W. Patrick Creber and Pat D'Arcy*

New Zealand  11
*Fred Johnson*

United States  14
*Stephen Tchudi*

**1. New Directions in Teaching English**             **17**

Conscience and Teaching  18
*Jean Blunt (England)*

Helping Children Make Sense of Their World  20
*Bruce Hammonds (New Zealand)*

How Many Trees Does It Take to Educate an
American?  23
*Elaine Snowden (United States)*

The English Primary School  25
*Andrew Folker (England)*

Megatrends in English Teaching  28
*Candy Carter (United States)*

Restoring the Imagination in Secondary
Education  32
*Debbie Myhill (England)*

New Directions for the Eighties and Nineties  35
*Jo-Anne Everingham (Australia)*

My English Teaching in the Eighties  37
*Meryl Jennings (Australia)*

## 2. The Teaching of Literature and Reading  43

On Not Teaching Literature and Reading  44
*Steve Bicknell (England)*

The Uses of Literature  46
*Lesley Pasquin (Canada)*

One Teacher's Approach in a New Zealand
Primary School  49
*L. Jeanne Biddulph (New Zealand)*

Letting Fantasy Go Free  51
*Elaine Snowden (United States)*

Personalized Reading Programs  54
*Richard E. Coles (Canada)*

Engaging Students in Reading  57
*Candy Carter (United States)*

Reading in the Secondary English Classroom  61
*Shauna O'Connor (Australia)*

English and Reading in the New Media  67
*Jo-Anne Everingham (Australia)*

Introducing Poetry  71
*Jean Blunt (England)*

Making Evaluative Responses to Literature
Through Imaginative Writing  75
*Peter Adams (Australia)*

Teaching Dated Junk  79
*James Lalley (United States)*

Literature and Vision  82
*Trevor Williams (New Zealand)*

Teaching the Bard  84
*Robert Squires (United States)*

## 3. The Teaching of Writing  89

Writing as Discovery  90
*Peter Adams (Australia)*

Making It Real—Reading to Write and Writing to
Read  93
*Carol A. Stamm (Canada)*

Teaching Written Composition as Process  98
*John Heenan (New Zealand)*

Approaches to the Writing Process  101
*Nancy J. Johnson (United States)*

The Skeleton in the Cupboard  104
*Debbie Myhill (England)*

Successful Strategies in Teaching Composition  108
*Bruce Hammonds (New Zealand)*

Essay Writing  112
*Mike Marshall (England)*

The Experience of School as a Writing Topic  116
*Jean Blunt (England)*

History Through a Child's Voice  120
*Cora Five (United States)*

Beyond Writing: Extending Revision
Strategies  125
*Cora Five (United States)*

Writing: From Motivation to Correction  128
*Jocelyn Tarrant (New Zealand)*

Punctuation  131
*Peter Forrestal (Australia)*

A Secondary Writing Programme  133
*Marian Hobbs (New Zealand)*

Personal Involvement in Writing  135
*Charlotte Jones (United States)*

**4. Oral Language and Drama**                                    **139**

Learning Through Talking  140
*Christine Chick (England)*

Classroom Drama—Another Approach  142
*Noel Price (New Zealand)*

Dramatization: One Modality for Oral
Language  147
*Cora Five (United States)*

Oral Language Literacy  149
*Nancy J. Johnson (United States)*

A Secondary Oral English Programme  152
*Shauna O'Connor (Australia)*

Teaching Oral English and Drama  153
*Jocelyn Tarrant (New Zealand)*

Living Theatre   156
*Robert Squires (United States)*

Drama and the New Media   158
*Sue Irving (England)*

Writing in Role   160
*Noel Price (New Zealand)*

## 5. Language and Learning   163

Language and Learning   164
*Jocelyn Tarrant (New Zealand)*

"Good" Language   168
*Lesley Pasquin (Canada)*

Opening Doors Through Language   170
*Marian Hobbs (New Zealand)*

Teaching the Language of Media   171
*Jo-Anne Everingham (Australia)*

From the Barricades   174
*Helen Watson (New Zealand)*

Teaching a National Language   177
*Bernard Gadd (New Zealand)*

International Perspectives on Language
Learning   179
*Jonathan Swift (United States)*

## 6. Multicultural Education   183

English and Multicultural Education in New
Zealand   185
*Trevor Williams, Jocelyn Tarrant, and Bernard Gadd (New Zealand)*

Sound and System   195
*Malcolm Reed (England)*

A Reading Centre for the Kahnawake Survival
School   200
*Nancy Eddis and Beverly Pyke (Canada)*

Education in Alaska: Innovation or a Star Wars
Approach?   204
*Elaine Snowden (United States)*

Linguistic Diversity in a U.S. College English
Class   207
*Charlotte Jones (United States)*

Whole-Language Approach in Native
Education   211
*Philip D. Pedersen (Canada)*

## 7. Classroom Management 219

Resources and Constraints 220
*Jean Blunt (England)*

Questions and Curriculum 221
*Richard E. Coles (Canada)*

Organising for Television Study and Use 224
*Jo-Anne Everingham (Australia)*

A Context for Teaching 227
*Lorraine Cockle (Canada)*

Individualizing Approaches to Poetry 231
*Rudi Engbrecht (Canada)*

Cronus, the Timekeeper 234
*Candy Carter (United States)*

## 8. The English Curriculum 237

An Alternative to English 238
*Sharon Gladman and Bill Mowat (Canada)*

An Australian Planning Model 242
*Peter Forrestal (Australia)*

Real World Curriculum Development 245
*Betty Swiggett (United States)*

An Australian Senior Secondary Programme 249
*Barney Devlin and Janet Rickwood (Australia)*

The Evolution of a Global Studies Program 255
*Jonathan Swift (United States)*

## 9. Evaluation and Assessment in English 259

Classroom Assessment 261
*Mike Marshall (England)*

The Other Side of the Coin 265
*Debbie Myhill (England)*

Evaluation and Assessement in Queensland 268
*Shauna O'Connor (Australia)*

The Evaluation of Fifth-Grade Writers 272
*Cora Five (United States)*

The Language Profile 279
*Trevor Williams (New Zealand)*

Bloom's Taxonomy and Assessment 283
*James Lalley (United States)*

Evaluating a Whole-Language Secondary-English
Curriculum: A First-Year Study   287
*Betty Swiggett (United States)*

External Examinations in New York   293
*Robert Squires (United States)*

Certificate Examinations in New Zealand   295
*Bernard Gadd  (New Zealand)*

**References**                                     299

# Introduction

*A Recent History of Teaching English
in Five Countries*

# Australia

## GARTH BOOMER

I suspect that Australian English teachers are like English teachers anywhere:

When they are good, they are very, very good
And when they are bad they are horrid.

Of course, the teachers placed in each category will vary according to the ideological eyes of the beholder. Those who preserve culture in aspic and who look backwards and forwards with fervour to a golden age of correct, standard, "Queen's" English, would find the Australian teachers represented in this book to be a menace to civilization; a threat to good order; a kind of genetic aberration in the line of English teaching.

In my view, by contrast, they represent the cutting edge of Australian education. They epitomize the reflective, self-critical practitioner dedicated to the continual making of culture through intelligent action, together with their students. They view language as dynamic, evolving, and as diverse as the contexts and localities in which it is generated. Their drive is to help students to control an ever-widening repertoire of registers and forms for more and more purposes.

Literature to them is matter for comprehending and for relating by students to their own dreams, anxieties, and challenges. It is also a means of helping them to act with more control and subtlety in their daily lives. It is for cultural literacy.

Since the reader now has access to some of my values, it is safe for me to extol the virtues of our best teachers, and to make brief reference to the front-line issues faced by our bravest and our best.

In primary schools our best teachers are past the euphoric stages of "Graves-itis," the rapture of discovering kid watching, conference/process writing, and autonomous meaning-making by students. This is not to decry Donald Graves and his effects in this country. The effects have been magical and inspiring. It is, however, to sound warnings about the dangers of taking a too naive, apolitical view of the learner. The best Australian teachers (primary or secondary) have a sharp apprehension of the political, social, educational structures which contain, shape, and, in many ways, determine the behaviour of their students. And they take political, collective action to offset their worst effects and to capitalize on their best effects.

They realize that "to process," to read, write, speak, and listen is not in itself empowering. They therefore pay attention to the "what?" of processing and the "why?" They take in good, gutsy, challenging texts and set about helping their students understand, question, and respond with a purpose. They make demands which stretch and prod, in the interests of empowerment, knowledge, and know-how. They are deliberate teachers, dedicated to making students progressively more independent of them. The role of facilitator or some kind of midwife to the birth of ideas is too irresponsible and neutral for them. They acknowledge their responsibility to teach what they are, what they know, and what they can do. For these brave, self-critical teachers in both primary schools and secondary schools, I'd say the major issues are:

1. How to organize a classroom where rules are negotiated, curriculum is coplanned, assignments are contracted, and evaluation is commissioned by learners rather than imposed by teachers.
2. How to teach for social coherence around common themes with whole class discussion and group work as opposed to a private enterprise regime of "individual progression" on preset assignments and exercises.
3. How to find texts which will collectively be the makings of an inclusive curriculum (of girls; of those of non-English speaking background; of working class children; of indigenous people).
4. How to throw off the contamination and pressures of a pervasive, behaviouristic learning theory entrenched in school and system management structures, in textbooks, and in testing systems.
5. How to develop alternative, vigorous assessment practices which are not based on competition and ranking and which allow all children the chance of success through effort.

I'd also say that the most worrying thing about most of our teachers tends to be their guilt. We've had over a decade now of brilliant rhetoric arising from the wonderful tales told by people like James Moffett, Jimmy Britton, and Harold Rosen; a rhetoric legitimated and made orthodox by systems' curriculum guidelines and the journals of our English teachers' associations. By and large, we have convinced most teachers of what ideally they ought to be doing. The vision of a perfect "language and learning" classroom serves to remind them how comparatively shabby, petty, and confined their actual practice is. The result is either guilt, self-flagellation, and growing despair, or guilt, defiance, and cynicism. Too often teachers blame themselves for falling short. It must be their lack of skill, they think, which leads to the failure to implement group activities.

By contrast, our finest teachers are aware that to implement group work, for instance, is to go against the whole tenor of western schooling, which historically has been devoted to dividing, controlling, and privatizing. Instead of guilt about themselves, these teachers will harness a concerted anger at the worst effects of systems and society to make strategic gains *towards* what they imagine to be possible and desirable. They can accept the present compromises because their principles remain alive and they are determined to win new footholds.

I suspect that none of this is specific to Australia. Recent discussions at international conferences suggest that for all of us this is a time for vigilance and struggle against instrumental notions born of rat psychology and desires for increased gross national product. I think we are fighting common enemies. At our best, we are winning in Australia.

# Canada

MARY MAGUIRE

Many Canadians think of their country as unique in the extent and nature of its ethnic, geographical, and linguistic diversity. So much so, that when I first thought how I would select 10 teachers for this book, the metaphor of "the giant Canadian ice cube tray" came to mind. Ten teachers from each of the 10 provinces would slot nicely into some kind of vertical or horizontal mosaic of cultural diversity and Canadian English education. But this seemed a too chilling metaphor to situate, clarify, and illuminate English teaching practices within these pluralist hinterlands.

What does the ideal English teacher in a nation committed to bilingualism and multiculturalism look like? The answer is reflected in the diverse ways English teaching is realized in Canadian classrooms and the ways in which Canadian teachers in the various provinces come to grips with some of the limitations inherent in the Canadian educational system and their constraints on human learning. In this collection, we see different profiles of English teaching from varying angles, distances, and even elevations. However, these contributions are not meant to reflect a global interpretation or picture of the patterns and trends within the Canadian English teaching profession. To attempt such a unified picture of English teaching would be as hazardous as trying to survive a blizzard in the northern tundra alone. To even negotiate a footpath through the labyrinth of assumptions which underlie Canadian English-teaching curricula would be an equally hazardous journey.

Unlike the Australian Association for the Teaching of English (AATE) and the New Zealand Association for the Teaching of English (NZATE), there is no one cohesive educational system that we can distinctly label as Canadian English education. In general, education is a provincial domain; in each of the provinces syllabuses exist which articulate the aims of English teaching. For the majority of the provinces, they advocate more holistic, integrative approaches. However, these curricula can do no more than point to general directions which are interpreted variously by different school officials and teachers. The works of James Britton and James Moffett have been important influences in the shaping of many of these provincial English/language arts curricula. In many provinces, teachers are left with a good deal of freedom to orchestrate learning in their classrooms to suit the diverse needs and interests of their students, for many of whom neither English nor French are mother-tongue languages.

Given such provincial diversity, it is surprising that many Canadian English teachers have shifted away from the mechanistic, reductionist models of language and learning. There are teachers who have been responsible for melting down the provincial barriers and continuing the quest to work collaboratively in their teaching and learning. What motivated this shift?

Some were perhaps motivated by the French Canadian nationalism, which started a trend of French immersion as a way of schooling in Canadian schools and as a consequence limited the number of contact hours in English language arts instruction. Many English language arts teachers began to reflect on how they could use the 50 or so minutes of English instruction more productively. Something had to be deleted from their curriculum; for a good many teachers, spellers and basal readers were placed outside the doors of classrooms. Some were influenced by the Pearson Commission on Bilingualism in the early seventies. However, rather than focus on these more public trends and bills which have no doubt influenced Canadian teachers' perspectives on language and learning, there are some important people who have guided the journey and provided alternative visions of what is possible in Canadian English education.

In the late sixties, Merron Chorny, recently retired professor from the University of Calgary, began the Canadian movement of teachers as learners, knowers, and explorers. In 1967, post-Dartmouth, he created the Canadian Council of Teachers of English. In addition to founding this professional organization, Chorny established summer institutes at the University of Calgary on the teaching of English. It is through these institutes that Canadian teachers became aware of such internationally recognized scholars as John Dixon, James Britton, Margaret Meek, Nancy Martin, James Squire, and Miles Myers. Chorny's institutes were not American and British tea parties on Canadian soil. They focused on teachers, students, learning, teaching, and human development. It is largely because of people like Chorny that the authors in this volume are making statements of their beliefs and understandings of language and its role in teaching and learning. All these authors focus in one way or another on the learner and attribute to language a central role in their coming to know and to discover. In a sense what Nancy Eddis and Beverly Pyke want for their native Indian students at the Kahnawake Survival School on the south shore banks of the St. Lawrence River is what many Canadian teachers want: pride in one's culture and self, a need for survival as a people, a community spirit of interdependence.

This shift in Canadian teachers' perspectives on English teaching has not come about quickly; it has occurred more so in geographical pockets of the country. For example, in the late seventies, Ian Pringle and Aviva Freedman hosted an international conference on writing at Carleton University, Ottawa. This celebrated event in the history of the Canadian Council of Teachers of English revitalized classroom teachers and exposed them to leading writing theorists and researchers such as Janet Emig, James Britton, Donald Graves, Donald Murray, Ann Berthoff, Richard Young, and many more. Many teachers who attended the event returned to their classrooms encouraged to make more expansive use of the Canadian educational terrain. It is hard to tell how many teachers actually shifted towards a process approach to writing. And there were other teachers, like Lorraine Cockle in this volume, who had moved even further away from garrison terms like *reading* and *writing* to more hazy boundaries of language and learning. However, there is no doubt that the conference led many teachers to reexamine what they did in their classrooms. From the authors in this volume, we see many moved towards more personalized reading experiences, even embedding something specific like the study of the novel within broader classroom themes and integrative approaches.

Although many provincial curricula allow for various degrees of input at the classroom level from teachers, students, and communities, teacher influence is subject to potential constraints. Lists of authorized texts exist in many of these provincial documents. These lists have not only curtailed some teachers' use of self-selected reading materials in their classrooms, but prevented some students from being exposed to Canadian classics. For example, Margaret Lawrence's book, *The Diviners,* has been subject to much censorship debate.

Evaluation is an equally thorny issue in Canadian English teaching. At the elementary level, there are still many school boards in Canada which hold great faith in The Canadian Test of Basic Skills. At the secondary level, systems of external examinations influence what and how some teachers teach. In some provinces, however, there has been a move towards the implementation of alternate assessment strategies, while others are still battling or even succumbing to the pressure of standardized testing. Another constraint facing Canadian teachers who want to fly with their new-found freedom as professionals, is the narrow, sometimes even erroneous interpretation given to provincial syllabus statements. For example, in some areas of Canada, there are school officials who believe they can successfully marry clinical models of instruction, like the Madeline Hunter model of time on task, with provincially recommended, holistic, integrative approaches. Fortunately, there are teachers who are insightful enough to see how both these models of learning are derived from a different set of assumptions about language and learning in classrooms. As one Canadian teacher put it, the clinical model attempts to supervise teachers and control the learning environment while the latter attempts to empower children and teachers working collaboratively and endorses the tacit dimension in human learning.

Chorny's institutes have provided Canadian teachers with a good model of human learning. I cannot say that only a few of our Canadian English teachers are using prescribed texts, sitting students in rows, teaching phonics, spelling and grammar, and other such trivia. I would venture to guess that we have like other countries too many teachers still clinging to the residual effects of ineffective teacher training. We have our debates about standards as well. For example, should we teach Canadian children British or American spelling patterns? These issues are further confounded by the ever-increasing ethno-linguistic mix in each of the provinces. We have reason to hope that external examinations, at least in some provinces, will eventually cease to exist. The policy on evaluation and testing published by the Canadian Council of Teachers of English is gradually making its way into the hands of school board administrators and teachers.

However, teachers need time to work out their philosophies and to examine the assumptions which underlie their teaching. As Cockle says in this volume, more and more teachers are beginning to see there are things they can do to help. Ironically, many are returning to the very institutions which trained them; this has forced some Canadian faculties of education to explore new ways of helping teachers not only as learners but as researchers in their own classrooms and communities as well. It is becoming clearer to teachers how research can augment their search for new teaching strategies and lead to exciting and significant learning.

This book, as Stephen Tchudi conceptualized it, has teachers both across and within nations sharing and talking to other teachers. These interactions bring an added dimension; to use the words of two Canadian authors in this volume, Sharon Gladman and Bill Mowat: "the stirring up of wider ranging connections permits us to create more comprehensive patterns and meanings from the world in which we live."

# England

### J. W. PATRICK CREBER

I sometimes do not know whether a sense of tradition is a good thing, for it seems too often to be a concomitant of less appealing characteristics such as imperviousness to argument or simply inertia. Tradition in England maintains a suspiciousness towards intellectual enquiry per se, and consistently undervalues the intellectual and indeed the aesthetic aspects of such important activities as engineering and teaching. As a teacher-trainer for many years, I am reconciled to being shot at, but I cannot get used to the consistent, institutionalised, and government-backed undervaluation of teachers. Bernard Shaw with his "those who can't, teach" has a lot to answer for. His slick shallowness has to be set against the fact, for example, that teaching is a deeply cherished aspect of the life of many great musicians, many eminent scientists. To say nothing of the fact that Christ saw himself as a teacher. In the present climate, one has to say that this is not the worst aspect: if it is reprehensible to undervalue the teacher, it is criminal in a nation ostensibly bent on national recovery to undervalue its most important asset—its youth.

In the palmy days of the late '60s and early '70s, I remember visits from English educators in other countries and quite particularly from New Zealand. Somewhere in the unmanageable heap that I call my filing system, there is a file called "New Zealand English Curriculum" which contains a series of early drafts of the kind alluded to in Fred Johnson's essay which follows. Even at that time, when we, too, had high hopes, this material evoked my wholehearted admiration, not merely for its intrinsic quality, but for the kinds of cooperation between official or inspectorial authority and teachers in the classroom to which it bore witness. It is very hard, coming from the country which, 10 years ago, produced Bullock, to speak confidently about what we have since achieved; and all too easy to be depressed, for example, by what seemed, even in a brief series of teacher workshops in Australia, to be a much more general and intelligent and strenuous awareness on the part of both advisers and class teachers of the importance of language.

Last year the National Association for the Teaching of English (NATE) celebrated its jubilee with a publication called "The First 21 Years," and reading the testimony of several of the key figures of the early days it is hard to avoid a feeling of pessimism. As Harold Gardiner put it, reflecting on the time from 1974 when he was staff inspector for English, "educational change is slow and resisted." "I wish," he said, "I could feel that satisfaction outweighed frustration in the memory of those years."

Rather similarly, Jimmy Britton in the introduction to *Reflections on the Bullock Report* (Ward Lock) wrote, "I don't believe that 'enlightened education' (meaning in its true sense 'progressive education') is part of any bandwagon, fashion cycle or pendulum swing; it is a slowly growing movement with philosophical roots way back in the past and pragmatic roots deep in the intuitive wisdom of the most successful teachers of today. It has not been tried and found wanting: it has, as yet, barely achieved a foothold in the schools of this country."

It would be easy at a time when our teaching profession is unprecedentedly demoralised to continue in this vein, but perhaps it is more important to hang on to the notion that progress in a culture such as ours is slow but real. Three areas seem to me to offer hope: (1) development in the approach to examinations, (2) new ways of encouraging response to literature, and (3) the increasing involvement of practising teachers in teacher training, testifying to the beginnings of a new, and for decades longed-for, cooperation between training institutions and local authority.

Under the first area, I would cite the significant achievements in methods of examining at A-level largely inspired by the work of John Dixon. His own efforts—as he would be the first to point out—have been underpinned over many years by less eminent, but steadfast souls who have, in meetings about examinations at C.S.E., 0-level, and A-level, by their remorseless fidelity wrought a slow but real change. Members of NATE and the Schools Council examinations subcommittee deserve special mention in this respect.

As far as the second area is concerned, a superficial observer may see the growing emphasis on "response to literature" as in some way displacing an emphasis on the importance of language in the classroom and returning to literary considerations which helped the English teachers of yore to feel a sense of purpose and identity. Thus, in the jubilee publication from which most of my quotations are drawn, George Allen said, "If I have a single personal wish for English and for NATE, it is that the great tradition incessantly reinterpreted may take literature, above all poetry, into our present and future."

It seems to me, however, that this reference to the enduring great tradition does not adequately reflect recent developments. Certainly many teachers have returned to the notion of placing literature at the core of their activity, but if one examines the tendencies in their current practice, it becomes apparent that these pay more and more attention to what has been learned about language in the classroom, about small group exploratory talk, for instance, from the work of such people as Britton and Barnes. In other words, I believe that a real growth in awareness of different talk techniques may have been obscured because it appears to come hanging on the coattails of literature, rather than as a full frontal linguistic assault.

Those teachers who have rediscovered their confidence in literature as central to their distinctive activity are in effect carrying on the "new ideas" with which NATE, in the early palmy days, was associated. As Peter Medway put it: "The 'new ideas'—new in terms of a century of public mass education—are about what English should be in the experience of the majority of the country's children. They represent a radical break with two long traditions, of grammar school and elementary school English. They assert, against both, that language in the class-room should not be produced, passed and inspected like counters: it should *mean*. In talking and writing children should say what they mean and mean what they say; in literature they should find their own meanings and say what those are and not mouth conventional sentiments."

The third hopeful development may be illustrated by my own recent experience. At the second of a short series of introductory lec-tures on language to our first year B.Ed. students—all fresh, green, and eager to teach—there were present five local, primary teachers who were sharing the input, discussing it with staff subsequently, and using it as background in their attempts to guide students on school observa-tion. These teachers have been freed by the local authority for a day each week, in the first place to acquaint themselves with our proce-dures, and in the second to prepare themselves for supervision of stu-dents in the school. This is one of the most helpful developments in teacher training that I can remember, and current signs are that we will be able to build on these small beginnings with the backing of the De-partment of Education and Science and of local education authorities, sometimes using more sustained teacher input over short periods such as a term.

The testimony of the contributors from England to this volume does, I believe, support my notion that progress, although slow, has not stopped; several show what I believe is just the right blend of intel-lect and playfulness. There is still, however, as Gordon Hodgeon put it, a need for "much change: to respond to, to set in motion. The coun-tries that exist need much improvement if they are to be fit places for young talkers and listeners, young writers and readers."

In 1965 I began *Sense and Sensitivity* with a quote from John Stuart Mill. Its relevance in 1985 seems undiminished. "We must aim at too much to be assured of doing enough."

### A Footnote by Pat D'Arcy

As a "local education authority" adviser, working with teachers in schools after they have moved out from excellent university depart-ments of education like Exeter, Southampton, Bristol, or the London Institute of Education—to name only the ones with which I am directly familiar—I find myself in total agreement with many of Creber's com-ments. Yes, teachers (young, middle or old) do find themselves under fire and shot at in our present system—on all sides.

Calls for teacher appraisal are receiving understandably ambivalent responses. On the one hand, the demand for a professional way of map-ping pupils' development in talking and listening, reading and writing is to be welcomed as a move beyond "one off" examinations—which must involve a more detailed, continuous assessment of what happens in the classroom. On the other hand, the apparent implications of the newly proposed General Certificate of Secondary Education (GSCE) combined examination at 16+—that performance can be stratified into seven clearly distinguishable grade levels—*has* to be a nonsense that no self-respecting teacher can possibly accept!

The move towards classroom-based research—where reflective teachers can be given even a minimal one-day-a-week breather away from actual practice to contemplate what is actually happening in their day-to-day involvement with pupils—is a positive move forward, allowing for an analysis of the interaction between teacher initiatives and pupil responses which may well lead to the formulation of better contexts—and strategies for learning.

Paradoxically, the current obsession in England with increasingly detailed checklists of what to expect before any interaction in the classroom occurs, may well constrain such classroom-based initiatives—if not totally castrate them.

In England at this point in time, both possibilities are "on the table." There are more opportunities for classroom-based research on offer to teachers on secondment to universities across the country, but there is also the present government's steamrolling plans for the new GCSE which appear to be demanding a superficial agreement under pressures of time, about so-called "criteria" which have to arrange themselves conveniently into seven "levels" for every subject. This could well make a nonsense of the complex, reflective, and analytic documentation of learning development that our best teachers in primary and secondary phases of education are gradually beginning to build.

I suspect, perhaps hope, that the statutory obligation to define GCSE 7-level criteria in any workable sense, will end up in a muddied confusion when it is presented to real teachers. If that happens, our classroom-based researchers will have a platform for alternative ways of approaching assessment which could also have a national platform.

If on the other hand the GCSE steamroller trundles through regardless, as movements from the centre tend to do, we shall be back to sniping from the trenches . . . *Plus ça change* . . . ?

# New Zealand

FRED JOHNSON

Teachers in New Zealand often teach 23 hours out of a 25-hour day. They have been used to doing a highly professional job for moderate financial reward and with a level of ancillary support and conditions of service that need improvement. According to what few comparative international studies we have, the standards New Zealand teachers enable their students to achieve are more than respectable. This is probably the result of the excellence of the teachers themselves and the particular context in which English is taught in this country.

New Zealand has a small, cohesive education system through which it is possible to pass ideas fairly quickly. Two examples well illustrate the point, I think. Twenty years after the Dartmouth Conference of 1966, the language growth model of language acquisition has not yet become the norm in English classrooms in the United States or England. In this country, in the dozen or so years following the formation of the National English Syllabus Committee in 1969, both primary and secondary teachers of English have adopted syllabus statements implementing that model and have undergone major changes in their own teaching. This was accomplished by the happy combination of the Department of Education and teachers themselves previous to the formation of the New Zealand Association for the Teaching of English (NZATE) in 1981.

The second example is the more remarkable because of its speed. In 1982, NZATE and the Department of Education combined to bring to the NZATE conference that inimitable exponent of process writing, Donald Graves. Three years later, largely as a result of the impact of that visit and videos made during it, primary schools have made process writing their own, and I can hear Donald's words coming back at me through my 10-year-old's work at our local school. Likewise, as a former secondary head of department, now principal, remarked to me this year, the secondary school that is not doing something with process writing these days in really "dragging the chain."

So, New Zealand teachers of English, or "Language" as my primary colleagues prefer to call it, are in general heading in the same direction on the same track as it were. The cohesive factors are syllabus guidelines in the form of "Statements of Aims" (their official titles), firstly, in terms of general education goals, and then in terms of the language aims of:

1. Increasing the students' abilities to understand language and to use it effectively.
2. Extending the imaginative and emotional responsiveness to and through language.
3. Extending the awareness and ideas and values through language.

These aims are underpinned by language "modes," all of which teachers are expected to work in. They are, as it were, "production" and "reception" modes paired thus: speaking and listening, writing and reading, moving and watching, and shaping and viewing. The activities which flesh out these modes are suggested, and ways of integrating and planning programmes have been communicated to teachers through in-service work evolved through 10 years' practice. Guidelines for assessment have also been given.

All of this leaves individual teachers with a good deal of freedom, under the guidance of their professional superiors, to produce programmes suited to the needs and interests of their students, with much latitude in the choice of resources. Few teachers of English in New Zealand these days would use what could be called a "course book" with any consistency. Such a system treats teachers as professionals, capable of assessing their students' needs and of designing and implementing programmes that meet those needs.

Under such a system, debate over whether standards are the same from school to school, or from one end of the country to the other, or even whether they should be so, is inevitable, and is vigorous in this country at the moment. In the past, New Zealand secondary education has put its students through external examinations in each of the latter three years of high school. Teachers have been working for a long time to change this, and with a new government in power since 1984, the changes have begun. From 1986, external examinations at the end of the penultimate year cease, and it seems clear that they cannot survive very much longer at the end of the year before that. This is so for all subjects in the curriculum, not just English. The present government has, in fact, engaged in a comprehensive programme of public discussion and debate over curriculum and assessment issues.

So the freedom experienced by teachers of English in New Zealand has certain corollaries. One is the consequent debate about consistency of standards in a country jealous of its reputation in reading and literary achievement, and of its egalitarian tradition. Likewise, for a system such as ours to work well there must be a high degree of professional contact between teachers so that there is a constant cross-seeding of ideas. Without this contact, as we have experienced in the early '80s, teachers often do not see beyond the islands of their own classrooms or schools, and, unless they are highly inventive and resourceful individuals, their teaching tends to become stereotyped.

The teaching of English in this country, then, tries to place the teacher and the students and their needs at the centre of its concerns. Programmes can therefore reflect not only the different academic needs of students, but their differing interests, their cultures, their levels of maturity, their differing needs as females and males in what is still a basically sexist society. In the best of what we do, they do.

As teachers of English, we enjoy the freedom we have, but as so often happens, that freedom is extremely demanding. We are no more classroom managers going through the motions with a textbook. It is our task to assess our students' needs, design the programmes to meet them, and increasingly assess both the students' progress and achievement and the programmes themselves. We can be creative exponents of the art of teaching. The New Zealand teachers in this volume will be recognized by the reader as such exponents.

# United States

STEPHEN TCHUDI

The "recent history" of English teaching in the United States begins with the Russian launching of Sputnik in 1957, a technological achievement that began the space age, set the U.S. back on its heels, and led to more than two decades of scrutiny of public education. That the Russians beat "us" into space was perceived as a national defeat, and, as often happens in such situations, the blame was placed on education. Within two years of Sputnik, the U.S. Congress passed a National Defense Education Act (NDEA) to improve what was seen as a deteriorating educational system.

At first, the NDEA provided funds for curriculum development and teacher retraining only in the areas of mathematics and science, because those fields were perceived as leading more or less directly to improved national rocketry. However, lobbying by the National Council of Teachers of English (NCTE) persuaded legislators that literacy, too, was important to "national defense," and in the early '60s, English was added to the NDEA. A series of Project English centers was created around the country to study and conduct research into the teaching of English and to create new curricula.

Views on the effects of Project English differ. One of the legends surrounding the Anglo-American Dartmouth Seminar of 1966 is that the American Project English people came to the conference promoting spiral, sequential, incremental curricula patterned after the "new math" and "new science" curricula only to be taught by the British that the child, not the discipline, ought to be the center of schooling. In fact, the Project English centers offered diverse perspectives on English, including writing as process (e.g., Wallace Douglas's center at Northwestern University) and contemporary literature taught by themes and issues (e.g., Marjorie Smiley's Hunter College "Gateway English"). In retrospect, the greatest impact of Project English was not any particular curriculum plan or design "process" or "product," but broad recognition by the English profession that "the tradition"—meaning literature from a chronological perspective, writing taught by rhetorical forms, language study as grammar—had failed and needed to be replaced.

Unquestionably the Dartmouth Seminar and the "growth through English" model powerfully influenced U.S. English teachers. Simultaneously, they were intrigued and even enchanted by the narratives of a group of so-called "romantic critics" of education, including Herbert Kohl, Jonathan Kozol, James Herndon, George Leonard, and John Holt. These men didn't know much about language learning, but they did understand kids and general learning. They argued that U.S. schools were too strongly oriented toward subject matter teaching, and they offered the notion of giving students freedom and choice in learning. Into this equation must be factored Daniel Fader at the University of Michigan, whose *Hooked on Books* (1966) offered the thesis that kids would learn to read better if they were allowed to select from among a wide range of paperbook books.

At the secondary level, these various movements found a practical outlet in the idea of elective curricula for high school English. In the late '60s and early '70s, electives swept the country, and almost every school found a way to bring in a range of course selections—from *Sports Literature* to *Death and Dying* to *Shakespeare.* Although there were many weaknesses in the electives movement (Hillocks, 1972), this was a golden era for U.S. English teachers, for they were given autonomy to plan and develop their own courses rather than being required to follow prescribed curricula or conventional textbooks. The tradition was by no means gone (as subsequent events were to prove), but for a time it appeared that personal growth curricula, through electives, might change the shape of U.S. English education permanently.

In 1975, however, the climate changed. The Educational Testing Service, maker of the Scholastic Aptitude Test, a college admissions examination, announced that from 1964 to 1974 verbal (and mathematical) scores had been on the decline. The media interpreted this as representing (yet another) decline in public education and quickly blamed the "new education." The "back-to-basics" movement was born, and conservative thinking amongst the public and the press has placed teachers in general, and English teachers in particular, on the defensive ever since. The elective curricula are gone, and, in a great many elementary and secondary schools, the conventional textbooks are back, textbooks which look remarkably similar to those which were found wanting after the Sputnik era.

There are some bright spots in U.S. English education. Interest in writing has grown enormously, and it appears at this point that composition may come to be seen as the equal of literature in the curriculum. The National Writing Project (NWP) has helped to spread the word, and teachers all over the country have been engaged in and excited by the NWP summer institutes. The work of Donald Graves and his colleagues at the University of New Hampshire has been especially helpful in popularizing the "process approach" to writing, and the reading research of Kenneth and Yetta Goodman at the University of Arizona has had wide influence in changing perceptions about the

nature of the reading act. The "language across the curriculum" movement, initiated in England, has spread to the U.S., and there are hopeful signs that it will become a permanent part of our educational
scheme.

Still, these are difficult days for the teacher who is committed
to a *personal growth* or *experience-centered* or *student-centered* or
*process-oriented* approach to English teaching. Although such teachers
have the force of research and professional organizations like the NCTE
behind them, they are often alone and lonely in their schools, their
cities and towns, and their states, struggling against conservative forces.
It is my particular hope that this book will be useful to such teachers,
showing them they are part of an international community of teachers
that is much larger than many of us have suspected.

# 1.
# New Directions in Teaching English

The essays by classroom teachers in this part of *English Teachers at Work* show a set of common concerns and influences. It is apparent that similar "breakthrough" ideas have been powerful in the five countries, and the names of James Britton (England), Frank Smith (Canada), and Donald Graves (United States) are frequently cited, as are such names as Margaret Donaldson (Scotland), Margaret Spencer (England), and James Moffett (United States). Although John Dixon (England) isn't directly cited, it is evident that the "personal growth" philosophy of *Growth Through English* has permeated all five member countries of the International Federation for the Teaching of English. In one essay after another, primary and secondary teachers remark on the decline of workbook and drill in favor of language activities which deeply and directly connect with pupils' lives. At the same time, there is a rhetorical shift in several of these pieces, from new directions as they are *perceived to be taking place,* to *calls for action,* urging fellow teachers to adopt new ways. As one writer—Candy Carter of the United States—phrased it, we are here reading about changes that "will (or should) take place." There is a gap, then, between what these writers see as the best of the new directions and what is actually happening in many schools. Even so, there is throughout these essays a common concern, also as phrased by Candy Carter, for using "the arts and literature as a means of reaching students and giving them the human understanding they will need to cope with a future in which relationships are increasingly fragile."

# Conscience and Teaching

JEAN BLUNT
*(England)*

I started teaching English in the '60s in a new school, and there was plenty of money and enthusiasm for education. My training had been fairly halfhearted, so I had to learn by my mistakes, and I picked up teaching techniques as I practised. I suppose I lived in hope that the books I ordered, the topics I covered, and the way I covered them were appropriate and effective.

In the early '70s I read two books, *How Children Fail* by John Holt (1969) and *Lost for Words* by J. W. Patrick Creber (1972). I was taken by their irreverence for the school system and their concern for the products of it. Those books gave me a conscience about my own teaching. The way in which we talk to children in school and the way in which we ask them to talk to us and to each other is so important.

In the mid-'70s I went to Birmingham University and listened to Leslie Stratta. I spent a year there just after the publication of two seminal books, Britton's (1970) *Language and Learning* and Barnes's (1969) *Language, the Learner and the School.* Those books made an enormous impact on me as a teacher of English—much more than did *The Bullock Report.* The ways in which we use words could exclude our young learners from experiences they should be sharing. The implications are far-reaching.

This awareness of the interconnection of language and learning and the various attempts to pinpoint what mental and verbal processes are involved in the business of learning is reverberating into the '80s. The attempts to evaluate our practises might mean we no longer have to go on living in hope. However, I am baffled that only teachers of English apparently need to know that language is inextricably bound up with learning. School language policies, I think, are still viewed with suspicion outside English departments.

There is little educational affluence now. Schools have lost their comfortable ambience. Financial constraints will limit resources more and more. Fewer books are published because money is not available to buy them. Yet the new ones I have seen are exciting, informed, attractive. What a shame that purchasing books, hiring video programmes, and buying cassette recorders is becoming more and more difficult because of the shortage of money.

The British practise of examining children at age 16 is still a major concern for teachers of English and will be for a long time to come. Even in the light of all the exciting recent theory, the writing of set essays is still by far the most important component of any English examination at 16. The uncertainty about how the language ability of school leavers should be assessed has made progress here very slow. Though the examining boards may rename the exams, they still have the same format. Their mark schemes have changed but little in the past 10 years. I believe schools could manage their own assessments much better. Some have been valiantly doing this for a long while, sometimes requiring far too much of teachers and pupils.

I think we all have a lot to learn. I still do far too much marking and not enough reading for myself. Grading and commenting on written work takes a long time simply because the evaluation is more considered. We seem to have more ideas about what we are looking for. Knowing more about the learning process has given us much more work. Organizing small groups within a class of mixed ability and giving those groups a purpose for talking and learning requires a lot of energy. Being aware of all the different uses of language and providing for practice in all of them requires a lot of organization. I am sure that the task will get even harder.

Still, if in the '90s the vital emergent theories of the '70s and '80s can be built on, then pupils and teachers can look forward to a much more effective learning situation . . . at least in the English lessons.

# Helping Children Make Sense of Their World

BRUCE HAMMONDS
(New Zealand)

School is an experience far too many children would rather not have to face. Too many leave school achieving little of value to them, and for many it is a place of real failure. Traditional schooling itself, not the failing students, must be seen as the problem. We have treated pupils as pawns in an educational game of passing on knowledge, producing in the process negative attitudes towards learning in many children—children who in many cases are simply not able to understand. Recent research in a number of fields provides us with the knowledge to help all children to continue and extend the natural confidence brought to the learning situation by the preschooler.

As it is presently structured, education seems locked into approaches which do little to help many children make sense of their school experiences. From the point of view of the learners, study is broken into arbitrary and disconnected subjects. The views that children bring to any learning situation are ignored, while what is being asked of them seems beyond their comprehension. The role of the teacher in helping the learner to develp a reflective approach to learning through meaningful interaction has not been appreciated. Little will be changed unless teachers are made aware of the findings of current research. To help all children realise their potential for independent learning means we will have to make considerable changes in style and content to tailor learning to the needs of the students. At present, many children, through no fault of their own, have no choice but to fail.

Possibly the strongest argument for the development of reflective thinking through children's language is to be found in Margaret Donaldson's (1978) book. Donaldson argues that many children fail because they do not develop the skill of being able to pause, stand back from their experiences, reflect, consider the possibilities and alternatives, and then make appropriate choices. Those who develop this ability (and some enter school with this skill already developed) are able to control their own thinking and will succeed. Unless helped to see beyond their immediate response, the others will fail. The teacher's role in the development of reflective thinking in all areas of learning is vital, but it must be seen as a means to help children become independent learners.

Research that reinforces and complements the reflective thinking skills developed in Donaldson (1978) is revealed in the findings of the Learning in Science Project (LISP) (University of Waikato, 1984). Science educators throughout the world have become concerned that unless the views that the student brings to any experience are valued and used as a starting point, little real learning can ensue. Intensive research has shown that children have many ideas, developed from their own experiences, that make sense to them, but which are not in line with the traditional, "scientific textbook" views. The assumptions behind the LISP approach are that:

- From a young age all children try to make sense of their world.
- The ideas children hold, though often in conflict with those taught by teachers, are sensible and useful from the children's points of view.
- It is the task of science educators to help children make better sense of their world.
- Knowledge cannot be simply transmitted or developed by experience alone—pupils and teachers must interact and discuss ideas.
- Various skills related to questioning and investigating need to be developed in context.
- Children can take responsibility for their own learning, but only in an atmosphere where pupils' ideas are respected and where children feel free to express their personal views.

Such teaching requires that children be helped to separate themselves from their ideas (Donaldson's "reflective thinking") so that questioning of ideas, possibilities, alternatives is not felt by the children to be a threat to self worth. The LISP program is essentially devoted to developing children's thinking and idea development through language, and the findings are relevant to all areas of learning. Their publication outlines in detail practical examples of how to put their ideas into practice.

The interaction style of teaching depends on the teacher valuing children's ideas. From a teacher's point of view, this begins with a genuine desire to know what a child thinks, and why. A brief outline of the approach is as follows. The teacher must:

- Establish a learning situation of interest to the pupils which will challenge pupils to ask questions.
- Have children answer their own questions to identify children's views—many of which will be in conflict with "traditional" ideas.

- Provide exploratory activities to challenge children's thinking and define further questions.
- Select questions as focus for further investigations/research/ experiment.
- Help children reflect on their findings and consider alternative points of view.

The message is clear. Teachers in all subjects must listen to the views of the learner and then arrange situations to help children develop their ideas. This is in direct opposition to much traditional teaching based on the transmission of knowledge. The findings illustrate the need to develop new, personalised teaching strategies to help children modify their ideas in ways that make sense to them.

Research from a variety of subject disciplines has also been concerned with how children develop their ideas and the role of the teacher in this process. Such an emphasis is not new, but there seems to be a building up of research which is making a focus on exploring the viewpoint of the child in learning.

Frank Smith (1979) has made us aware that readers bring their own meaning to the written word and that the very act of reading is a personal and creative interpretation. Donald Graves (1982) and Smith again (1983) tell us that it is the personal concerns of the children that provide a sense of voice and an element of reality so necessary to produce children's writing of sincerity and personal meaning. Graves particularly is concerned with the teacher's role in the writing process.

Harlen, Oliver, and Boyd (1977) find along the same lines as New Zealand's LISP, but with greater emphasis on helping children develop the process skills of problem solving. Britton et al. (1975) encourage teachers to use language, not to test what children know, but as a means to help children learn and make sense of things themselves. Rosen and Rosen (1973) illustrate the role of language across the curriculum in helping children make sense of their experiences. Creber (1972) expands the theme of this article.

The Oxford Pre-school Research Project and Tough (1973) illustrate the teachers' role in developing the reflective aspects of children's thinking through language.

There are, no doubt, a number of equally important research findings which I have not space to include. Clearly, the focus on the use of language to develop children's thought is growing. The challenge to teachers seems obvious. We need to work to create a class, or preferably a school community, which is conducive to encouraging children to make sense of their experiences. We need an environment where all children can grow in self-confidence, where children feel safe enough to take risks, where their thoughts are valued, and where all children are given the appropriate help to develop personal meaning-making skills. Through dialogue or interaction, teachers can help enlarge children's areas of choice by sustaining interest, elaborating and enriching children's thoughts, and opening up new ideas for consideration. Reflective thinking—the ability to pause, consider, and choose from a range of possible alternatives—should be available to all children. Language plays a key role in all these developments, helping children make connections and realise their ideas. If schools were to change, no child need leave school feeling a failure. To achieve any qualitative change for failing learners will require considerable teacher growth, courage, and perseverance. For the sake of the children who fail through no fault of their own, we have no choice.

# How Many Trees Does It Take to Educate an American?

ELAINE SNOWDEN
*(United States)*

Teaching in the '80s and '90s will require teachers to seek new directions. Just as the world is emerging from an industrial age and moving into an informational age, so must teachers emerge from their lecturing, monitoring, and testing methods of teaching to more exciting and innovative methods of teaching.

For too long, American elementary school students have been inundated with mindless activities of workbooks and dittos. The volume of paper that elementary schools use is mind boggling. For example, one school purchased a new copying machine and went through 88,000 sheets of paper in two months.

John Goodlad (1984) states that the atmosphere in schools is "emotionally flat," and the students he has interviewed felt teachers' questioning techniques are geared more to classroom control than to stimulate critical thinking. The implication of Goodlad's statement is that training in thinking and imagining begins in the elementary schools. It is time for teachers to acknowledge the new information society and to provide students with the tools that help trigger their thinking. Indeed a new 'R" should be added to the existing 3 R's; that "R" should be *reasoning* skills.

John Naisbitt (1982) speaks of America as living in "the time between eras." He suggests, ". . . the most formidable challenge will be to train people to work in the information society. . . . Today's graduates . . . cannot manage simple arithmetic or write basic English."

To help students make a successful transition into this new era, teachers need to be aware of the tools available to them. One is developing techniques in all areas of the curriculum to challenge students to think and be able to reason. The other tool is the computer.

To foster critical thinking in students, I use discussion groups for reading. There are only three rules: (1) everyone must have read the chosen selection; (2) any answer to a question is acceptable as long as it can be backed up with words by the author; and (3) the teacher cannot give an opinion as to how he feels about the selection.

Another technique I use for teaching thinking skills in reading is to give the students a short selection to read, have them read half of it, and then ask them to write the ending. After they are finished, I put them in small groups and select one person to finish reading the original story ending. After the reading, each person reads orally his ending, then he explains why he thought it might have ended the way he wrote it.

Writing is another area of the curriculum where I teach thinking/reasoning skills. As a matter of fact, writing *is* thinking, for in writing students put down meaning in detail and they are forced to focus their thoughts. They create something for themselves and they find out, by writing, what they didn't know they knew.

For too long English teachers have wasted the valuable time of their students by having them study about language. Students do not learn how to write by using textbooks and ditto sheets to add or change words and punctuate sentences devised by someone else. Indeed no book or ditto sheet can ever replace the students' composing their own feelings, thoughts, and experiences.

One of the newest and possibly most interesting directions education is taking in the United States is in the area of computer-assisted instruction. However, computers present teachers with a dilemma. On the one hand, it takes time to evaluate the software; on the other hand, there is the realization that computers are the wave of the future and proper use of them could enhance instruction in the classroom.

Computers can be used in three ways: (1) to teach (by using drill and practice, problem-solving lessons, simulation, etc.,), (2) to provide management aids for the teacher (such as record keeping), (3) to provide utility programs (such as word processing).

The advantages of the computer are many, but one of the most important is that it can individualize. Students can work at their own speed, and the computer frees them from the embarrassment of repeatedly being wrong or having constantly to ask the teacher for an explanation.

In my fifth-grade class, I use the computer principally for writing. A parent volunteer comes in and instructs the class on how to use the word processor. Since computers are relatively new in our school, I first have the students write out their story, put it on the computer, and save it on a disk. When they finish, they load it on a computer with a printer to obtain a copy.

Other computer programs in our school offer open-ended questions to generate ideas and to develop critical thinking skills. We even have simulation games in the area of social studies, like the old Oregon Trail, challenging students to make decisions on journeys.

As I stated before, one of the dilemmas with computers is evaluating the software. If one isn't extremely careful, one could wind up with "garbage in—garbage out." Therefore, close examination of software is very important.

Teachers must also be careful not to use computers exclusively for drill and practice. If drill and practice lessons are used, it is important that teachers integrate them with teacher-presented materials such as vocabulary from an assigned story.

Computers do not take the place of "busy work" activities and certainly should not replace human interaction. Teachers must become "computer literate" and make informed judgments about both the appropriateness of the software and the use of the hardware.

Thus U.S. education in the '80s and '90s presents many new and exciting directions. It is my fervent hope that teachers will head in the direction of developing the thinking/reasoning skills of their students by using computers and developing new techniques to challenge their classes in this new era of information. We need to cut back on the "paper chase," so that the public will cease to wonder, "How many trees does it take to educate an American?"

# The English Primary School

ANDREW FOLKER

*(England)*

Perhaps the most exciting new direction that English teaching is taking for me in the English primary school is paradoxically the way that the subject "English" is disappearing from school timetables. In its place is an awareness of how central the role of language is to the whole curriculum and that attempts to compartmentalise and separate the various strands are self-defeating. The growing awareness of how experience is permeated through language has led many teachers to substitute the subject of "English" with that of "learning." It is not uncommon to find children being asked to explain by talking and writing how they have solved problems in mathematics, or to use historical and geographical starting points for their creative written work.

The growing acceptance of the totality of language has brought with it a greater awareness of the need for realistic reasons in school for talking, reading, and writing. Tests and exercises are gradually being phased out in favour of more appropriate types of work. As it is widely accepted that schools are microcosms of society, so this has meant all types of "real situations" are available in a school context. Children write letters to arrange coach trips and museum visits, invite guests into school, and send reports to the local press as part of their normal school activities. They see for themselves the purpose and results of their own actions; the organisation of their own learning becomes within their own control rather than being directed entirely by others.

Another gratifying aspect of this process is how many primary teachers now encourage a far greater depth of study of one particular area rather than attempting a superficial covering of many areas. To a certain extent this is due to a confidence in the skills which are being developed by an in-depth study rather than relying on an arbitrary programme laid down by "authority." Thus, it is not unusual to find children involved in topics at a depth which means their teacher is also a learner. Children are discovering for themselves how to research because they want to know the answers. "Higher order reading skills" become mastered by being used rather than being based on sterile, faded work sheets concerned with irrelevancies from the child's point of view.

There is a growing sense in all language work of the importance of audience. Children are being encouraged to write for others to read. Availability of photocopiers has meant children can easily share their writing with others. Once it is understood that your words will actually be read rather than ending their days in a dog-eared exercise book at the back of a drawer, a whole new dimension is added: presentation and accuracy are motivated by an internal, personal desire to make writing the best possible. The comprehension texts and gap-filling exercises, which were often children's entire perception of "English," are gradually being replaced by far more individual and deeper responses to real situations. The way in which real writers write is increasingly the way in which children are approaching their written work.

In reading, too, the same pattern of development can be observed. Once, carefully controlled vocabulary was perceived as more important than meaning; now there has been a dramatic growth towards a variety of books which children want to read themselves. Reading for pleasure has become a valid method of teaching reading. Children are being encouraged to choose from a wide range of literature. The reading schemes still used (more for teachers' than children's benefit) have started to become whole books rather than series of disjointed words that conformed to one particular person's perception of progression in reading.

Another encouraging aspect has been the closer partnership between school and home, particularly in reading. Teaching reading is now no longer seen as the sole prerogative of teachers—in many schools parents are required to engage in a close partnership with school to foster and improve a child's reading, and research findings support this general improvement. Parents in classrooms listening to and discussing reading with children have become a common sight in most English primary schools. Many schools have become involved in the Parents and Children and Teachers (PACT) reading programme, where parents are actively involved with their child's reading. This regular communication between home and school has given an added status to children's reading and made parents aware of how the school views reading development. I see this partnership aspect as a most exciting development, and, as schools respond in a positive way, they will be able to tap a vast potential resource for themselves and to use parents to support their own efforts.

Another major new direction in England has been the growing realisation that children can learn as surely by talking as they can by reading and writing. The value of talk in the learning process has been accorded a much higher status in recent years. Children are increasingly being encouraged to discuss with and learn from each other. A growth in the awareness of how thinking skills are dependent on experience of language skills (and vice versa) has led to teachers' encouraging children to represent their thinking orally. Children's oral language is increasingly being perceived as a positive resource to be harnessed, rather than as a hindrance to children learning. Children are being encouraged to give voice to their misunderstandings as a way of moving forward, rather than being repressed into silence in order to follow the "correct" path.

My feeling, then, is that generally "English" is becoming seen in England as permeating every learning experience. It is also becoming recognised that different individual responses to situations can be equally valid. Teachers are constantly working towards capitalising on their students' interests to give depth to learning. Schools are using the real world as their raw material rather than attempting to work with contrived stimuli. It has become realised by many that learning does not follow a neat, logical pattern which is the same for all—the skill and challenge for the teacher is to recognise and extract the educational potential from every situation.

# Megatrends in English Teaching

CANDY CARTER

*(United States)*

In his book *Megatrends,* John Naisbitt (1982) draws a picture of the upcoming high-tech/high-touch society. Much of what he describes has serious implications for teaching—both in terms of style and content. Whether education can change and modify to keep up with the change from an *industrial society* to an *informational society* remains to be seen. I believe the following changes will (or should) take place in education over the next two decades.

## The Importance of Time

The proliferation of classroom management workshops for teachers in the United States in recent years is no accident. We are more conscious than ever of the massive amounts of material we must "cover" to create "successful" students with "marketable" skills. Research has also shown that the more time students spend in successful practice of an acquired skill, the higher the achievement. Surprised? We shouldn't be.

A legislative or administrative answer to this research finding is to extend the school day or school year, and this is being done nationwide, perhaps worldwide. But what is the use of spending one more week or five more hours in time-wasting classroom situations? This is why the classroom management movement has stepped in with changes that can have far-reaching effects: the teacher directs the classroom, while the classroom activities themselves are student, not teacher, centered. Hence, teaching, in the words of California science educator Harry Wong, "is the process of arranging learning experiences to facilitate student achievement."

Managing student learning is difficult, however—far more difficult than lecturing, leading discussions, or having students work their way through textbook exercises and questions. It requires teachers to be highly organized and knowledgeable about classroom pacing. The emphasis on effective time management has also brought about an interest in structure in the classroom—not of material, but of the manner in which it is presented. The research and the classroom management experts emphasize that clear instructions heighten student achievement, that order and a sense of direction provide a comfort level to students that allows them to proceed with the learning process.

### The Explosion of Knowledge

It is almost frightening to contemplate the extent to which human knowledge has expanded in the last decade. As Naisbitt (1982, pp. 16, 19) says, "We now mass produce information the way we used to mass produce cars. . . . The new source of power is not money in the hands of a few but information in the hands of many. . . . In our literacy-intensive society, we need basic reading and writing skills more than ever before." Returning to the importance of time, we see that our responsibilities as teachers to bring the tools of knowledge to our students have mushroomed in proportion with the knowledge itself; there is no time to waste.

However, is it realistic to assume that we can, in the course of a school year, or 12 to 16 years of them, teach everything to students that they need to know? Of course not, and even if we could, much of that information would be antiquated within a decade. We can, however, give to our students the know-how they must have to be adaptable to an ever-changing society. In fact, the trend is amazingly away from specialization; specialists become obsolete within their lifetime, while generalists can continue to grow in their chosen occupations— and growth in turn leads to greater income and/or job satisfaction.

### Increased Expectations

For many years, American education has wallowed in "minimum competencies," the lowest common denominator that all students can attain in basic skills. While the minimum-competency movement did set some expectations for students, it fell far short of the requirements needed to outfit students for the knowledge explosion. Within the last few years, the alarming reports on the conditions in schools, particularly secondary schools, brought into the American public consciousness the high price of the tax-cutting reforms that decimated funding for public schools. The new reform reports have emphasized, however, that simply putting money into education—increasing teachers' salaries, giving education more money to purchase supplies like computers and standard supplies like books—is not enough. We need to increase our expectations for learning.

Like many U.S. teachers, I have come through the *Age of Relevance* (the late '60s and '70s) to the *Age of Basic Skills and Minimum Competencies* (the late '70s and early '80s) to the realization that, quite simply, if you expect things from students, and if those expectations are reasonable and clear, they will try to meet those expectations. The clear statement of goals is critical: too often teachers have a hidden agenda, an expectation that is never really revealed to students until it's too late. If, however, teachers structure assignments and goals, they will at first be surprised, then pleased, at how students will really try to meet the necessary requirements. There is, after all, satisfaction in a job well done.

Naysayers will complain that some students will never try, that they don't care, but for too long we in education have let those few students (and I do believe they are in the minority) set the pace for the rest. Elitists will argue that we can never set high but realistic goals for everyone. Perhaps, however, we in education should listen to Mortimer Adler's quiet response on a "Firing Line" TV program to William F. Buckley's sneering statement that not all students could learn. Adler said, "I would rather live with my hope than your doubt."

## An Appreciation of Cultural Diversity

The Spanish-speaking population of Los Angeles is second only to that of Mexico City. Fewer than half of the kindergartners in the Los Angeles public schools are native English speakers. This cultural diversity exists in other areas as well: Selma, Alabama is home to 120 Hmong tribesmen from Laos. Two thousand Tai Dam, a Southeast Asian tribe, have settled in Iowa. While the American reaction to waves of immigration in the 1800s was to quickly and almost brutally disenfranchise new Americans from their cultural heritage, the response in the 1980s seems to be to change the American landscape to include our recent citizens. Hence, we see ethnic diversity in all areas of our everyday life, from our eating habits ("What do you feel like? Chinese? Mexican? Italian?"), to entertainment ("Let's go see the new German film."), to sports (for example, the upsurge of interest in soccer).

As educators, we would be remiss in not celebrating ethnic diversity along with the rest of the nation. No child in that fourth-period English class will ever forget the time the Vietnamese boat girl told the story of how she came to America. Few students in San Jose will knowingly or even unwittingly slur a Hispanic student. Rather than being threatened by the new cultural diversity, we need to consider it an increase in options. Naisbitt (1982, p. 247) quotes Ralph Tyler, the American educator, as saying that "you can tell you are being educated if your options are increasing, and that the reverse is happening if they are decreasing. Similarly, a society can tell it is growing if the options for its citizens are increasing." These options and our new, colorful ethnic-American landscape, make this country exciting—perhaps frightening—and dynamic.

Improvements in the speed of travel and communication also make it increasingly important that we bring to our students an appreciation of other cultures. Even in the heartland of the nation, thousands of miles from a coast or a border, one can fly to another country within hours, or dial a friend on another continent by simply pressing a few more buttons. It is absurd, therefore, to insulate ourselves from the civilizations and life styles of all the world's people. Global education and global understanding may be the only ways to avoid global destruction.

### The Marriage of English and High Tech

English teachers are almost pathologically frightened of science and technology. Yet the computer has the potential to lighten our workload as no reader or reduction in class size has yet to do. Have you had a student lately who has used "Spellstar" or "Wordstar" on a home computer to correct spelling or identify synonyms? Have you had an opportunity to allow students to edit their papers on a word processor? If your school doesn't have this software yet, it probably will within the next decade. Soon computers and word processors may be as much a part of English classes as blackboards. It is fatuous not to use computer technology. Just like the use of calculators in math class, computers, when accompanied by an understanding of basic principles, simply make life easier.

English teachers might be threatened that a computer will replace them. However, with high tech also comes "high touch," and this is where we come in. Again from Naisbitt (1982, p. 53), "the more high technology around us, the more the need for human touch." Rather than putting us out of work, the computer will free us to spend more time bringing the humanities and arts to our students, because in our high-tech society, the humanities will add the needed "touch" to education.

Heightening the emphasis on the humanities in the schools will also provide the needed forum for communication in a society that is becoming increasingly individualized. Only seven percent of America's society fits the profile of the typical nuclear family, with a breadwinning father, two children, and a mother who remains at home. Teachers today face students with an amazing range of family backgrounds: single-parent families, never-married mothers, two-career parents, a working mother and a "house-husband," a blended family with step-siblings and half-siblings. In addition, our students are more likely to live alone when they enter their adult lives. One of four people today lives alone, compared with only one in 10 in 1955 (Naisbitt, 1982, p. 233). These people who live alone are the unmarried young, the elderly, and the divorced. Sometimes I find these changing relationships horrifying; it seems as though many of my students' parents dispose of their family responsibilities like Kleenex: children are bounced from grandparents to stepparents to cousins to older brothers and sisters as soon as things are not going smoothly. Yet, as a teacher of English, I have an advantage over the teacher of math or science: I can use the arts and literature as a means of reaching students and giving them the human understanding they will need to cope with a future in which relationships are becoming increasingly fragile.

### Teacher-Friend

In the '70s, we entered a period when all of a sudden we as teachers imagined we were supposed to be "pals." This didn't work. Many teachers started off the year as friends and ended up with dissatisfied students who had a great time but complained they hadn't learned anything because they had had no classroom discipline. This led to a period of intense cynicism and bitterness among my colleagues. The students became "the enemy," and this was no healthier than the "pal" period for either the students or the teachers.

I feel I have come full circle with the "teacher-as-friend" dilemma. Now I tell my classes, "I am your teacher first; then I am your friend." Friendship and the respect that accompanies it must be earned. Now I find that not only I, but many other teachers, say openly, "I like being with kids." The statement is made unashamedly. I enjoy the company of young people. They keep me young and let me see the future. I just appreciate that they have given me an opportunity to take part in the shaping of a new world.

# Restoring the Imagination
# in Secondary Education

DEBBIE MYHILL
*(England)*

In the imagination of man exists the seeds of all moral and scientific improvement . . . the imagination is the distinguishing characteristic of man as a progressive being.

*S.T. Coleridge*

In the '80s, many classroom trends are obscured by national concerns for computers, technology, and unemployment. It is an age of brutal realism in England, with television pictures of bomb victims, famines, and on-the-spot war reports. No misery is spared, no picture rejected in a thirst for representing the truth. In this atmosphere, fantasy and the power of imagination are all too often equated with escapism and dishonesty. Many English secondary syllabi now confine the imagination to neat boxes, opened for a quick jog through some creative exercises, and then locked closed again during other written work and reading. The analytical mind is much admired, and with older children, in particular, a considerable amount of time is allocated to detached assessment of literature in an examination-oriented timetable.

Despite the undisputed value of critical analysis, and indeed of confronting the world with a balanced awareness of its harsher realities, there is a more fundamental reality. The inner reality has been sacrificed to more tangible, accessible facts. The fully responsive imagination allows the children to transcend mere fact and order their experiences into a comprehensible form. Being overconscious of and overdependent on facts and evidences is inhibiting and restrictive. For me as for Frank Smith (1982), "Imagination is not reality manipulated, reality is imagination constrained." Through the imagination it is possible to attain a greater understanding of self and others. Surely this is the basis of comprehension, the ability to read and understand what the writer is saying, how the characters felt, why they might have opted to act as they did, and indeed what one might have done in the same situation. Too many comprehension exercises are concerned with facile observations on the surface meaning of the language and are directed toward one specific, correct answer rather than an open-ended, imaginative response. The pleasure we get from reading Hardy, for example, is not in recalling how many sheep Gabriel Oak lost over the clifftop, nor in paraphrasing Bathsheba's letter to Mr. Boldwood, but rather in understanding and empathising with the tangled web of relationships and emotions.

English literature teaching, which can be as dry and dull as old bones, can be given new life by a more considerate exploitation of imaginative powers. Standard character analyses are often far better tackled using some kind of empathetic technique involving seeing the character from an angle other than that of detached observer. Role playing and improvised drama based upon characters or incidents in a book may illuminate new shades of meaning, and writing playlets can also be useful in underlining aspects hitherto unnoticed or ignored. An average, comprehensive, secondary fourth-year group which was initially unimpressed by *Lord of the Flies,* the set text, came on in leaps and bounds after dramatising the pig-killing scene. There was surprisingly little dependence on the actual phraseology of the text, but very close synchrony with its intended meanings. Several of them picked up the ritualistic chanting and used it with considerable dramatic effect, whilst others concentrated more on the barbaric savagery of the incident and the grotesque delight in the killing—"The blood's warm, really warm. Feelit."

Appreciating and understanding poetry is also better approached by harnessing imaginative skills. Translating poetry into another medium—a sketch, a letter, a piece of prose—can display it in a new light. Imagining one's own response in a given situation may provide a useful contrast or comparison with the poet's viewpoint. Writing war reports based on some of the great war poems, compiling a sound tape to back a poem such as Roger McGough's "The Lesson," making a colour collage which captures the moods of Tennyson's "Mariana," rewriting Coleridge's "Rime of the Ancient Mariner" as a pop song, all use the imagination to perceive the inner rhythms and shades of poetry far more effectively than redundant lists of metaphors and similes.

The power of imaginative empathy should not be underrated. Not only is it invaluable in literature, as we have seen, but it plays a crucial role in the exploratory self-discovery which English teaching seeks to affirm. Understanding oneself and understanding others go hand in hand, and using drama or writing to work out responses and reactions in a variety of situations allows the child the possibility of not being himself for a few brief moments. It gives the image-conscious adolescent an opportunity to see things as other people do, to experiment with new encounters, and to consider his position free from the rigid framework of his adolescent self. In a society replete with breakdowns, industrial confrontations, and political misunderstandings, the ability to appreciate a situation from every angle, rather than just the purely personal, is a gift indeed.

For the infant and the young child, imagination is an instinctive faculty, the natural way of resolving inner tensions and working out problems. The border between imagination and reality is very fluid, and the child can shift from one domain to the other with absolute ease. The child's imagination acts directly upon his world, manipulating, challenging, and confronting in an effort to understand and control it. Fear and aggression are common in infant play and this is widely accepted as a means of coping with pent-up emotions: "The child is able to externalise his strong feelings which might otherwise be repressed from his conscious mind and experienced in the form of anxiety" (Roberts and Tamburrini, 1981).

It is play which forms the basis of the young child's imaginative activity, but the ability to see, believe, and transform in pretend play diminishes through childhood. The adolescent, with his awareness of adult life around the corner, has often forgotten this realm of experience. The imagination is no longer tied to play, but is a mental process for which language is an excellent outlet—and it allows the exploratory and manipulatory benefits of play to continue. Sadly, our respect for reality is often so strong that the imagination is relegated to a minor status in the curriculum. As Sartre (1940) insists, without the imagination to see things as they are not, or as they might be, man has no power to change his world. The imagination is the tool of progress, for both the individual and for mankind.

# New Directions for the Eighties and Nineties

JO-ANNE EVERINGHAM

*(Australia)*

After groping towards important new educational ideas and practices throughout the '70s, Australian English teachers began the '80s with an exciting new methodology (the writing process approach) and the challenge of new directions to explore in communication (the new electronic media).

In 1969, Postman and Weingartner and others were warning that schools must be changed and that the "new" education had to meet three criteria: to be *student-centred, question-centred,* and *language-centred.* They threw out a challenge to English teachers to clear from their schools "trivial ways of studying language which had no connection with life." The '70s saw most of us making genuine, committed, but often tortured attempts to do just this with little basis from experience or training. Teachers attempted, with mixed confidence and success, to individualise instruction; to use inquiry methods of learning: and to value creative writing, talk, listening, and other previously under-rated languaging skills.

These attempts to implement new educational philosophies suffered many teething problems which were frequently aggravated by harping cries of "back to basics" by those who saw the parsing, analysis, and punctuation books collecting dust. However, the '80s have seen the philosophies realised and the three criteria met in at least one aspect of English teaching: they have combined to give an almost magical formula for the teaching and learning of written expression—the "process approach," of which Donald Graves is probably the advocate best-known to Australian teachers (Walshe, 1984).

The practices now working so excitingly with respect to writing and which are starting to permeate other aspects of English are:

1. Shifting our emphasis from "product" to "process."
2. Learning controlled by the student (in writing, this applies to choice of topic and choice of revision alternatives to implement; in other aspects of English, it is characterised as negotiating the curriculum).
3. Realising the importance of questioning as a tactic for observing and interpreting communications. This involves consideration of alternatives (the basis of revision in writing and of awareness in all communication).

4. Using talk as a powerful interaction to promote learning and personal growth (as in the writing conference).
5. Emphasising activity-based learning; demanding a creative input from students.
6. Providing opportunities for students to show what they are capable of doing, rather than exposing what they can't do.
7. Encouraging self-evaluation of the effectiveness of students' work.
8. Promoting a student-teacher relationship in which the teacher is a facilitator rather than a judge or expert.
9. Valuing an audience which is not just the teacher but includes peers, parents, and others.

These are also the essential principles underlying, and indeed demanding, an extension of our students' literacy beyond the almost exclusive concern with print media which has characterised English classrooms for four centuries. This, too, was perceived by Postman and Weingartner (1969) who pointed out that if it is "the essential function of schools to develop literacy and sophistication in the languages most important to the students then media study becomes critical in the new education."

In this respect, there have also been faltering advances during the past decade in English classrooms. In the mid-'60s—with increased access to television and wide popularity of films—came a concern among educators to protect students against the ill effects of the media while teaching them to enjoy what was evaluated as the best of the art form by traditional aesthetic criteria. As a result, in Tasmania, a generation of Diploma of Education graduates taught a generation of students a film study course which required analysis of three fiction, three documentary, and three animated films. Increasingly through the '70s, English teachers diversified media studies to include other aspects: production of school newspapers and super-8 films, and the study of advertising.

English classrooms are now becoming the scene for many questions and activities which form a systematic investigation of all forms of symbolic codification. That is, language, in its broadest sense, is the focus of student inquiry. For instance:

- Students are negotiating the topics they will study: "What can we find out about our favorite television serial?"
- Students are observing techniques used to convey meaning and interpreting their conventional use: "Why is the newsreader always in a suit and tie and talking straight to camera?"
- Students are realising the importance of audience and that individuals bring to communication products a selective and interpretive process: "What knowledge of my own can I apply to the subject of this documentary?"

This important shift of focus which English is taking in most Australian states (and, I gather, in other English-speaking countries) broadens the traditional language-literature dichotomy to the study of communication. This study is based on the insights of semiotic, cultural, and other theoretical approaches to textual analysis.

There remain some challenges for Australian English teachers to contend with, especially attitudinal ones with respect to the most pervasive communication medium, television. There must be a breakdown of the negative attitude of all teachers (not just English teachers) who overwhelmingly show distrust and hostility towards television and lack of respect for those who teach about it. We also need to abandon some long-cherished approaches in English teaching, especially our notions of "quality" and "appreciation" that have grown out of a particular tradition of literary criticism.

However, over the next 10 years, I hope we can shoulder what the UNESCO Declaration on Media Education called, "the responsibility of preparing the young person for living in a world of powerful images, words, and sounds." UNESCO believes, "Children and adults need to be literate in all three of these symbolic systems, and this will require some reassessment of educational priorities. Such a reassessment might well result in an integrated approach to the teaching of language and communication." This will require action by education departments and authorities to initiate and support media education programs and develop teacher training courses. During this time, I hope media studies will move from the peripheries of the curriculum towards its centre. I hope the characteristics of the highly successful, process-oriented approach now being applied to writing will be extended to all aspects of communication and especially to exploration of the electronic media which play such a huge part in our students' out-of-school life. If my hopes are realised, the sorts of activities described above will become widespread.

# My English Teaching in the Eighties

MERYL JENNINGS

*(Australia)*

If there is one trend in secondary English teaching in South Australia at the moment, which I hope without reservation will continue into the next decade, it is the trend towards honesty in the dealings between teacher and student over the content and methodology

of subject English. Much has been published in the past 10 years on
the topic of "crafting" as a concept in writing. In the course of that
discussion, emphasis has been placed on the relationship between
teacher and student and on the nature of the writing process. English
teachers have been led to consider the master/apprentice concept in
the teaching and learning of writing; writing for specific audiences;
"real world" writing; drafting and editing with their cutting, pasting,
and rejecting; writing files and conferencing, and the notion of ownership of a piece of writing. I have certainly felt both a lessening of the
pressure of being expected to have all the answers and at the same time
a need, which has quickly grown into a personal desire, to model the
writing process for my students.

A similar awareness of the reality of reading situations and an
honest self-appraisal of my reading habits and responses have taken
my practices as a teacher involved with literature in a new and, I hope,
more honest direction. I recognize that literature is "manipulative" in
the broadest sense of the word and not necessarily taken in a pejorative
way. That is, I believe that words "do" things to receivers of them and
that writers craft and construct their works to achieve responses from
readers. Hence, my underlying aim in the treatment of literature in the
school situation is no different in kind from my personal aim in reading: to open up the opportunity for interaction between the texts and
the voices behind them, and the students and the voices within them.
Because I want to extend that mutual contact as much as possible, I
am concerned to make the meeting points and springboards as smooth
as possible and point ways to increase recognition of the voices mentioned above.

In the January 1984 issue of *Notes Plus,* the following reference
appeared under the heading, "Talking and Writing about Literature":

> It is not fortuitous that when the Carnegie Report addressed the
> priorities of the high school curriculum, it listed literature first
> (Boyer, 1983, pp. 95–97). As Boyer puts it, "Reading, writing,
> speaking, and listening—along with computation—are the basic
> tools of education. But the mastery of language means more than
> acquiring these essential skills. During high school all students dis-
> cover how language is a part of culture, probably the most impor-
> tant part. They should learn about the variety of ways civilization
> is sustained and enriched through a shared use of symbols.
>
> As a first step we recommend that all students, through a study
> of literature, discover our common literary heritage and learn
> about the power and beauty of the written word. . . . Literature
> addresses the emotional part of the human experience. It provides
> another perspective on historical events, telling us what matters
> and what has mattered to people in the past. Literature transmits

from generation to generation enduring spiritual and ethical values. . . . As great literature speaks to all people, it must be available to all students." There can be no more important activity in the curriculum than reading literature—and talking and writing about it.

The descriptions which follow are of a couple of my teaching practices which are working out well with my classes. I think they are all part of the new direction of honest, real, and process-focused English teaching. Possibly they are not "new" as activities, but are now being justified by a sounder theory or are more clearly seen as developing learning in the language arts area.

I borrowed my title for a reading/writing programme I have developed as a result of some of these trends from the shared book experience concept of Don Holdaway (1979).

Shared reading responses involve the class and me in reading a story together and stopping along the way to write and then share with partners our individual responses. At the end of the reading/responding stage, we consult with our writing partners about directions in which we could go to develop a piece of our own writing arising from our reading experience. I have used this method from Year 8 to Year 12 and, with necessary variations, in the study of drama and poetry as well as prose.

It is important that the experience is a shared one. (Remember my comments about openness and honesty.) Most teachers who have talked about their own experiences of life or read their own pieces to a class know that rapport is established by something like this. Students listen with rapt attention to personal revelations from a teacher. What's more, modeling a way of commenting about response is important, as is sorting out aloud what you as teacher might write. The whole reading/writing process is demystified.

As students share immediate impressions, they gain all sorts of understandings: I read differently from others but I can gain added insight into meaning by using another's responses to the same material; my experience is significant, as is the author's; I have stories in me and ideas and personal descriptions which can become literature for me and for others.

It seems to me this is a legitimate, honest way of responding to literature, because it values the uniqueness and worth of individual reading; it allows insight into individual differences, including the teacher's; then it allows time for reflection on the whole experience of the reading; finally, it opens up ways of writing in response to the reading which allows for ongoing interaction between author and reader, who now becomes author. It doesn't stop the reader at the stage of rewriting, often badly, the original piece, but allows him to stay with part of the reading if necessary or move away into areas perhaps only fleetingly suggested by the reading. I like the idea of the "continuation of literature" that this process suggests. It's a way of linking reading and writing which has been emphasized by a number of people here in South Australia and elsewhere.

Judith Langer (1982) indicated a similar emphasis amongst American teachers of literature. Referring to a report of the National Assessment of Educational Progress on the 1979–80 national assessment of reading and literature she writes:

> The students were asked to read a passage, respond to a range of multiple-choice items (primarily dealing with their reactions to what they had read), and then respond in writing to either an open-ended or more focused question—to evaluate, analyze, explain, or elaborate upon why they had reacted to the text in the way they had. What is so refreshing about this approach is that it represents an attempt to view reading comprehension and response to literature as interwoven and naturally occurring reasoning, understanding, and communication phenomena. (p. 337)

The practice is honest because it confesses to what *we* do when we discuss our reading or reflect on it privately. We don't make summaries or precis, or write book reviews, or even dash off a dramatisation or model of it. (The only person I've known to do the latter was one of my colleagues—a mathematics teacher with a love of good science fiction. After reading Arthur Clarke's *Rendevous with Rama*, he attempted a scale model of the spaceship described by Clarke!)

A second example: the concern to open up paths into valuable literary experiences led two of my colleagues and me some years ago to develop a method for encouraging the reading and enjoyment of Shakespeare by students from Years 10 to 12. The essential element of our programme is a series of "act-outs" of main events in the play by means of contemporary scenes improvised by the class divided into small working groups.

We have found that such introductory work before viewing, hearing, or reading each act of a Shakespearean play greatly aids students' appreciation of the unfamiliar language of Shakespeare and their understanding of plot and character interaction. We first used this method with Year-12 matriculation students, but soon extended it to Year 11, and have now successfully employed it at Year-10 level. The method is, of course, applicable to any drama study, and I have also used it with the study of novels. Its extension into other areas of education can be readily imagined.

I could go on with other developed methodologies which have become part of my teaching because of "new" ways of looking at secondary English teaching. They would not all be innovative, but they would all, I hope, be seen to spring from a desire to level with students while at the same time maintaining the centrality of literature and its special use of words in any English programme. I use the term *literature* not in the sense of only those works which have formed the traditional canon of good writing. Literature for me is defined by its peculiar creative and imaginative use of language which would rule out what I am engaged in now as I write this paper—the difference which enables one to talk of some verse as "prosaic"!

As we move toward the '90s, I would like to see more real credit given to the value of students' response to literature from a personal, subjective point of view. Examination questions are still couched in academic terms, demanding by their tone a more sophisticated response than a 16-year-old is capable of. At the same time, I would like to develop ways to help students move easily between writing from "inside the reading experience" and "outside" critical writing. I see much evidence of an understanding of mood and tone and meaning in literature by my senior students, even the poorest of them, when they write *as a character within* the book and so on. Yet the majority of students write awkwardly and obtusely *about* the same aspects of a literary work.

I would like to see much more record keeping by teachers of the way students' writing, talking, and reading have developed—an extension of the writing files which a number of secondary teachers and a good many primary language arts teachers are using in South Australia to monitor student progress.

Finally, I would also like to see a concerted publicity campaign to inform the general public about the excellent things that are happening in schools to make better readers and writers out of many more school students than ever before in this state and nation.

# 2.
# The Teaching of Literature and Reading

Steve Bicknell of England begins this part by stating that "it is nonsense to suggest that books can be *taught* to children." [Italics added.] He goes on to articulate what appears to be a more-or-less common philosophy among our contributors: "Instead of talking about literature and reading teaching, let us instead talk about how we do our best to encourage children to enjoy reading literature." The essayists do just that, describing reading/literature programs in primary and secondary schools, and offering insights into their own methods and approaches. Yet beneath the common philosophy, there appear to be alternative views of how best to approach the task, and some nagging questions remain unanswered: What do we do about the skills of initial reading? How do we teach in states and provinces where examinations focusing on so-called basic skills are employed? How does one mesh the required basal reader or set text with the ideal of individualized reading programs? Too, there is a tension evident between the ideal of individual reading for pleasure and the traditional, cultural heritage model of teaching common texts. One senses a struggle on the part of these teachers (representing English teachers worldwide, no doubt) over "classic" literature—"dated junk" as one contributor labels it— and ways of making reading appeal to students. It seems clear that among and within the IFTE member nations there remains a great deal of study, research, and experimental teaching to be done on the "teaching" of reading and literature.

# On Not Teaching Literature and Reading

STEVE BICKNELL

*(England)*

Literature and reading are not taught in my classroom, and I believe it is nonsense to suggest that books can be taught to children. What does happen though, is that children acquire a love of reading and literature.

Before I go any further, however, it might be advisable to destroy yet another commonly held notion that reading and literature are somehow separate. For children to love literature, they must also enjoy reading and vice versa. Instead of talking about literature and reading teaching, let us talk about how we do our best to encourage children to enjoy reading literature.

If teachers accept that literature has a central place in the primary school curriculum, they will have taken the correct stance to achieve our goal. A start will have been made. Literature has to be obviously valued; it is no good saying it is important if it is not promoted from the position of "the end-of-the day, gap-filling, child-pacifying story"! I believe literature should occupy a central place in the curriculum because it does more to the developing brain than most other experiences available inside or outside our classrooms. Apart from providing the reader with entertainment, it also gives the "consumer" the opportunity to think and communicate. Literature gives readers the chance to experience (albeit secondhand) more than ordinary life. If teachers value literature they will do all they can to give their audience a broad selection of books of the highest quality. Where possible and appropriate, it can be valuable to give copies of the book to the children so that they can follow the text during the reading. It is also advisable to think carefully about the time of day when the book is to be read (or in the case of picture books, read *and* shown). There seems little point in reading a demanding work at the end of an afternoon; some time in the morning is much better if the children's attention is to be engaged. I find it is usually better, especially with younger children, to have them sitting comfortably on a carpet in the book corner during the story. This somehow adds to the "magic" of the occasion. If literature is so important, let us make a fuss of it and then perhaps our customers will believe in it too.

Once a book has been read to a class, the worst thing that can happen is for the children to return to other activities. Literature must be discussed. It is only by discussing with others who have experienced a book that new meaning can be effectively constructed. The discussion should not take the form of guessing what the teacher has in mind, but should proceed from children describing their reactions, puzzles, opinions, and observations. If children acquire this habit, they will gain much more from the book than if it had simply been read to them and no more. It will acquire further dimensions and meanings and, probably, become memorable. (Try this out for yourself, at your own level!)

Finally, if children's positive attitudes towards literature are to be maintained and enhanced, it is obviously desirable that a school policy for the promotion of literature be formulated. Consistency of approach is not vital; children can gain a lot from one committed teacher in one year; but, if the whole staff works towards a common aim, the benefits for the children will be immeasurably improved.

# The Uses of Literature

LESLEY PASQUIN

(Canada)

An interesting incident happened in school one day. It was decided that the free flow (resource) teachers would be responsible for teaching a group of Grade 4 boys their language arts for next year. These boys have been free flow candidates every year. Most have repeated a grade somewhere along the road. Some are disabled readers; all are disabled writers; and some suffer from language deprivation. Now the interesting aspect of the situation is this—the entire order of materials which the teacher had originally assigned was scrapped. No remedial readers, no mechanical phonics, and no workbooks for them. If they are to become readers, then above all they must read for pleasure and understanding. Literature would be the tool.

What is reading? What does it mean to be a "reader"? Frank Jennnings (1965, pp. 3–4) says, "Reading is older than printing or writing or even language itself. Reading begins with wonder at the world about us . . . starts with the recognition of repeated events. . . . You are dealing with ideas and concepts that have no material matter or substance and yet are 'real.'" Northrop Frye (1985) emphasizes that reading has to be continuously active. If you call yourself a reader, think how actively you participate when you delve into a new novel or crack open the latest English journal. Readers are people who read voluntarily, who are interested in books, and who apply what they have read to their lives. Glenna Sloan (1975, p. 1) calls the literate person, ". . . one who reads: fluently, responsively, critically, and because he wants to. Reading involves an engagement with print and an active personal involvement with the ideas expressed in it. Children will become readers only if their emotions have been engaged, their imaginations stirred. . . ." Will workbooks and remedial readers and phonics drill do this? The answer is obvious.

Some curricula tend to set aside a pocket of time for literature, rather than using it as a base for reading and writing programmes. The value of literature is limitless. We are frequently told that instruction should begin where the child is, if it is to be successful. Imaginative literature is exactly where he is (Sloan, 1975, p. 2).

A good story invites the reader in. Four forces seem to be taking place: (1) identifying with the characters or the setting, (2) projecting the reader into the work, (3) undergoing a catharsis, and (4) gaining insight into our own world and that around us. Thus, literature can provide an outlet for emotional needs. Literature shows human motives for what they are, inviting the reader to react to a character. We understand the motives and can justify the deeds (Lukens, 1976, pp. 2–3). Even as adult readers, we *know* why Peter Rabbit could not resist Mr. McGregor's garden; we hold our breath as he is caught in the gooseberry net; we shed a tear with him as he finds the locked door in the wall with no room for a fat little rabbit to squeeze underneath. Literature gives shape to human experience and develops sympathy and empathy.

Literature also trains the imagination. We can know what it is like to be dancing with wild things in Sendak's *Where the Wild Things Are,* or to be deep in the dungeon with Richler's *Jacob Two-Two and the Dreadful Hooded Fang.* This is particularly important for children who have not had a stimulating language background, or for children who are passive television watchers and are not in touch with their own imaginative powers.

Literature helps us look at life and sort out the world. Says Lukens (1976, p. 4), "... little, if anything, is outside the province of literature ... friendship, greed, family sacrifice, childhood, love, advice, old age, treasures, snobbery and compassion are set before us." The archetypal quest, a recurring theme in literature, helps the reader to develop the ability to recognize and define problems and to speculate on possible solutions. Discussions which center around such questions as: "What would you do next? What do you think will happen? Would you agree with the actions of _____ or would you have done something different?" will help the reader understand that there are different ways of solving problems that confront us in life.

Finally, literature provides us with a zest for life. It leads us on adventures of the mind and spirit. "Reading gets us out of our own time and place, out of ourselves; but in the end it will return us to ourselves, a little different, a little changed by this experience" (Huck, 1976, p. 706).

Using literature to teach reading requires a reversal of the typical learning-to-read sequence. Traditionally, the child is taught to recognize printed words and to pronounce them when he sees them in print. As the child masters word recognition, the emphasis is shifted to understanding. Then, the child is taught about books. It certainly makes more sense to reverse this order: that is, to foster a love of books, to understand what a book is telling us, and then to recognize that print represents oral language and so learn what the words represent. This can begin when a child is but months old. Rhymes and games like "This little piggy" and "Pat-a-cake, Pat-a-cake" are essentially stories that an infant can understand and appreciate. They have sequence, theme, and characters. With the wealth of picture books available, it is an easy task to find entertainment, for what child does not enjoy an adult's undivided attention?

One morning, my four-year-old daughter woke us by coming to read to us. This is her favorite activity. She reads in the car, to her dolls, before bed. Another morning, she brought her book to the breakfast table because "You read the paper." Her selection that morning was A. A. Milne's *When We Were Very Young*. She chose the poem "Market Place" because "It is a poem about a boy who wants a rabbit and if I went to the market, I would want to buy a rabbit too." She is a reader—a lover of books. This is because books are part of life for us; reading is an important part of our day. There is always time for a story. At first, Lisa would recite much of the text of the simple picture books from memory. As time went on, she began interpreting the symbols and recognizing words. She has advanced to more sophisticated books with not so much as a single phonic lesson.

I am convinced that this same exposure to print and books can be used in classrooms, even with a group of disabled readers. It is essential that we get suitable books into the hands of children. Two things are important: knowledge of the students' needs and interests, and knowledge of books. The first requires a sensitive teacher. The second requires development of criteria for choosing appropriate literature. In order to do this, the teacher must read books. Sebasta and Iverson (1975) and Lukens (1976) provide good guidelines which I summarize here.

*Theme*: Is it important? Is the author asking a significant question? Is what the author says honest and important? Does the theme contribute to the reader's growth and discovery?

*Character*: Do the characters invite identification and projection? Do they present the chance for exploring outcomes and discovering alternatives? Do the characters resolve their conflict and come out the better for it?

*Setting*: Does the work give a sense of place? Is there psychological as well as physical reality to the setting?

*Plot*: If the story is a narrative, does it make the reader want to turn the page to find out what happens next? Does the plot illuminate the theme and the characters? Is there a danger of sensationalism? Is there a lack of conflict?

*Style*: Does the style tie the book together with some significance? Is it trite? Is it stimulating?

*Point of View*:: Does the point of view provide the opportunity for projection?

It almost goes without saying that getting the books into the hands of the students is only the first step in a long road to becoming readers in a complex society. As Sloan (1975, p. 6) says, "The experience of literature is a great teacher, but it is not the only one however. It is our task to set imaginative literature at the center of [a child's] education."

# One Teacher's Approach in a New Zealand Primary School

L. JEANNE BIDDULPH

*(New Zealand)*

I don't regard "reading" as simply a subject to teach. To me it is a personal meaning-gaining process which is inextricably bound up with a child's experiences, oral language, and prior achievement in reading. For example, a child who has not experienced a visit to a farm will have difficulty making sense of "milking cows," and a child who does not have "highway" in his vocabulary will not find it easy to attach the relevant meaning to that word. Because children in any one class differ widely in the experiences, oral language, and reading knowledge and skills that they bring to the reading task, and because reading needs to develop a generalized ability that can be used in many different contexts, I use a range of teaching strategies to help children learn to read rather than basing reading instruction on, for instance, a series of graded readers.

The most significant components of the programme I provide are:

## 1. Continuous monitoring of children's development.

By continuously identifying each child's strengths and weaknesses in reading, using procedures developed by Clay (1979a, 1979b) and Nicholson (1982, 1984), I can assist each child to develop more adequate, appropriate strategies. For example, a young child who has directional confusions is helped to read from left to right and top to bottom. An older child who relies almost entirely on visual cues when faced with an unknown word in a text can be helped to consider meaning and structural cues while reading. Another child who uses context clues well but who fails to use visual cues to check guesses can be encouraged to do so. The continuous monitoring of children's reading development enables me to provide and discuss reading materials which are meaningful to the children and easy enough to ensure success. Assistance that may be needed with word analysis is provided within the context of a story or article being read by the child, not in isolation.

## 2. Guided reading.

Regular guided reading of material which is not too difficult, and is of interest to the child or children involved, is an integral part of my programme. Important aspects of the story or article are discussed with the children (either individually or in a small group) before it is read silently by them. Additional ideas are explored during a follow-up discussion, and further related reading of suitable material is often encouraged. New Zealand teachers and children are fortunate to have an increasing range of fiction and nonfiction materials from which to select.

Particularly valuable are the *School Journals* and *Revised Ready to Read Books,* published by the School Publications Branch of the Department of Education in Wellington. These contain stories and articles written by some of New Zealand's best authors. Efforts have been made to ensure that the content of the journals and books is relevant to the experiences and interests of our children, and that the language patterns in the books match the oral language patterns of the children. Such material makes it possible to capitalize on and extend the unique set of experiences and ideas which each child brings to school. Because reading is an important way of helping children to explore new ideas, and to make better sense of the world in which they live, it is not confined to a particular period each day.

3. *Reading to children and shared reading.*

As part of my programme, I frequently read new and well-loved stories and verse to the children. In my experience there is a place for this at all levels of the primary school. I also use shared reading techniques to encourage all children to participate in the reading, and this leads to independent reading of these stories and poems. Singing known and new songs, the words of which are recorded on charts, is also an important part of the daily programme.

4. *Language-experience.*

Discussing and writing about some of the many experiences which the children have had as individuals or as a class group is an integral part of the programme. This writing and subsequent reading of stories by the children aids their reading development. I find that it is particularly helpful for low-progress readers.

5. *Independent reading.*

In my view, opportunities to read independently for pleasure are an essential part of the total language/reading programme, while reading for information is an integral part of all curriculum areas. I therefore encourage and support frequent independent reading by the children, both at home and at school.

6. *Parent support.*

I have developed a special programme to assist parents to provide their children with encouragement and effective help in reading at home (Biddulph, 1983). This supports the work done by the school in the language/reading areas.

### 7. Classroom environment.

After many years of working with children, I am convinced that a nonthreatening and noncompetitive classroom environment is essential if all children are to experience success and satisfaction with language and reading rather than frequent failure and frustration. I work to establish such an atmosphere as my part of the programme.

Finally, I should mention that the programme I have outlined is based on (1) an interactive view of reading (see, for example, Nicholson, 1984); (2) a constructionist or generative view of learning (see, for example, Wittrock, 1981); (3) my belief that each child attending primary school can learn to read, given appropriate help; and (4) my view that the role of the teacher should be one of providing the support, resources, and environment that will enable each child, as a fellow human being, to develop competence in language and reading.

# Letting Fantasy Go Free

ELAINE SNOWDEN
*(United States)*

"Kids are missing a tremendous part of life if they don't read," states Caroline Bauer (1983). "You have to get them started early so that it becomes a habit."

Children should experience the magic of fantasy that books bring into their lives. Stories of fantasy allow them to pursue the wild things in the forest, to join Mole and Water-Rat as they explore the river world, and to enter the secret place of Jesse and Leslie as they cross their bridge to Terabithia.

How do we get young children to take these "fantasy journeys"? How can we as teachers extend those journeys and ensure that our students are "hooked on books"? The key element of this process is best stated by Bernice Cullinan (1977): "Books can play a significant role in the life of a young child, but to the extent to which they do depends entirely upon adults. Adults are responsible for providing and transmitting literary heritage. . . ." Although there are many theories about the teaching of reading, there is general agreement among researchers that adults do play a positive role in encouraging children to read. Anne Forester has cited numerous studies in which "common features emerged" in children who are already reading when they enter first grade. Those features included *oral reading*, a *variety of material available in the home*, and *parents who are willing to answer children's questions about reading.*

There is also a correlation between teacher effectiveness and student achievement in the area of reading skills instruction. Fran Lehr (1982), reporting on teacher effectiveness research projects concluded ". . . that teachers do indeed make a difference. Effective teachers structure their classes so that students have ample opportunities to learn . . . and they are active participants in the teaching/learning interaction."

In recent years a new debate in reading has emerged. This time it is theoretical, and the focus is on what the process of reading is. Jean Otto (1982) states, "Researchers now debate whether reading is a bottom-up or top-down process."

The theory of learning which underlies the bottom-up process is behaviorism. These skills-oriented people advocate that reading should be taught from part to whole. At the other end of the spectrum are the top-down people, the psycholinguists who view comprehension as central, teaching reading in a "whole language context, rather than focusing on isolated skills" (Goodman and Burke, 1980). Somewhere in between these two theories is a middle ground referred to by some as the interaction approach. Pearson and Johnson (1978) contend that "comprehension is building bridges between the new and the known"; in other words, comprehension is a dialogue between the reader's knowledge and the text.

The philosophy of teaching reading in the Anchorage School District falls somewhere in this middle ground. Basal reading series are used at all grade levels. A "basal" reading series, as described by Sandra Forsythe (1981), "is a series of graded reading books from one of many American publishers that presents reading skills sequentially by a look say, phonics or eclectic methodology. The series or program usually includes many supplemental aids: records, tapes, charts, workbooks, testing materials, and comprehensive manuals for the teachers."

However, most Anchorage teachers use literature to supplement the basals. At my school, the basal reading program covers the skills component. To assist teachers with students who have difficulty in reading, there are additional certified staff personnel, such as a remedial reading teacher, a learning disability resource teacher, and an oral language development teacher.

The library in our school enhances the reading program in a number of ways. There is an annual, teacher-monitored, reading competition sponsored by a charity organization, the Muscular Dystrophy Foundation. (Last year our students read over 7,000 books.) The library is open for students at all times during school hours; however, teachers are encouraged to allow students to visit the library daily where they can check out books for that day's reading. Once a year, a famous author of children's books is invited to spend a week in the school, and before his or her arrival students are encouraged to read the author's works. (Recently we had Steven Kellogg and Martha Alexander.) There is a continuing program of celebrating famous authors' or poets' birthdays. (This is done by setting aside a special section in the library and featuring the author's books.) The big continuing event each year is the Young Reader's Choice Award. (This consists of a list of 12 to 15 books chosen by the Northwest Librarian's Association that are read by fourth-, fifth-, and sixth-grade students. Once the students read all the books on the list they can vote for the one they liked best.)

In my classroom, the main emphasis of reading is literature. It is my belief that children should become acquainted with their heritage through literature. To accomplish this goal I have a parent come in three or four times a week to read out loud to my fifth graders. She recently read *Wind in the Willows* to the students. Each day after she finished reading she had them summarize, in a sentence or two, what she had read. Using *Wind in the Willows,* she had the students list the main characters and decide on the problem and the resolution of the story. When she finishes a book, she has the students do follow-up activities, such as dioramas, mobiles, or analyzing story characters.

I feel students should realize that reading is for their own entertainment and that it can be a lifetime enjoyment. To accomplish this I introduce them to the Newberry Award books and the Young Reader's Choice books, and I have a program of sustained silent reading.

Another aspect of my literature program involves acquainting students with the Caldecott Award books, which have been recognized for excellence in illustration. I believe teachers have the responsibility to help stimulate the aesthetic development of students. To do this, teachers can use Caldecott books to concentrate on the skills of aesthetic expression and impression.

To summarize, my reading approach has strong support from our district-sponsored library resources, the assistance and backing from the parents, minimal censorship of reading materials, and my own continued love of literature. The "kids" are indeed taking those "fantasy journeys." Monica, a fifth grader, says about books, "Some teach me stuff and some let my fantasy go free."

# Personalized Reading Programs

RICHARD E. COLES

*(Canada)*

"Wow! this is the best book I've read," declares Nelson, a student in a Grade 5/6 classroom. "I wonder if this guy has written any other books." Eagerly, he moves to another group of students to discuss the story with Joe and George. Paula, Fatima, and Cassandra are quietly moving around the classroom selecting a new book to read. Tammy is curious about the pile of new books on the teacher's desk. "When will these books be available to the class?" she asks. The teacher has just completed a reading interview with Lan and he is recording some of his observations in an annotated record book. Soon a selected group of students will meet at a table for a reading strategy lesson. The rest of the class is engaged in reading, browsing at the book display, or working on a variety of art, writing, or drama activities, dealing with the literature they have read.

Students in this classroom are actively involved in their reading and learning. They read—at their desks, in comfortable chairs, on a soft rug, or at the library, throughout the school day. They discuss their work with each other. Books covering a variety of interests are everywhere in the classroom. Displays illustrate scenes from novels, cardboard cutouts of popular characters, original book jackets and surveys of favourite books and authors. Activity centres, containing crossword puzzles, word searches based on familiar literature, collections of jokes, tongue twisters, riddles and poems, are also part of the literate classroom environment.

Students select reading materials that reflect their interests and reading development. The teacher assists the students with their selections, monitors their progress through individual conferences, and discusses with each reader appropriate follow-up activities. The teacher also develops a psychological climate that encourages children to read a variety of materials and to express their reactions to these selections. The students have an opportunity to read an assortment of literature and to explore new ideas and interests. They are also developing their ability to comprehend a variety of texts and to become readers for life.

In many multicultural communities in Canada, teachers come in contact with students of different educational experiences, interests, background knowledge, and expectations. The challenge for teachers is to provide each student with appropriate, interesting learning experiences across the curriculum. This sort of personalized reading program I have described is in use in several schools with multicultural populations in the Toronto area.

However, a personalized reading program requires an understanding of the reading process by teachers. The psycholinguistic model of reading maintains that the goal of reading is always the identification of meaning. Reading is viewed as a language process (Goodman, 1975). Language is used for communication and as a medium of thought and learning (Goodman, Goodman, and Burke, 1978). Readers use their understanding of language and knowledge of their world to obtain meaning from print. They actively interact with writers through print (Goodman and Goodman, 1977). From a reader's prior knowledge of language there are three sources of information: the graphonic, syntactic, and semantic that are used "simultaneously and interdependently" (Goodman, 1973). Reading involves the use of recognizing, sampling, predicting, confirming, correcting, and terminating strategies to make use of the graphonic, syntactic, and semantic cues.

Based on this psycholinguistic model, the purpose of reading is comprehension of meaning. The three cue systems—graphonic, syntactic, and semantic—are not separated for instruction (Goodman and Goodman, 1981). Rather, the students read whole, personally meaningful, relevant materials. Readers develop their reading strategies while interacting with whole texts that have the characteristics of real language.

Self-selection permits students to choose a variety of materials that are meaningful and relevant to them and best suited to their reading development. Such experiences encourage a commitment on the part of the student to complete the reading of their own selections (Lee, 1983). Students have expressed a preference for self-selected materials rather than those assigned by the teacher (Coles, 1981).

Each class member has a reading folder which is kept in one of the student-designed boxes throughout the classroom. The folders contain a personalized reading contract sheet, a file card, and a video or cartoon character name tag displaying the student's name. The *contract sheet* indicates the name of the material the student is reading, the agreed-upon assignment, and the due date for the next conference. These dates are fairly flexible, since field trips, visiting theatre presentations, and other special events take place throughout the school year. Both the teacher and the reader sign the personalized reading contract sheet. On the *file card,* the students record the names of each book they read and the authors. This information assists the teacher when suggesting new books for the students to read. These cards also indicate the kind of reading materials that should become part of the class library. The *video* or *cartoon character name tag* is placed on a special bulletin board display when a student wants a reading conference. A quick glance indicates to the teacher who requires a conference.

The teacher has an appointment book, which indicates when each student requires a conference, and provides the materials that are necessary for the students to complete their displays based on their readings. The teacher also keeps an annotated record book. Each reader has a separate page in his book. During the course of each school day or after a conference, the teacher comments about a student's reading development and interests. As the program is set in motion, students select their reading materials from many books in the classroom or library. These books cover a variety of interests and are suitable for students with different, developing reading abilities. When the students have read the books and completed their assignments, they place their name tag on the display board, indicating the need for a reading conference.

The reading conference is the keystone of the personalized reading program. Each conference takes place at a table in a quiet corner of the classroom. The student brings to the conference his or her reading folder and assignments. The conference begins with a discussion of the assignments. Next, the teacher asks the reader to briefly retell the novel or short story. This question brings out basic information about the characters, plot, and setting that is required for answering additional questions. The teacher employs a variety of questions and probes to determine the student's comprehension and personal response to the reading material. Students are provided with enough time to formulate their answers and are also encouraged to ask the teacher questions. Christenbury and Kelly (1983) and Barnes (1979) have developed questioning strategies that can be adopted for a personalized reading conference. The final part of the conference involves the teacher and student discussing and agreeing upon the date and the assignments for the next personalized reading conference.

Evaluation involves the teacher's being aware of the various materials the students are reading and their ability to comprehend them. This requires the teacher to know the class members, the reading process, and how the students learn to read. With this knowledge, the teacher is a "kid watcher" who observes and monitors the reader's progress (Goodman, 1978). The teacher is looking for evidence that the students are using reading strategies that focus on comprehension. The teacher becomes aware of the materials students are reading by observing the self-selection process, the students' reading in class, and by checking their file cards.

The teacher monitors the students' progress during the personalized reading conferences. On some occasions, the student and teacher can follow the miscue analysis procedures (Goodman and Burke, 1973). Even on an informal basis, the teacher now has a description of the students' reading strategies. This information is used by the teacher when forming a small group of students with a specific problem for a reading strategy lesson.

Although this is a *personalized* reading program, there are many opportunities for the students to discuss and share the excitement of their reading experiences. Students form small groups in different parts of the classroom. Each reader chooses a selection from his or her file card and discusses this material with the group members. Another method involves groups of students who have read the same kind of novel such as a mystery or an adventure story. Class members who have read the same story during the course of the year can form a group and discuss this book. Art displays provide another means for students to express their reactions to their reading materials. Coody and Nelson (1982) offer many creative suggestions for integrating art and reading.

In a multicultural community, teachers encounter children with a variety of backgrounds and interests. A personalized reading program based on a sound rationale is a successful means for helping these students develop as readers.

# Engaging Students in Reading

CANDY CARTER
*(United States)*

When I first began teaching in the late '60s, the cry in the United States was "Johnny can't read," and this, in turn, spawned countless reading programs, some based on old-fashioned phonics, others on programmed learning, still others on comprehension drills. All were presented as "sure cures," and all attempted to create order out of chaos. The fact that nearly all reading programs were not the panaceas they purported to be is not the issue; very few of the materials took into account the desirability of presenting students with good literature while at the same time improving their reading skills. When small children eagerly start school and want to learn to read, they aren't simply thinking of the cereal box. Rather, they want to break the secret code; they want to enter into the adult world of books.

In the U.S., the reading hysteria has died down. Students were performing better on measurements of reading competence through standardized tests (and, by the way, the reading programs were excellent at improving test savvy). Then the writing hysteria took over. Students supposedly couldn't express themselves on paper, probably as a result of all the multiple-choice answers on the reading programs! New approaches to the improved teaching of writing were developed by writing projects throughout the nation. Students wrote and revised and rewrote and proofread and critiqued—essays, stories, poetry, letters, journals.

However, in spite of all the good done by the writing projects, one frightening trend surfaced. Literature was still on the back burner. Students were writing more and writing better, but teachers were forgetting to give them something to write about. Whole senior classes were leaving high school saying, "Moby Who? The Scarlet What? MacWhosis?"

No one, not even the most seriously deficient reader, should be denied the opportunity to be exposed to good works of literature. If a student can't handle the vocabulary level, the teacher can put the book on tape; there is no shame in being read to. For a teacher to take it upon himself or herself that a student is too "slow" a reader to be given a chance to tackle a good book is a serious disservice to another human being. Literature, like everything else in school, must be taught with joy. True, the remedial reader cannot be handed *Huckleberry Finn* and told: "Here, this is a good book and you should read it. Take the test in two weeks." But that student could be told, "This is a book written over 100 years ago about a kid a lot like you, who didn't like school and probably doesn't read much. But he had wisdom beyond his years like you do. Let's experience this together."

In my class, I commit what some teachers would call a heresy, because I tell students *not* to look up every word, to skip things that are dull for them. If I were teaching dedicated English majors, or even honors seniors, that would be one thing. But I'm not. I have a mixed group of 13-year-olds, and I just want to make readers out of them. I want them to understand the difference between trashy pleasure reading and good literature, and to know the place of both in our book culture.

To accomplish these goals, I do a lot of work on "speed" reading, learning how to skim, pinpoint ideas, and draw conclusions. Try this experiment. Pick out a page from a difficult piece of literature. (I use the paragraph about Oliver's request for "More" in *Oliver Twist.*) I have students quickly read the passage without benefit of dictionary and write down the basic story line of that incident. Next they identify five or so words that they don't understand or know. Then they look up the five words in the dictionary and write down the definitions. Now, do the students have a significantly better understanding of the passage? Probably not, and probably their first impression was correct. My message: "Be comfortable with ambiguity. You do not have to understand every word."

I also don't discourage students from reading "trash." English teachers have a real obsession with good books, but every one of us probably reads some form of trash—bad science fiction, obvious romances, corny mysteries. The key comes in helping students learn the difference between trash and lasting literature and understand the place of both. One way I accomplish this in my eighth-grade class is to have an independent novels unit that lasts four weeks, during which students must read 500 pages from a prescribed reading list. Reading lists are abundant; most local libraries have them. Students must complete a review sheet on the book and must have a conference with me on each book they read. For a conference, the student brings the book to me, and, after flipping through the pages and identifying major characters, I ask questions about the book. This is a good opportunity to get to know my students through books.

During this independent novels unit, I also show videotapes of films based on books on the list—*The Three Musketeers, A Tale of Two Cities,* and *The Count of Monte Cristo,* to name a few. A teacher may say, "Well, after they've seen the film, they won't want to read the book!" or, "They'll try to fake a book report based on the movie." However, many students do want to read the book, and the rest will at least know who D'Artagnan, Edward Dantes, and Sidney Carton are. Also, teachers can always say, as I do, "I know all the tricky questions to ask to see that you aren't just going by the film."

Why is it important that all students, from the most gifted to the least academic, be exposed to good literature? Literature gives us something in common with others, a heritage, if you will. Recently, a group of teachers from my school district met to adopt literature texts for our students. We were a diverse group, different in age, sex, race, political leanings, social backgrounds, geographic upbringing, and even in educational level. Not all of us were English majors. Yet as we looked through those books, we had something in common. "Oh, I remember that story!" "Oh great, this book has *Romeo and Juliet!*" "I memorized that poem in the eighth grade!" Suddenly, the conversation flowed. We had all shared those pieces of literature, and it gave us a connection with one another that transcended our school association. Some might say that in our pluralistic American society such connections are neither attainable or desirable. My own view is that the variety in people just makes our literary base richer. This rich literature will in turn bring us together and help us to realize that in spite of our differences, we all feel and want the same things.

Literature takes work, too, and that's another aspect of the teaching of reading that has been neglected. Somehow in the last decade or so, American teachers got stuck on the idea that students had to "like" everything, not realizing that part of our job was to help them like it. Where in my teaching credential does it say that my students can and should like everything? I have come to the point that I would rather have them grapple with a concept and enjoy a work of literature upon completion than experience perpetual pleasure with unsubstantial material. Reading difficult literature, if nothing else, teaches students to use their minds and to feel a sense of pride and accomplishment in that task.

In spite of what sometimes appears to be overwhelming indifference, our students, too, realize the value of "hard books." They may make you drag them kicking and screaming through *Hamlet,* but when all is said and one, they'll recite 20-line soliloquys with feeling (and never forget the verse for the rest of their lives), and write with understanding and sympathy for a young man who, like themselves at times, feels out of joint with the world. One of my remedial students expressed this desire to read in the following "letter to myself,"

> Dear Gary,
> I don't know how to understand what I reed after I'm doen.
> I dont know the big words like habitat and words like that.
> I would like to know how to reed Big words and to reed big
> books like smart people do.
> I wood like to reed fast as a normal person.
> I wood like to have a stack of fifty books that I have read in the
> past.

My hope is that now that Johnny and Jane can read and write, or at least now that the hysteria is directed elsewhere, we will return to literature as a part of our human heritage. Perhaps it is my own hysteria when I say that we seem to have lost our literary commonality. Our world is on the brink of a disaster as great as a nuclear holocaust because we have lost our sense of contact with others. We risk becoming isolated, and, with isolation, all communication stops. In his message, "Welcome to the English Department," Stanford University English department head Robert Polhemus (1981) summed up the importance of literature in the world:

> Reading imaginative literature . . . can and should give you speaking mirrors where you can find a self and a world given new clarity and an articulate voice. . . . Literature can make you see and even feel the drama, joy, horror, and intense reality of other beings not yourself . . . you'll find your deepest soul touched and defined, you'll sense an explosion of meaning in yourself, and you'll better know your own humanity and what it might signify. There could be no better educational purpose or experience.

# Reading in the Secondary English Classroom

SHAUNA O'CONNOR

*(Australia)*

It is extremely valuable for English teachers to stop, now and then, and take stock of what they are doing. This has recently been a worthwhile exercise for me. What I do with my students from Year 8 to matriculation is a reflection of my underlying principles, either articulated or subconsciously held. At the same time, activities which I used to engage in but no longer do, or activities which I've started doing in my classes but didn't do before, are pointers to changes or developments in principles, aims, and values over my years of teaching. In some instances I have found that I continue to share particular activities with my students, but after this evaluation process I hope I now know why I believe they are worthwhile experiences in my classes.

I am indebted to Dennis Lawton (1973, p. 11) for sharpening my awareness of the points made in my opening paragraph. He writes: "Questions about the content of the curriculum are surprisingly rare even in informed discussions of education. Although the efficiency of various *methods* are [sic] often called into question, the assumption is often made that if something has been taught for a number of years by schools it must inevitably remain on the timetable."

When I first started teaching in 1962, my senior expected me to take a lesson for each arbitrary division of the English curriculum. It was to be set out in my programme as a methodical, systematic approach to cover fairly and regularly all aspects of English. This approach was strongly reinforced by the fact that all my own schooling and tertiary training had been thus subdivided and categorised. I would ask students to read aloud around the room, with my own oral reading interspersed; stop and explain "hard" words; or ask questions to gauge attention and "comprehension." Weaker readers were cut short after a lot of assistance from me to get through a few sentences. In a hazy way, I was aware that oral reading gave some indication of a student's reading competence, and I thought every student should have the chance to demonstrate this, even when it held up the smooth flow of the story. I confidently used novels and short stories as the main (often only) reading material. Like most of the population I had been accustomed (by the school system, I think) to regard "reading" as synonymous with "reading fiction."

The class and I read "the novel" as an isolated experience, mainly because I saw this activity as a separate aspect of a range of discrete areas covered by the subject "English." After the reading, I usually required a piece of writing, typically a review or summary of the whole or specific parts of the story. I confess I was taught that way! I remember my intermediate English teacher dictating summaries of the chapters of *Kidnapped,* so that we could use them for revision purposes before the examination. In my own teaching, I thought that an accurate summary was a sure indication of comprehension of the material read. In many cases, it may have been—but it treated reading fiction as a mechanical study, with emphasis on content comprehension rather than concept grasp/development and enjoyment of the many facets of a literature encounter. I felt no compunction about giving headings such as "characters," "plot," and "setting" for notes about the book read. This was tied up with ideas about total comprehension of the book by analytical methods. I insisted, especially in reading aloud, on word accuracy, and, in silent reading, on reading every bit of the story. I thought that good readers read every word and that comprehension depended on total word intake. I thought reading was about getting meaning from the actual words on the page, and that students should be required to look up all unfamiliar words in the dictionary.

These practices probably sound familiar to English teachers of my era. Obviously for some secondary students, they are limiting rather than directly damaging. But I suspect those students are ones who like me had other rich experiences of literature and the reading process beyond the classroom activities. To bring some of the rewards and constant delights of reading to more and more of the students, my practices have been modified over the years. I have been influenced by the accumulating publications in the areas of understanding the reading process, response to literature, shared book experience, teachers as models of reading behaviour and so on.

So, for my first principle:

*Reading is not an isolated language activity*—nor is writing or listening. If the language arts are to flourish, they must grow together. They need each other and they must be seen to be interrelated by the students as well as the teachers. I now take a book or language issue as the basis for reading/writing/discussion/performance, arising out of the original shared language experience.

A unit of work I teach at Year-10 level, centred on Steinbeck's *The Pearl,* begins with my telling a fable to the group seated on the floor. We discuss the concepts of "story" and "fable" and swap yarns. I then read the short introductory piece from the book and talk about the kind of language used there—its suggestions and implications for what is to follow. The students have the opportunity to complete a first reading right through, after which I ask them to record their immediate reactions and responses.

We then return to Chapter 1 and progress in a leisurely fashion through the book with time for reflection—orally, silently, in writing of various kinds, and in drawing. I read part of the story aloud, of course. The students' workbooks at the end of our study contain: those first comments and questions with personal comparisons and anecdotes; a "Song of the Family," which ends on a discordant note with some suggestion of the scorpion's sting and the doctor's indifference; a sketch of village life; a list (with comments) of "ominous images" from Chapter 2; the results of a pair-discussion of the visions Kino saw in the pearl. On the board, each pair has quickly drawn its "vision" radiating out from my hastily drawn pearl; a written answer to the questions: "When, in Chapter 3, do you begin to feel the evil of the pearl? How has this evil developed by the end of the chapter?" At this point, we experiment with mime and create tableaux of scenes in Chapter 4. When Chapter 5 has been reread, I ask the students to write as a first-person reflection either Juana's or Kino's feelings at a point in the chapter that they can select; at the end of Chapter 6, we discuss the tragic aspects of the story and the nature of tragedy in general. The final exercise involves looking at the ballad form, reading and discussing some examples, and then each of us composing our own "Ballad of The Pearl." I usually complete most of the exercises I ask of my students, so I, too, attempt ballad writing on the board to model the composing process. However, I have yet to complete my own ballad, since I am on urgent call for the budding balladists in my class who eagerly seek help with rhyme, rhythm, and structure. I am always impressed by the quality of the poetry produced, often mirroring the mood, themes, and even style of the book studied.

I allow for a lot of silent reading time, but also do a fair bit of reading aloud to the whole class group. During silent, sustained reading time, I read too.

*Reading is both an individual and a social experience.* I want the delightful book-sharing experience of beginning reading to continue into the secondary school. I am sad that the "TV generation" misses out on a lot because if a book doesn't "grab" them in the first few pages, they "change channels" and dismiss it as "boring." My oral (and dramatic) reading is a bridge between initial contact with the book and personal involvement in it. I never cease to be thankful that my father, who otherwise took very little part in our daily routine as young children, did spend lots of time reading to my brother and me. I'm sure it had a profound effect on my later development of reading interests, love of words, curiosity about words, word games, etc. It also biased me in favour of reading aloud for dramatic effect. I still have a very old, dull-looking poetry book which I got out of my grandmother's bookshelf when I was still in primary school. I must have used it to practise reading aloud from, as I have written in red ink beside some of the poems such instructions as, "To be read aloud, with atmosphere!"

I like reading aloud to groups of students, and only once in 11 years at my present school have I heard a student object to my reading aloud to a class. Other English teachers here have been been begged to continue reading aloud—and not only by "poor" readers either. Almost any book or story can be read aloud effectively, given the right situation and context.

*Periods of sustained silent reading give students the chance to get involved in reading.* When I think back over some of the most pleasant lessons I have experienced as a teacher, my mind usually lingers over the memory of those times, usually in winter, when I and a class have sat quietly through a 40-minute period—with the classroom lights on, the gas heater hissing out its warmth from the corner of the room, rain gently falling outside, and interesting books having their pages quietly turned by absorbed readers.

On most of those occasions the books have been part of an extension reading programme after we have, as a group, read together and discussed, and perhaps written about, one of the novels in a class set. Sometimes it has been a "free choice" of any library book for subsequent reviews. Stifling my initial guilt feelings about not "teaching" in those lessons, I, too, have settled down to some of my own personal reading, more often than not using it as a chance to read more of the children's literature in our school library. In the circumstances I am recalling, there was always an enviable hush over the whole room, and a sigh of disappointment when the inevitable bell rang. There was usually, then, some discussion amongst us, quite informal and rather animated, about the things we had just taken in. I would also find myself halfway through yet another book to add to the pile by my reading lamp at home, to be finished at the earliest opportunity.

I am sure such lengthy periods of quiet, involved reading are a prominent part of many an English teacher's programme in secondary schools, and have been so over the years, under a variety of names, such as "free-reading time," "library lesson," or "reading for pleasure." (Why else?) Since 1970, such delightful periods of real reading have become elaborately entitled "uninterrupted sustained silent reading" or some variation of that theme. The activity has been legitimised and I now see that I was right to stifle my feelings of guilt! To encourage a wider concept of reading, I let students use the library freely, read reference books, newspapers, magazines, comics, handbooks, posters, other children's writing, in fact any printed material. We talk about preferences and reasons for them, and I facilitate sharing of material so that students can meet new kinds of reading.

*Reading is a wider activity than just reading fiction. Discrimination and taste are developed by a wide experience of different kinds of reading material, of good and poor quality.* My class and I often "workshop" some of the situations/ideas in the novel, through improvised drama, before or during the shared-reading experience. We talk about personal experiences similar to those in the novel. I use films, related excursions, visits from writers, student-produced games and charts, and illustrations to link the novel with the readers' own reality.

*Reading flows from the rich experience of life.* And where the wider experience (either actual or literary) has not been rich, I want to provide something to give students some awareness of the connections between life and literature, some concept of the significance of creative, imaginative language in human experience.

*Reading extends interests and opinions.* The reading of a book can open up all sorts of areas of enquiry, research, activity, reconstructions by, for example, dramatisation, retelling from a different viewpoint, illustrating, and so on. I try to provide a wide range of follow-up activities to the reading of a book, including the obvious one of reading some more—by the same author, or on similar themes, or contrasting in style or theme or time. Students, too, suggest possible extension activities. I believe these follow-ups also demonstrate a grasp of the meaning of the reading and do so in a creative, productive extension of experience and thought. I still discuss with the class, small groups or individuals, different aspects of a book, such as the traditional "setting," "characters," "style," "themes." I encourage them to try their hand at writing in similar forms.

*Shared awareness of the structure of "story" facilitates comprehension of subsequent reading matter.* I hope this is a further extension of the way beginning readers build up predictions about "story" and talk about aspects of a book. I don't think analysis need be destructive. Greater understanding of parts can add to the enjoyment of the whole, which can still be viewed as more than the sum of its parts.

I want secondary students to realize that:

*Reading rates vary according to the purpose for reading,* and provided meaning is made from the material, there is no crime involved in skimming over irrelevant (for the required purpose) matter. In fact, survival in our society demands such discriminatory reading and it is part of normal, everyday information seeking—we don't read the telephone book from page 1 each time we make a phone call—as well as being one of the strategies of the "good" reader. I have now had it demonstrated to me that even I, who thought I was such an "accurate" reader do not, in fact could not, look at each word and still read as rapidly as I do.

*Reading strategies which emphasize meaning in context are more valuable than those which concentrate on single-word accuracy.* It is a valuable exercise for teachers (and students, too, I believe) to reflect on how we have built up our "meanings" for particular words. The importance of growing familiarity in context should be recognised. Why should a method which worked so well when we were first learning language be denied our students in school? Why should they be asked to stop reading and "look it up" as soon as they meet a new word, when very often if they went on reading, the context would make the meaning plain?

I discuss judicious skimming, scanning, and occasionally skipping where necessary, and talk about ways to cope with unfamiliar words, with emphasis on the use of context as the major cue for the meaning of individual words.

*Reading improves reading strategies.* I do all things possible to keep students reading. The "poor" reader is in a dreadful bind—he doesn't want to read because it is a failing situation and hence to be avoided; yet one of the surest ways to improve reading is to read. It is my task  then to encourage reading so that the vicious circle can be broken. It is a very difficult task. Any teacher involved in reading teaching is constantly aware that she or he often fails to really help the "poor" reader, and that there is no sure-fire way to "teach" someone to read. The secondary teacher is even more aware of entrenched negative attitudes towards reading and lack of understanding of the reading process—in both students and teachers! One of the biggest stumbling blocks is the assumption amongst secondary teachers that their students have been taught all there is to know about reading and how to read—or, if they haven't, the English teacher can patch up the gaps. When one remembers that the primary teacher was responsible for teaching a wide range of academic "subjects," one ought to be a little wary of assuming that the teaching of reading can be the province of one area of the secondary curriculum.

This is obviously a limited assessment of my current position, but I hope such self-evaluation will continue to be part of my teaching programme as I come to understand more about the process of reading and the multitude of activities which can foster its development in the secondary English classroom.

# English and Reading in the New Media

JO-ANNE EVERINGHAM
*(Australia)*

Television presents a challenging new medium which students must learn to "read." Typical teacher concerns which prompt them to start teaching about television include: "It occupies such a large part of students' life . . . more hours spent viewing than spent at school!" "Their viewing is so passive!" "They believe the world is really like what they see on TV!"

I wanted an approach which would respond to these concerns without denying my students' worth or tastes. Consequently, my first aim in teaching about television has been to develop the ability to "read" television by developing the ability to view differently. One very literal way of doing this is to show edited one-minute segments of a range of programs and note how much small and incomplete bits tell us. This is an awareness-raising exercise—particularly awareness of alternatives. Students have already seen thousands of hours of television; I don't need to show them more of the same. My role is to make them *do* something with their viewing by setting up questions about their experiences, encouraging reasoned points of view, and negotiating tasks or inquiries with them.

This year my students' favourite television programs were *A Country Practice* and *Sons and Daughters*—both Australian-produced serials that I would classify as soap operas. We decided to use these two programs as the basis for some of our media studies work. Our aims were:

1. To recognise some of the technical, organisational, social, economic, and political *motivations, controls, and constraints* on serial production teams.
2. To identify and interpret the variety of *techniques* used to create television serials.
3. To identify the *ideas, values, and customs* portrayed in those soap operas and conveyed by them.
4. To recognise how *audiences* engage in the process of interpreting television serials.

We explored production constraints using the finished product and anecdotal material from actors and producers. Relatively easy simulation or production exercises allowed the students to experience many of the limitations themselves. We started observing with a viewing checklist in which students kept records of studio and external sets as well as regular and "guest" characters. Students were allotted simple tallying and noting tasks. After pooling the class information from school and home viewed episodes, we made a simple exercise of "statistical analysis" ("What things are the same for each program?" "What are the differences?" "What patterns do you notice?"). These allowed a number of generalisations to be made:

- The number of guest characters is low and about the same for each program.
- There are many more indoor scenes than outdoor ones.
- There are some sets used in all of the programs, and the number of studio sets is about the same for each program.
- The amount of time outdoors is very similar for each program and so is the number of external locations.

These answers helped us pose our first key question: Why did these patterns or limits exist? Was it just because the story went "that way"? Students suggested time and cost as constraining factors. This was reinforced by the document "Guidelines for Scriptwriters" provided by one production house and a storyline editor's article from a popular women's magazine describing her job. Finally we acted out a simulation of the recording of one scene with students in various production roles. I had them face such last-minute constraints as: an actor is ill and not available for this scene; the wombat cannot be induced to wake up and walk around as required.

By involving the production crew, we effectively raised a second question: "How is a program put together?" We viewed a film outlining various production tasks ("The People Behind *The Sullivans*"), then viewed again part of one study episode, while each student detailed the contribution of one particular crew member to the scene (for example: the makeup person). The emphasis was on the deliberate selections these people make. To the same end—namely deconstruction or reversal of the production process—we drew up a storyboard by asking: "What was this section's storyline?" "What pictures were used to show that?" "Why were those images the ones chosen and not some of the possible alternatives?"

While I want my students to realise that the narrative is shaped by filmic conventions, such as camera shots, angles, and editing, and I want to demystify some of the technical tricks of the television trade, I don't want this to degenerate into "spotting the edit"—the old "spot the simile" trap of poetry dissection days. I tend to approach the concept of visual, verbal, and sound codes by examining traditional narrative conventions—familiar ground to an English teacher—*setting, character, conflict,* and *resolution.* Here's where the freeze-frame and fast-forward buttons on our videotape player really aid us in viewing differently. We note the everyday settings which are nevertheless visually interesting for the viewer; the frequent changes of setting to give variety; the use of changes of film shots to add variety; the means of establishing characters and their relationship to one another (e.g., dinner table shots); which characters we like or dislike, why, and whether this is fairly commonly agreed among class members; any characters who seem to do the wrong thing all the time; the tendency to have only two to four characters on the screen at once. We view the scene before each ad break to see the establishment of conflict; we switch the sound off and choose the most attention-holding pictures; we find out if the people *show* their feelings or *talk* about them; we turn the pictures dark and notice how there's a lot of talking, but each person's language is brief and conversational; we compare the contributions made to the story by sound and pictures; we listen for sound that's not part of the story (music, for instance) and discuss why we accept that and what its effect is; we view an edited version with segments jumbled and try to work out the sequence; we view initial and later scenes of a story and guess what came in between. Quite a game can be made of these exercises, and a *lot* of teacher effort goes into preparing cues for the videotape! There are also many opportunities in examining television production techniques to compare with our techniques in writing: "showing" rather than "telling"; the emphasis on the dramatic; the choice of ways to begin and end; adopting a point of view for telling a story; using dialogue to carry the story forward and reveal character. We can even ask if students experience their writing visually (that is, see it in their minds before they describe it in words).

During this examination of technique, some of the students' observations are often about how many choices are made to convey a certain meaning. This is the third important question: "What are the prevailing messages of the program, especially those about our society? This is an area of difficulty for secondary students, and I find it helpful to create a checklist in which they examine behaviour of the television world to compare with the real world. This often reveals some startling biases which students find hard to accept if they are simply *told* them. For example: 60 percent of male characters in soap operas are represented as doctors, lawyers, businessmen—only five percent of females perform such roles—while 62 percent of females are nurses, secretaries, and housewives. This leads to questions of stereotyping: messages about women, rich people, employers, and family relationships were all contained in our study episode of *Sons and Daughters*. *A Country Practice* is very interesting to study with respect to stereotypes as the program directors have chosen to challenge some stereotypes by having a male nurse, a female vet, and one couple living an alternative lifestyle. The producers of this serial also publicise the fact that they deliberately select social issues to represent in the programs (like anorexia nirvosa and alcohol abuse). This is known by the students and is a convenient, explicit acknowledgment of the social comment which is implicit in all serials.

The fourth area we investigated concerned audiences. In our exploration of this, we broadened from our focal serials to consider the television genre as a whole. We worked with program guides to find answers to such questions as: "What kinds of programs appear on television? Which types are most common on both commercial and national stations? What is the mix of drama, comedy, sports, news, children's, educational, religious, cultural, current affairs, documentary and informational programs? At what times are various programs screened? At what kinds of audiences are these types of programs directed? What products are advertised during the programs? We reinforced our findings by playing a version of the board game *Commercial Break* (Munro, 1982). The final question for us as audience and students can then be posed: Do we *notice* all we've been studying as we view? Why not?

There have been many doubts about television expressed by educators. One is that the language of the medium tends to be glib, rehearsed, and planned with little room for tentativeness or hesitation. There is concern for the predictability of speech in given situations and devaluing of language by using words to repeat rather than supplement visuals which results in viewers paying less attention to the words. These are the sorts of fears held by Marie Winn who claims that television is taking us away from verbal or language ways of thinking and encouraging nonverbal, nonlanguage ways of thinking. However, other writers have spelled out the language character of the medium in more detail and in ways that are familiar to English teachers who have come to terms with linguistic codes in children's talking and writing since the accusations of Bernstein.

Grant Noble claims that television is in the "restricted code" but that it therefore provides greater communication possibilities by serving as a common symbolic structure and facilitating interpersonal speech. Fiske and Hartley (1978) develop this Bernsteinian notion further. They distinguish between *oral* and *literate* modes of communication with these characteristics:

| *Oral modes* | *Literate modes* |
|---|---|
| dramatic | narrative |
| episodic | sequential |
| mosaic | linear |
| dynamic | static |
| active | artifact |

| *Oral modes* | *Literate modes* |
|---|---|
| concrete | abstract |
| ephemeral | permanent |
| social | individual |
| metaphorical | metonymic |
| rhetorical | logical |
| dialectical | univocal/"consistent" |

These writers argue that television discourse by nature of the medium is an oral mode. However, most of its program makers are deeply committed to literate modes so these play a strong part in the final form of television culture as well: "TV is the first and so far the only medium which has institutionalised the interdependence" of oral and literate modes.

This clearly indicates that television provides unique texts for language study and analysis. The conflict or tension is *within* the medium, not between it and the literate values we English teachers hold dear.

# Introducing Poetry

JEAN BLUNT
*(England)*

Something happens to classroom English when our pupils move from third to fourth year in the secondary school—roughly ages 14 and 15. The freedom and fluidity allowed through looking at interrelated topics is suddenly lost. There was a time when pupils could confidently offer their own asides, opinions, irrelevancies, as the minutes ticked away. What wasn't finished one lesson might be worth remembering in the next, or perhaps some other story might be worth the telling. By the fourth year, this becomes extravagance. In the British schools, there are texts to read, essays to be written. The brighter children should now have acquired a mature response to reading. It must have happened during the summer vacation when they were 14 and threw away their bikes and *The Secret Diary of Adrian Mole,* and picked up boyfriends, girlfriends, and *Cider with Rosie.*

But it doesn't really happen like that, does it? It has occurred to me that we expect too much from not just our reluctant readers but our brightest and keenest ones, too. In England, they need to be helped towards this maturing response to the literary works which examining boards have chosen for them. I have found that an awareness of all the psychological elements called into play during the reading process has helped me to help teenage pupils to read more responsively.

Teaching poetry is perhaps the most difficult area. Yet a poem is a piece of fiction and we read it as a representation of events, feelings, interactions. Wouldn't a knowledge of D. W. Harding (1962) on what happens in a mature reader's head as he engages with a work of fiction help me to encourage young people to not just appreciate a good poem but also like it?

A fundamental truth has first to be recognised. Poetry usually has very low status in teenagers' values. "Dipping into" the set poetry book and rapidly reading half a dozen poems from the first section does more harm than good. That first meeting with the first chosen poem is so important. It is worth being well prepared. Readers have to be *invited* to the event. Harding (1962) has told us of the vital importance of the role of the spectator. Students have to spectate willingly at something relevant and interesting. The scene for the early poetry readings needs to be carefully arranged. Adolescents, even the brightest, need to be enticed to participate in the show. I think a poem should take them by surprise.

Before reading "Street Accident" by Richard Church, the members of the class were invited to recall their own experiences of traffic accidents. One or two had been directly involved. A girl remembered being knocked from her bicycle and not wanting to tell anyone her address. She felt people around her were intruding and wanted them to go away. Others talked about accidents they had seen and the curiosity they had felt as they passed by. Then I read a newspaper report of a recent fatal traffic accident. It had happened a short distance from the school and some students had known the victims. Only after we had talked for 20 minutes or so did I read the poem. They did not know it was coming. They listened without looking at the text, then asked to hear the poem again. There was evidence here that they were "attending willingly." They then wrote down their immediate direct responses, whatever came into their heads. The first jottings about that first poem were the beginnings of the appreciation which I was able to help them shape up. Their own first reactions were valid and they were to be made to feel that. Looking through their notes, I found that all the elements of the full response were there, though perhaps crudely. There was elementary understanding. One writer imagined the scene vividly enough:

> Poem about a road accident. A stretcher, a battered figure, age, sex, uncertain. Ambulancemen like vultures over a carcass. A blanket. Another person, pale, shocked, head in hands. Who is it? Nobody knows. Companion of the victim? Lover? Thrown together by this twist of fate? Nobody appears to be talking to

them, yet there are plenty of people around. A crowd had gathered like ghouls on Halloween.

There was empathy also:

> To me the poem was very distressing. It makes me realise how awful a road accident can be. Everybody going past and having a good look, not thinking about stopping to ask if they could help, just having a good look, standing there like "posers" looking down on the bleeding body. I wouldn't like to be stared at.

There was also some evaluation of what those present at the scene did. There were opinions expressed and measured against what they imagined their reactions might be:

> The poem left me feeling quiet within myself. It was a good poem because it made me think about things I take for granted and how even though we watch and stare at such accidents we're often glad it's not us.

There was even some evidence of readers seeing the poem as an artifact created to comment on human experience:

> It is a powerful poem, depicting a typical road accident in a style which "puts you in the crowd," watching the events. It tells of reactions to events, how people act under pressure, how would *you* react?

These first half-formulated comments were highly personal. The students had not been told how to react, what to look for, what to like or dislike. Their reactions were fresh and very close to the full response. Some needed to see the work as a highly crafted piece telling us more about the human condition. Yet they had already perceived this. Setting the scene for the poem had, I think, been well worth the precious minutes it had taken. I read with interest the comments of the girl who had been knocked from her bicycle, and I realised she had measured the ideas and images of the poem against her own experiences and appreciated it all the more.

> The victims are described as being isolated in grief, as if nobody in the crowd gathered around can come in contact or understand the kind of sorrow and pain that the people involved are feeling—
> No touch is felt, no coaxing word
> From the outside world is heard.

Foisting poems on teenage readers is a difficult business. Teachers of English have somehow to lure the readers into wanting to read them. Without this willingness, a superficial, half-hearted response will result. Opening up the subjects of the poems before they are read seems to me to be the best way of introducing other people's choices. I think it is worth the time and trouble.

I introduced Peter Chamkin's "A Modern Hero" with an examination of desk graffiti. Did it mean anything to anyone? Did anyone know the "artists"? Or was it just a vain attempt to be noticed, remembered? "Nowhere Man" (Lennon and McCartney) was played and discussed before the poem was read.

For "The Horses" by Edwin Muir, we read a little about James Herriot's "glorious draught horses emanating their almost tangible vitality and power." I told the class about Edwin Muir's love of the land and his boyhood memories of working horses. What did they remember from their childhood? If forgotten treasures were to reappear, wouldn't they seem all the more precious? In considering their responses, they may have been helped to a fuller appreciation of such powerful lines as:

> Now they were strange to us
> As fabulous steeds set on an ancient shield
> Or illustrations in a book of knights.

The first responses were expanded, rewritten, embellished, and final essays were produced. I was pleased to see that first reactions were included and then modified. Even in the writing of the commentary, the response was growing:

> When the poet first mentions the strange horses the reader is inclined to think that they are some kind of horse with five legs or mutants created by the war. They frighten and mystify. But a lost ancient companionship between man and horse slowly brings them back together again.

From humble beginnings, the response was growing and, though awkwardly expressed, this 15-year-old saw the poem as something like a conversation full of attitudes and assessments for the reader to consider.

> The poem returns the survivors to nature—a sideways glance at the writer's hopes? Are there memories from his childhood love of his home-island farm animals? The poem is not so much about war and how man will destroy himself but more about a way of life which has been lost.

The method of introducing a poem to adolescent readers, then, may critically affect its appreciation. A cursory reading and a later analysis, I believe, is inconsiderate to both poet and reader. For the sakes of young readers, a great deal more care and some understanding about what might be going on inside their heads is needed.

# Making Evaluative Responses to Literature Through Imaginative Writing

PETER ADAMS

*(Australia)*

Stories are only stories when they are moving and acting in the imagination. . . . (Jones and Buttrey, 1970)

Earlier this year, my Year-10 students read Robert O'Brien's *Z for Zachariah*. Their responses to the novel were immediate and powerful: they were outraged by Mr. Loomis, whose behaviour towards Ann affronted all their conceptions of ordinary decency and gratitude. They were puzzled to account for his actions. "Is he mad?" they asked. "Has his mind been affected by the radiation sickness?" Their sympathies largely lay with Ann, of course; yet there were times during the novel when they were sharply critical of her, too—critical of her fearfulness, her passivity, her willingness to enslave herself.

When they reached the end of the book, they were divided in their opinion of Ann's decision to leave the valley, just as they were divided over whether Ann should have taken the risk of speaking to Mr. Loomis for the last time before her departure. Some thought Ann should have fought to stay in "her" valley; others, while understanding why she felt she had to face Mr. Loomis, found her determination foolhardy rather than courageous. As for Mr. Loomis, while they conceded the magnitude of the sacrifice he made in letting Ann go, they were curiously unmoved by it. "Too little, too late," someone remarked, "and in any case, he's going to revert to type as soon as she's gone." They hoped Ann would find the birds Mr. Loomis pointed out to her and the valley with a schoolroom full of children waiting for her to begin teaching them, but no one felt very confident that this would happen.

These sorts of remarks, arising out of the buzz of lively, untidy, and sometimes heated discussion generated by the book, clearly represent evaluative responses to some aspects of the novel. But they are *ad hoc,* immediate, and provisional responses—rather like the kinds of comments one might expect to find in a response journal (Jackson, 1980; Brown, 1982; Brown et al., 1983), embedded among the speculations, memories, private associations, and reflections that together make up students' running commentary upon their reading. While one might expect some of these responses to be modified by further reflection (and we need to provide the opportunities for that to occur), there are other responses, especially those which involve "reading against the grain" of the novel, which we would expect to be confirmed and extended by further thought. Yet these responses, the ones that call into question some of the novel's implicit valuations of the experience it presents, are precisely the ones we don't give our students a great deal of help in exploring and articulating. For many of my Year-10 students, the ending of Z for Zachariah was especially problematical:

> Now it is morning. I do not know where I am. I walked all afternoon and almost all night until I was so tired I could not go on. Then I did not bother to put up the tent, just spread my blanket by the roadside and lay down. While I was sleeping the dream came, and in the dream I walked until I found the schoolroom and the children. When I awoke the sun was high in the sky. A stream was flowing through the brown grass, winding west. The dream was gone, yet I knew which way to go. As I walk I search the horizon for a trace of green. I am hopeful. (O'Brien, 1976)

In the absence of any qualifying irony, it seems as if Ann's optimism has the novel's weight behind it. What difference, then, does it make to your sense of the novel, if you find you don't share Ann's hopefulness, as most of my students didn't? The novel ends with an affirmation—if you reject it, what is there left here that you can affirm?

To pursue these sorts of questions speculatively, in the abstract, is to invite bewilderment and despondency. But there are other ways in which such matters can be pursued, concretely and specifically. To illustrate what I mean by that, here is the ending of a continuation of Z for Zachariah, written by a 14-year-old boy of average intelligence who nevertheless has quite serious problems with reading (he wouldn't have completed the novel unless a good deal of it had been read to him) and who experiences great difficulty with written work. I have summarized the story up to the point at which the extract begins.

> [Demoralized by the desolation of the world through which she has been traveling, Ann has decided to return to the valley. On the way back, she has accidentally punctured the safesuit and injured herself. Aware that her life is in danger, she makes her way back to the valley in the hope that Mr. Loomis will look after her in her need as she looked after him in his. At the point where we take up the story, Ann has just reached the valley, and, ill and weak from exposure to the radiation, has made her way to her house.]

When I opened the door I saw that Mr. Loomis was not there. I figured he was picking up supplies. I fixed up my cut and lay down in my father's chair. I waited and waited.

Finally I got the strength to go upstairs and look out of the window. From here I could see the whole valley. I got the binoculars that were on the mantelpiece in my room. I got up on my bed and looked out. Firstly I looked at the store. I saw nothing. Then the fields. There was one more place. The corn crop on the side of the hill. A cold shiver went down my spine. I was right. I saw the tractor on its side.

I fell back on my bed.

This is my last entry in my diary. I grew up in the valley and I am pleased I can die in the valley. I hope someone will find my diary and see what we really went through.

I am afraid.

*Sam McClure*

Simple and moving this may be, but in what sense can it be said to represent an *evaluative* response to Robert O'Brien's novel?

We might begin to answer that question by noting that we seem to see this piece of writing from a double perspective. On the one hand, the voice we hear in these words is recognizably Ann Burden's, and we feel that the way in which she meets the extremity of this situation is completely consistent with what we know of her from the novel. On the other hand, we sense a quality of strong personal engagement in this piece of work, and an accompanying seriousness. It is as though, in finding the words in which to imaginatively realize *Ann's* experience, the writer is bringing to definition something that has an intimately personal value *for himself.* Furthermore, the significance upon which he is bent discloses itself to him only insofar as he is able to dramatize *Ann's* consciousness—he could not state that significance for us abstractly or discursively. So, what Ann stands for in the novel, the human potential she represents, is taken not as something given (immutable and essentially outside the writer), but as the means by which he can imaginatively enter into, and make real to himself, something that he values—in this case, a particular kind of response to defeat and the desolation of irrevocable loss.

We might, at first sight, say that what is being affirmed here is a kind of emotional restraint. We notice, for example, that Ann says nothing about her feelings until the very last line—the emphasis has fallen entirely upon actions and physical sensations. Yet the restraint of the utterance is eloquent precisely because we feel that there *is* something there to be held in check. In the second paragraph, for example, Ann's mounting dread, as she begins to guess that Mr. Loomis is *never* coming back to the house, is very powerfully conveyed by the bare, stating manner of the prose. What is *not* said is as telling as what is: reading aloud, we find we have to pause after we say, "Then the fields," and in that pause we hear the silent expiration of Ann's last hope. When she turns to look at the cornfield, it is in the expectation of finding Mr. Loomis dead.

But we are not offered this laconic restraint as a value in itself, as we might be in Hemingway, for instance. These very powerful feelings, of dread and horror and growing despair, are kept under such tight restraint because Ann's whole conscious being is focused upon a single act of attention—to *know* what her fate is. She has, of course, already guessed it, but those feelings which threaten to engulf and overwhelm consciousness are kept at bay until the guess is confirmed, until the worst is known: "I was right. I saw the tractor on its side." When this effort of attention collapses, so does she: "I fell back on my bed."

Yet the diary does not end with Ann's abandonment to feelings of grief and despair. What remains is the need to find some kind of fitness in the ironic pattern that her existence has assumed, *and* the need to bear witness, even in a world in which there may be no one to hear her testimony. And what her diary testifies to, it now appears, is not simply what she uniquely experienced, but "what *we* really went through." She and Mr. Loomis are enfolded in a single vision of mutual suffering. The dance has only led them both to the same end.

All that remains is to acknowledge her vulnerability and fear in the face of death. The rest is silence.

What is being affirmed here is a particular kind of human dignity, or courage, or integrity. The right words are hard to find because what is enacted here is complex and subtle. It is easier to say what it is not than to say what it is. It's not the kind of self-conscious toughness that has its roots in a fundamental distrust of the life of feeling; nor is it the kind of stoic fortitude that springs from philosophical conviction, with all its attendant temptations to a subtle form of egotism. The absence of any consciousness of self as more than an experiencing centre may remind us of some of Lawrence's last poems, such as "Bavarian Gentians" or "The Ship of Death," although Lawrence's undertaking in these poems clearly required a personal courage and disinterestedness that do not apply here.

An *evaluative* response to the novel? Yes, emphatically. It is as if, in this piece of work, the writer were responding to the implicit question, "What am I moved to affirm as a result of my experience of this book?" and the answer that comes is not merely stated but enacted and embodied, discovered in the act of being given form.

# Teaching Dated Junk

JAMES LALLEY
*(United States)*

When I was a young and inexperienced teacher, fresh from graduate school with my tons of neatly typed notes on the New Critics, time lines and charts for the historical background on authors and literary periods, and the texts of novels and poems nearly obscured by the copious notes in the margins, one question from a student would stop me dead in my tracks. I would be discoursing eloquently on the sterility images in "The Hollow Men," flinging an occasional question at a dozing student when some impudent, sarcastic cretin seated in the back of the room would ask the dread question: "Why are we studying this junk anyway?"

The question angered and frustrated me. It angered me because I loved this thing called "literature." It frustrated me because I really didn't know the answer. Or, at least, I didn't have an answer that would make sense to them. It angered me because I was supposed to know all the answers—that was what graduate school had been for. It frustrated me that I couldn't articulate what was so obviously special to me.

All the "close reading," all the "textual analysis," all the tracing of archetypes helped me understand literature, but they weren't what made me love literature. The insights into the self, the glimpses into the souls of others, the hint at the purpose of existence were the *literaria* that touched my soul. The valorous Beowulf, the lusty Wife of Bath, a confused Holden Caulfield, a brooding Marlowe, a rebellious Huck had triggered something in my imagination and had touched my being. Alexander Pope said: "The proper study of mankind is man." The proper focus for the teaching of literature is humanity.

Over the years, the question still surfaces, but now my answer is simple. Literature helps us understand ourselves, others, and the world in which we live. My survey course in British literature always begins with a discussion of the characteristics of "serious literature." This year I had four:

1. *Serious literature says something significant about human nature, values, and the world in which we live.* Beowulf shows us courage, loyalty to friends, and the problems of aging. *Macbeth* stuns our notion of self with its scattering insights into "vaulting ambition" and the abuse of power, and the human's limitless potential for evil.

2. *Serious literature reflects the age and culture that produced it.* Beowulf shows us fifth-century Scandinavian society with its long boats, great wooden mead halls, and warrior society. Chaucer shows us

medieval England with a deeply religious and valiant knight, corrupt clergy, and lusty livers.

3. *Yet serious literature transcends the age and culture that produced it by saying something about the essence of human existence and the world in which we live.* Beowulf is still a human being trying to face his world. The Wife of Bath is still searching for the perfect mate. Huckleberry Finn sorts and challenges the values of the adult world that surrounds him.

4. *Serious literature has a form or literary genre which if we understand it will help us better get in touch with the meaning of the work.* The structure of the sonnet can clue us to understanding. Images and symbols clarify and intensify the meaning of works. Just as any discipline has its own specialized vocabulary, formulas, and techniques, so does literature, and an understanding of them makes comprehension possible and enhances our appreciation.

Let me show you how I approach one piece of "dated junk," *Pride and Prejudice.* (On the student survey at the end of the year, *Pride and Prejudice* ranked high in popularity.) What could Jane Austen teach my 16- and 17-year-old male students about life, about human relations, about what it is to be human?

I begin my instruction on *Pride and Prejudice* with a review of the elements of the narrative form: setting, characters, plot, narrative point of view, and theme. I follow that with a short history of the novel and then focus on the novel of manners, defined as a narrative that has as a major focus the manner, mores, customs, and values of a particular age. The students compare the novel of manners with such movies of manners as *Urban Cowboy* or *Saturday Night Fever.* Both of these rather popular movies offer insights in the customs, values, and attitudes of a particular group of people, yet they were entertaining also because they said something about human beings in these particular social groupings.

As students read the novel, I ask that they do a plot outline, tracing the relationship between various couples. I ask them to look at what values each person holds most dear and the results of living out those values. Students in small groups draw up character sketches of each of the major characters, Elizabeth, Darcy, Bingley, Mr. and Mrs. Bennet, Collins, Charolette, Lydia, Lady Catherine De Bourgh, Georgiana. The character sketches are based on actions, dialogue, and descriptions from the text.

I then show the first two episodes of the PBS production of *Pride and Prejudice.* The dramatization helps students visualize the setting, focus the characters, and appreciate the witty dialogue. Comfort, serene rural settings are new for my city boys. The beauty of the Bennet sisters, the lightheadedness of Mrs. Bennet, the pomposity of Mr. Collins come alive before the student's eyes. Lastly, dialogue, which when read seemed sterile and lifeless, now heard with proper inflection and tone, suddenly strikes the ear as fresh, vital, and clever.

After the viewing, I ask them to compare and contrast their interpretation of the characters with the interpretations as seen in the dramatic production. What a lively discussion that can be. In small groups, we discuss the manners, mores, customs of the period, particularly the courting and marriage customs. Students initially find the customs strange until compared to artificial contemporary situations. Our dances, proms, and parties can be just as artificial as the balls at Meryton. (Boys on one side of the gym talking about girls and girls on the other talking about the boys is still common.) A night spent playing Trivial Pursuit is just as "bizarre" as playing cards all evening. Fashion in clothes and culture is still a perennial topic of conversation.

But what in this book captured their imaginations? What insights into the self, others, and the world did it offer? I'll let my students explain in their own words:

> Elizabeth and Darcy are truly in love. They love each other not because of conventions or false perception only because they encountered difficulties, strove to overcome them, and ultimately because they saw in each other so much of themselves with all their pride and prejudices.

> At first I couldn't understand how Charolette could settle for so little in her life. To sell her happiness for contentment, to trade her independance for a life of material security seemed so foreign to me. Then I thought of my mother. She did the same thing. I wonder what the price of my soul is.

> How could someone as provincial as Jane Austen have such a keen insight into human nature. I have dated everyone of those Bennet sisters. The Elizabeths of my life scare me by their wit and self-assurance. (I still have not adjusted to the feminist movement.) The Kittys are too smart for me. The Lydias are too fast. You know it is much safer meeting these characters in a book than at the "Tulip Trot." Yet if anything, this book showed me that girls are really people.

> My mother is Mrs. Bennet's reincarnation. She talks and talks; my father hides from her; she wants to direct my sisters and my life down to the last detail. Yet just like Mrs. Bennet, she loves her children and that has to count for something.

Over the years, the question about reading this "classical junk" seems to be coming up less frequently. Perhaps teaching literature as human experiences precludes the question.

# Literature and Vision

TREVOR WILLIAMS

*(New Zealand)*

The first requisite on the part of the teacher structuring a litera-ture programme for a class is to have some idea of why he or she wants that book to be read by the class. If the teacher doesn't have that initial reason for introducing the book, then it's very likely that no one in the class will by the time the lessons have finished. A good literature programme, therefore, is a chance to provide perspective as well as pleasure. Careful thought has to be given to the content area so that the various aspects studied in one year knit well together and can be related to the following year's content. Let me explain by way of example.

Here is a scheme on the theme of *vision* for an able class of third formers. In the beginning, there was myth. Using *The God Beneath the Sea* (Garfield and Blishen, 1970) pupils were introduced to myth as the earliest form of literature. While these tales are enjoyable in them-selves, what should also be appreciated is that: myth is a way of seeing, an explanation of the nature of the real world and the nature of per-sonality (for example the story of Cronus or the story of Narcissus); and myth is a way of being—it represents the value system of a culture and delineates the limits of man acting under the gods.

In *The God Beneath the Sea,* pupils can learn to *see* through the tales the world as experienced by the Greeks and their observations on the complexities of human behaviour. "Why are we like we are?" is a question answered in the myth of Pandora. Even a third former can learn to see the peculiar contrast between the shattered, grotesque hulk of Hephaestus and his refined soul and dreams and in that contrast be led to see what the Greeks are saying about the origins of creativity.

Through the myth of Prometheus, a pupil can speculate on man's origin not as the workmanship of a benevolent God, but as a feat of daring and defiance on the part of a rebellious Titan. Man lives despite Zeus, not because of him. In the figure of Prometheus, too, lie the early elements of tragedy—defeat yet triumph, suffering, and knowledge.

The rivalry between Hera and Zeus typifies the eternal male-female struggle. Their rivalry probably has a basis in historical fact (Graves, 1955); perhaps it also describes society's adoption of time reckoned on the sun rather than the moon.

Sustained throughout *The God Beneath the Sea* is the theme of the dream. That theme is, of course, a dominant one in literature—whether we are thinking of the Arthurian legends or Shakespeare's *The Tempest,* Ibsen's *The Wild Duck,* or Hesse's *Demian.* At the end of *The God Beneath the Sea,* Hermes, the god of lies and illusion, the artificer in dreams, turns to Hephaestus, the god's artificer in gold and bronze and, as both of them regard the world, says, "Between you and me, eh? It is always between you and me."

Why that should be so and what can be seen in that statement is worthy of consideration.

Myths, then, are a valuable resource for exercises in creative "seeing." Pupils can learn to see not only how much is in an individual myth, but also how the world can be seen in mythic terms. Peter Smart's book on myths and legends provides further resource material for class exercises. Peter Brueghel's picture of the Tower of Babel provides another interesting perspective on myth that can form a creative writing exercise.

This class went on to read a selection of science fiction and *The Adventures of Sherlock Holmes* as a continuation of the idea that they were learning how to see. Of course this idea of *vision* isn't the be-all and end-all of the study. It provides the glue between the parts. Science fiction was a probe into the future, what Wells called "fantasias of possibility," and Conan Doyle's hero was presented as an expert in observation and deduction. Films, paintings, thinking exercises by De Bono were incorporated to demonstrate ways of seeing.

This idea was reinforced at further levels in the school but perhaps I can briefly refer to the seventh form to show how this initial work tunes in with later elaboration.

In the seventh form, the first two or three weeks are spent on investigating different perspectives on reality. Most worthwhile writers seek to show us a reality, and this reality may be a set of circumstances or beliefs, a society's way of doing things, an accepted code of behaviour, manners, ideals. The writer describes this reality to us. He or she may also analyse and question it or show the individual in conflict with it. Before we can venture into whatever realities our writers reflect to us, we should know a little more about our own from other frames of reference. The business of perception is subtle. In literature opinions can differ. Where do we turn, then, to feel confidence in perception? Science seems to have the credentials of truth today. What does science tell us about the word we see? Ideas from Newton, Einstein, and Heisenberg are considered; the models of the unconscious described by Jung and Freud are discussed; perception diagrams and the workings of binocular vision are demonstrated; then the world as created by language is witnessed through the extract from Orwell's *1984* (often studied the year before). Dicken's anthropomorphic descriptive opening to *Little Dorrit* is read in conjunction with this; Kafka's *Up in the Gallery* shows us the difficulty of resolving ambiguity, and Lewis Thomas's "Language and Human Communication" is seen to postulate that language is by nature ambiguous and ambiguity is the glory of the reality man creates.

This quick reference to other fields of thought serves to enhance the stature of literature in the eyes of science students especially. Literature is not just a private pastime without any relevance to the world of knowledge. It is concerned with many of the same problems of existence and knowing that the other branches of learning are. If the response from some students to the ideas which are met in literature studies is one of "bunkum" or "so what?" I hope I can show them a certain parallel—that an idea they might be dismissing in *Beckett* or *Hamlet, Slaughterhouse 5* or *Lord Jim,* is the literary expression of a scientific principle.

I think we do a disservice to literature when we reduce it to plot, theme, characterisation, structure, and background. Behind literature worthy of the name is a vision, an attempt on the part of people to see themselves in relation to their society, their times, and the universe. It can be taught.

# Teaching the Bard

ROBERT SQUIRES
*(United States)*

Whenever I wonder why I teach Shakespeare, a passage in Orwell's *1984* reminds me. Early in the novel Winston Smith reflects, "Today there were fear, hatred, and pain, but no dignity of emotion or deep or complex sorrows." Two paragraphs later he awakens with the word *Shakespeare* on his lips.

Surely the question is not why, but how, and in the November 1967 *English Journal,* Frank S. Hook of Lehigh University beautifully stated our objective. He wrote, "We are trying to get our students to respond to the excitement and beauty of Shakespeare's work. Our efforts should be directed toward removing the barriers that stand in their way and opening up this world of majesty and passion." His goal is a good one and, if we are sensible and realistic, a realizable one.

Over the last two decades, I have come to the conclusion that the teacher of Shakespeare must bring to the classroom eight skills. She or he must have skill as a "director," as an "actor," as a "theater technician," as a scholar, as an historian, as an explicator, as a critic, and, of course, as a teacher.

Reading a play, any play, is much harder than reading fiction, and is probably the reason that so few people do it for pleasure and why directors, actors, and theater technicians are among the few who do it easily and well. One of the most valuable skills a teacher can give students is the habit of reading a play the way a director reads it, but it is a habit that must be worked at, and a skill that the teacher must first possess. The teacher must continually exhort his or her students never to read a line without simultaneously imagining the action that goes with it. The reader who is his own director, who manipulates the characters about the stage of the mind's eye, who dictates their vocal inflections, facial expressions, and physical attitudes, is the reader who is beginning to really read the play. The reader who can take an active part in directing Romeo and Juliet at their first meeting, telling them how to say the lines and posing them physically on an imaginary stage, is the reader who has gone a long way toward understanding the impact of that scene and the personalities of its principal figures.

The role of teacher as actor is very like the role of teacher as director. The teacher who requires students to solve such problems as "How does Lady Macbeth say, 'We fail'?" or "How does Malcolm avoid making 'Oh, by whom?' sound silly?" is getting students to participate actively in a literary and theatrical experience, rather than merely receiving and recording a predetermined interpretation. The student who is required to risk a fresh interpretation of the "Tomorrow and tomorrow" speech finds himself engaging in character analysis without its being an academic chore.

Technical theater skills are perhaps the least essential of the teacher's bag of tricks, but they are useful ones, especially for motivation. A student needs to know nothing about perspective or costume design to construct an imaginary forest of Arden or to regally dress the court of Richard III. However, such problems as the blinding of Gloucester on stage, or the suicide of Brutus, or the cauldron scene in Macbeth can easily get some students to forget they are facing a complex and difficult play written in a foreign language.

And now I'd like to turn from those skills that enable the teacher to enrich the study of the plays as drama to those skills that help the teacher to treat the plays as literature.

First, I think, the teacher must be something of a scholar. G. B. Harrison, in the September 1963 *English Journal,* wrote, "When approaching a play of Shakespeare's we do not brace ourselves for an intellectual struggle in quite the same way as if we are about to translate a Latin classic . . . when we expect difficulties of vocabulary, idiom, and a different outlook. We subconsciously resent such difficulties in Shakespeare because he uses words which are still common, but he frequently uses them with different meanings and connotations. As a result we often miss his meaning, or—what is more exasperating—we produce a perfectly good sense which was not what he meant at all." Certainly the teacher owes it to the students to supplement the footnotes whenever scholarship gives her or him information that illuminates the meaning of the text. Hamlet's use of "nunnery" is a familiar example.

At the secondary level, the teacher of Shakespeare ought, I think, avoid playing historian for the fictional *Romeo and Juliet* and *A Midsummer Night's Dream.* But with a play like *Macbeth,* if students know something about James I, for example, they can better appreciate the significance of the many ambiguities and curious paradoxes in the behavior of Banquo.

The role of explicator is the one most familiar to a teacher of literature. The danger is that the teacher, who is most comfortable in this role, may explicate too much. Students of even average ability can perfectly well read and explain Macbeth's "Tomorrow" speech or Hamlet's "Oh, what a rogue" speech for themselves. Certainly they will not get everything, but if we accept that learning is attempting, then students must not be denied the opportunity for active participation. I am not at all bothered that droves of my students will go to their graves perfectly content without understanding every word and phrase of *Macbeth* as well as I do. On the other hand, there are many difficult passages in Shakespeare—difficult in vocabulary, syntax, and metaphor— and certainly the teacher needs to step in and explain the meaning before the action of the play and the progress of the class can move ahead. We old hands know that Mercutio's "Queen Mab" aria is a brilliant *tour de force,* but it is likely to be gibberish to adolescents encountering it for the first time.

When secondary teachers become critics, they are dealing with the trickiest and most delicate skill of all. But is is absolutely essential that they act the critic in the classroom. Even those students who may not understand much else that is happening will be quick to note when teachers express an admiration they do not feel or when they refrain from showing an honest passion. Teachers who refrain from finding fault with Shakespeare create resentment in students who do not understand a muddy metaphor or an unmotivated bit of behavior. Those who refrain from waxing enthusiastic run the risk of proving to their students that they too find Shakespeare an overrated bore. However, the teacher who confesses thinking Shakespeare must have been suffering from a monumental hangover when he wrote, "Oh, by whom?" for Malcolm and some of the stilted dialogue for Hermia and Lysander, or who extolls the rhetorical perfection of Theseus's "lover, madman, and poet" speech will find many satisfactions. The teacher may discover that honestly stated criticism, which suggests Shakespeare's fallibility, helps to make the playwright more human and therefore more approachable. Best of all, the teacher may find that naked admiration of a scene or a passage of exquisite poetry with the consequent vulnerability to mockery that any open admiration carries with it may encourage first one, then another, then many students to express enthusiasm for the bits and pieces that have appealed to them.

Finally, no matter what else they may be at any moment, teachers of Shakespeare are teachers. A teacher is sometimes a teller and sometimes a guider. There are certain generalities about Shakespeare's dramatic methods that teachers with their broader knowledge ought to share with their students who could never arrive at them on the evidence of one or two or three plays. For example, the opening scene of a tragedy, whether long or short, always establishes the presence of chaos on three levels: in the individual in the foreground, in the political arena in the middle ground, and in nature in the background. The final speech of a tragedy is always given to the character designated by Shakespeare to reestablish harmony and order. When I was much younger and more naive, I taught *Julius Caesar* four times before I discovered that the final speech is Octavius's, not Antony's. It was another few years before I came to appreciate the significance of that editorial excision, and I've harbored a resentment against that eminent publishing house ever since. However, I insist that the teacher who gives such generalities to students is helping them become involved. Such a general framework gives students a starting point, and rather than restricting or inhibiting their study, frees them to concentrate on the text. The student who has studied *Julius Caesar* in the classroom may well be motivated to attend a production of another tragedy to see how Shakespeare has arranged the opening scene and to try to guess the identity of the final speaker.

Teachers must be aware of all their students, and of their abilities and needs, psychological as well as intellectual. Honest teachers never allow questionable interpretations to go unchallenged, but they often permit a superficial or inadequate interpretation to stand. There are often times when teachers must recognize that a particular student has made, for her or him, a brilliant contribution, and they will not look for greater depth. I do not think I am being dishonest in suggesting this approach. If we accept Frank Hook's goal that "we are trying to get our students to respond to the excitement and beauty of Shakespeare's work," then we must often be grateful for modest steps in that direction, and not "turn our students off" by frequent reminders of the inadequacy or simplicity of their responses. And teachers must confess when they do not know or do not have an interpretation. Perhaps the greatest gift we can give our students is awareness that the teacher can be confused and unsure and still love Shakespeare.

If we aim for complete understanding and brilliant interpretations from our often immature and unsophisticated students, we are doomed to failure; but if we aim to break down the barriers that prevent understanding and enjoyment, then we *can* achieve our goal.

# 3.
# The Teaching
# of Writing

No area of the English curriculum has received more attention and effort during the past 10 years than the teaching of writing. A revolution has taken place, and in this part, one essay after another refers to the "process approach" to writing, particularly as described and taught by Donald Graves of the United States. If there is an "orthodoxy" in English education in the five countries, it is in the shift away from teaching composition through rhetorical forms toward letting students experience its essence. There is concern among the contributors that the idea of process has already begun to rigidify, that too many teachers speak of *the* writing process as if there were only one for all writers. Several essayists also address the perpetual concern of helping students find things to say, urging teachers to look beneath the surface ideal of "letting students write about any topic they choose" toward finding developmental schemes that help explain the evolution of personal growth and the selection of topics as these lead to increased power over the writing process. "Skills" remain a worry too, in part, as several writers suggest, because community expectations for correctness are often at odds with the aims of process-centered teachers, but also because the profession has not altogether resolved two fundamental questions: "How do I integrate correctness and personal expression?" "How do I teach expressive writing while preparing students for the transactional demands of society and school?" A major issue, alluded to in several essays, is the effects of external examinations, which, in all five countries, frequently force teachers away from the best writing programs they can imagine.

# Writing as Discovery

PETER ADAMS
*(Australia)*

We rarely use writing as mere communication. There is nearly always some element of exploration, of discovery, of finding out what it is we want to say. . . . (Britton, 1972)

Most forms of writing are ways of discovering thought, of finding out what we mean rather than merely recording or reporting what we already think. In itself, that is hardly a novel or a startling proposition: Was it E. M. Forster who said, "How shall I know what I think till I see what I say?" But, before I go on to show why this is so powerful a notion in the classroom, I think it is worth asking how it is that writing can function in this way.

Janet Emig (1977) has written about the way in which writing represents a unique mode of learning: "Writing serves learning uniquely

90

because writing as process-and-product possesses a cluster of attributes that correspond uniquely to certain powerful learning strategies." Rather than retread the ground Emig has explored, I want to explore the power of writing as a heuristic from two additional perspectives:

1. *Writing works as a way of discovering thought because it seeks to discover or create pattern and order; it reaches out towards closure.* This is as true of the imaginative forms of discourse as it is of the expository. Taylor Stoehr (1967) provides us with a marvellously compelling description of this process at work.

> Although one could imagine a writer carefully planning out an essay . . . preparing an outline of themes to be introduced and interwoven, and of effects to be produced, it is really very unlikely (that) writers plan their work so minutely beforehand. What ordinarily happens is that an idea comes to an author, and then another occurs to him, fired off by the first, and then still another, suggested by the last. Sometimes the idea is a natural development of the preceding one; sometimes it is a corollary notion suggested by some defect noticed in the original, or by some objection to it. One thing leads to another.
>
> At a certain point the sentences begin to have an overall shape or pattern. The writer sees a drift or tendency, probably only implicit, perhaps intended from the outset, perhaps not, but now clearer and more obvious. It is like watching an artist draw a picture: at a certain moment, with the addition of one more line, the object being represented suddenly becomes "visible," and just as with the artist, at this moment a whole new range of choices and possibilities opens up. Some parts of the work must now be deleted, as not contributing to the overall effect, while others must be elaborated, since they seem more crucial to the whole than first appeared. Empty areas are seen, gaps in the argument, which is fast growing to completeness now that it can be contemplated as a whole.
>
> In all this process the writer is, in a sense, at the mercy of his thoughts. He does not direct them at this or that point; instead he follows them with more thoughts, spontaneously, naturally. It is hard to say whether he has the thoughts, or they have him.

Significantly, this sense of shape or pattern is perceived as emerging *from within the writing,* rather than as something that is imposed from outside. It is this intuition of an emergent pattern which determines thought, which draws the writer on towards the completion of the glimpsed *gestalt.*

2. *Any good writing will be the result, to some extent, of a willingness to rely upon intuitive levels of thought:*

Writing is a human process whereby intuition (or illumination), to the degree that the concepts held in mind may be bypassed, can disclose itself. Writing doesn't lay out the notions that are lying dormant in the mind waiting to be displayed. Writing is the "seeing into" process itself. It is the tearing through the mind's concepts. The process itself unfolds truths which the mind then learns. (Mandel, 1978)

Whenever and wherever we consult the professional writer on writing—which we do with strange infrequency considering he is our most powerful primary source—we find it is the rare writer who admits to writing a wholly conscious and contrived piece.

The single well-known exception is probably Poe who, in his essay "The Philosophy of a Composition," tells how "The Raven" "proceeded step by step to its completion with the precision and rigid consequence of a mathematical problem." And, one might add unkindly, reveals all the hazards of inappropriate transfer, of fulfilling a poem as if it were an assignment in geometric ratiocination.

All other writers of whom I know convey implicitly or explicitly not only awareness that there is an unconscious actively performing in all their writing, but a belief—more, awe—in its importance, efficacy, and power. (Emig, 1983)

My two points are not actually as distinct as it would seem from the way in which I have stated them, but central to both of them is the concept of writing not merely as a way of recording or representing preexisting meanings *but of bringing meanings into being.*

My way of putting this into practice is to constantly reassure my students that writing need not be exhaustively and meticulously preplanned, that it's not always necessary or even desirable to know exactly where a piece of writing is going before one starts writing, that sometimes it's enough just to start writing and see what happens. I tell them to use writing to *find* ideas, rather than waiting to have ideas before they feel they are ready to write. I teach them to be alert to the moments when writing suddenly takes on a life of its own, when they are no longer pushing it ahead word by word, sentence by sentence, but seem to find themselves drawn irresistibly forward—and I tell them to respect those moments. I encourage daring and risk-taking: ". . . just push off from the shore, and see where you get taken." Sometimes I let writing incubate over quite long periods; sometimes I will suddenly apply the pressure of a stringent deadline or demand that they write *now.* I write in class about the things I set my students to write about, and share my writing processes with them—my excitement when it is going well, my frustration and despair when it's not. I talk to my students about their writing at every stage in its progress from the first draft onwards, and all the time I am trying to elicit from them a sense of the shape or pattern they think the writing might assume in its final form.

I have found that once my students experience the power and excitement of writing as discovery, there is a sudden depth of commitment to writing itself and an accompanying seriousness about themselves as writers that were not apparent before. The cry, "I haven't anything to write about," dies away. The more they learn to trust themselves to preconscious processes, the more likely it is that they will be surprised and delighted by what they find they have written, and so, the more they will recognize the need, in revision, to consciously shape and elaborate and delete in order to bring to completeness the whole they have glimpsed. So, a two-way traffic is set up between preconscious and conscious processes, and revision becomes a re-vision, a seeing again that is also a seeing into.

This does not mean that all my students have the same styles of composing: Robert mulls for days, and then suddenly pours words onto paper in an urgent spate; Lisa simply picks up her pen and writes to see what will emerge onto the blank sheet. But I felt I had to be doing something right when Philip came up to me to say: "These two people just walked into my story. One's pushing a wheelbarrow with a big wooden box in it. I don't know who they are." I remembered what William Faulkner said about the way *The Sound and the Fury* began—with a vision of a small girl in a pair of muddy drawers sitting in a tree—and I told Philip, "You'd better keep writing if you want to find out."

# Making It Real— Reading to Write and Writing to Read

CAROL A. STAMM
*(Canada)*

Teachers in Quebec are having the opportunity to take part in an exciting change in the approach to teaching language arts. After a number of years of consulting with teachers, consultants, administrators, professors, and others knowledgeable in the field, the Ministry of Education has developed a whole-language, child-centered, integrated approach to the teaching of language arts based on the theories of Britton, Halliday, Graves, Clay, Goodman, and others. A number of school boards have already begun implementing the new program, while others are just being introduced to it. I have been excited by the program because it supports beliefs I hold about the most effective way for young children to learn to read and write.

I have found the most exciting aspect of the teaching of this language arts program to be the writing the children have done in my Grade 1 classes. I developed a writing program geared to the needs of the children in my class, a program which is constantly evolving and improving. Each year the quality of the writing reveals children are much more capable than is generally recognized.

One of the most important elements in developing a classroom of writers is to make children believe that they are writers, that they have the ability to write, and that they have something important to say. Teachers do this by communicating to their children that they believe that the children can write, even as early as the first day of school.

To convey to the children the message that they could write, I gave each of the 24 children in my Grade 1 class a book which I had prepared, entitled *All About Me,* the first morning they entered my class. The children were to draw the pictures and to write something on the lines below headings which included "My Name is . . ." "This is My Family . . ." "This is Something I Can Do Well . . ." "This is What I Did This Summer . . ." I made it clear to them that they were to write what they thought the word looked like, that I did not mind if the word was spelled incorrectly, and that I wasn't going to tell them how a word was spelled. I knew from past experience that the whole process of writing bogged down when the children wanted a word spelled out and waited for the teacher to come around to help them, rather than working out ways of spelling the word themselves. I also knew it was an important aspect of the writing process for children to take ownership of their own writing.

Once the children realized that what they had written was considered writing, they became quite enthusiastic about writing under their pictures. Several children said, "I can't," and they had to be helped to see that writing "l" for *like* or "lt" for *little* was writing. Once the child had completed his or her book, I wrote my comments on the back cover (e.g., "You wrote a very nice book, Michael." "I like your picture of your bicycle."). A space was left for parents' comments and the books were sent home for parents to see.

I found it critically important to inform parents about the Grade 1 writing and reading program. On Parent's Information Night, which was held early in September, I stressed the writing program, distributed articles on invented spelling and referred the parents to the works of Donald Graves, James Britton, Susan Sowers, Tom Newkirk, Jane Hansen, and others. I had language arts journals and reference books with me to lend further weight to my position on functional or invented spelling.

I wrote monthly newsletters which explained to the parents what we were doing in class, and I had open house twice a month on Fridays for a half hour after school so the parents could come in and see their child's work or discuss the program. Many parents were not able to come every time, but even working mothers and fathers arranged to come in a few times. Grandparents, brothers, and sisters also visited. Many parents commented on how they could see the progress in their child's work from one visit to the next, and how much they appreciated being able to see what we were doing in school.

I included a place for parents' comments on much of the work the children did. This helped to make the parents aware of the activity as well as to provide feedback for me. More important, it was a message to each child that what he or she had done was important to the teacher and the parents.

Many of the children quickly developed a flow to their writing, while others took six to eight weeks before they developed enough confidence in themselves to take risks and commit themselves on paper, to write even a few of their thoughts.

There were many children in my class who were writing every day but who had not yet learned to read. Furthermore, they loved writing. I suspect that this was because they hadn't had previous experiences being unable to write, where they had with reading. I noted that the two processes of reading and writing were closely intertwined. As the children gained in confidence in themselves as writers, they felt more confident about themselves as readers. As they became more able to work out how to write words, they became more able to work out how to read words.

After the children have been convinced that they can write, the next step is to make reading and writing easy for them. I found that the "Big Books" were ideal for this. We started with Ginn's *Mrs. Wishy Washy*. After reading it through together several times, all the children could "read" it. We also read many little books with predictable story-lines. The children could "read" these books and so believed they could read. They were particularly enthusiastic about taking these books home to show their parents that they could read. The children started to use many of the words in these books in their writing. They knew the books by heart, and so knew where they could find a particular word. Often a child would be saying a word out loud as he or she wrote, and someone would announce, "I know where to find that! It's in *Three Little Ducks*," and the child would run and get the book.

I posted a list of words the children often used in their writing on a large wall space in the class, which was easily accessible to all children. These words were listed alphabetically, each letter on a different colour of paper, four or five words, numbered, for each letter of the alphabet. If a child wanted to find "friend," he or she was told by me or by another child, "It's under the 'f's' number 1." These lists stayed up all year and were referred to frequently.

Whenever we worked on a project, vocabulary words related to that topic were displayed. The words were written in different coloured inks, in alphabetical order to help the children locate a particular word. We also had bristol board cards on which I wrote frequently used words in categories such as "Family Words," which included *mother, father, grandparents, baby, cousin,* etc.; "Party Words," which included *invitation, presents, cake, candles, happy birthday,* etc.; "Hallowe'en Words," and so on. These cards were kept in a large box and the children took them out whenever they needed them. Through these approaches, the children were developing a sight vocabulary and were using this knowledge both in their reading and in their writing.

It is extremely important that reading and writing be real, and not artificial or contrived activities for children. The most obvious way is to have the children make choices about what they will write or read. We convey to the children that we respect their judgment by giving them many opportunities to make choices. The topics they choose to write about, the books they choose to read will be the ones which are the most motivating to them for they will be the ones which they know something about. It is through working with something familiar to them that children feel secure. They become confident decision makers, who can participate in decisions about their own learning.

The following are some strategies that I used in my Grade 1 class:

*Dates.* One of the most important routines the children learn is that they have to put the date on every page they write. In this way, the child's work can be put in chronological order, and one is able to see the child's growth and can point this out to the child or to his or her parents. One is able to see how long a child spent on a piece of writing, one can see patterns in writing—in fact, one can see the developmental process on paper. This is an important element in the evaluation of the child's work.

*News Books.* I found that having the children write news books entries about what they did on the weekend, or the day before, was the easiest kind of writing with which to start. Its context gave the children a security and a framework, and the children came to believe that their own experiences were important topics to write about. Occasionally, I had the children choose one of their favourite entries from their news books to read to a group of their peers. I then typed all of these on one sheet of paper, with each child's name beside his or her selection, corrected them for spelling and punctuation, and made a copy for each child. The children read their sentences as well as the entries of their friends. They had an amazing ability to remember what was said once they read the person's name beside it. We did reading activities with the sheet, finding certain words, finding rhyming words, looking at initial consonants, underlining all the times the word "went" appeared, circling all the words "my," for example. The children took their copy of the page home to read to their parents. The reading was predictable to them and the content was meaningful—their reading and writing activities were real.

*Writing Files.* Each child had a *working* folder and a *completed* folder. Often the children did write about their experiences in these but most wrote imaginary stories in them.

*Projects.* The children studied about whales and other underwater animals. They were able to organize this knowledge and write it in their own words. They also wrote an elaborate project on Indians and Inuit. During the course of this project, the children read many books to look up information which they wrote in their own words. This project included sections on vocabulary, research, communication, planning, decision making, forecasting, evaluation, and creativity, each with five to ten choices offered. Each child had to choose one or more items from each category. By this time, we had as a class learned a great deal about the topic and there were many books available to the children.

*Letters.* The children wrote dozens of letters—thank you letters, letters to ask people to save the whales, and letters to obtain information. The most popular were pen pal letters and each child was able, during the year, to write three letters to his or her pen pal in a Grade 1 class in Toronto.

*Reports.* We had many visitors in the school who gave presentations on a variety of topics. Following each presentation, we discussed the points the children remembered. I wrote some of the key words down, and each child wrote a report.

*Authors.* I found that when the children were writing every day, their reading improved even if we weren't concentrating on "reading." They spent time reading their work as they were writing it and most shared it with a few friends when it was completed. Authors also read their completed work to a group for peer-editing. The most borrowed books in the classroom were the published books the children had written. It was clear that the two areas could not be separated for "instruction."

*Book Club.* The class belonged to a Scholastic book club. Often I would order five or six copies of a book and a group of children would read it together. We had frequent silent reading periods during the week when the children were free to choose and read their own books, and they visited the school library at least once a week to read and select books to read at home.

In general, I found that the children learned skills when they needed them in their writing. Children who included a good deal of conversation in their stories saw a need to keep track of who said what, and were receptive to understanding a lesson on quotation marks. I also found that once the children were made aware of a convention or rule in writing, they tended to overapply it and that is how they learned about the many irregularities in our language. Many children put a silent "e" on *find, behind, for,* and *most,* for example. When some of the children were ready to learn about doubling the consonant to soften the vowel, a child asked: "What about 'rest'? Do you double the 't'? What about 'living,' 'coming'?" The children became aware of the irregularities ities not only through their writing but also through their reading. They perhaps noticed how words were spelled because they realized they would be using those words in their writing.

Research tells us that there is an association between being read to and being able to read. The children who are read to are better readers. Children who read stories and who have stories read to them come to understand the "storyness of stories"—they come to understand the language of books, which is very different from the language of conversation. This knowledge helps them in their reading and in their writing. Children who become aware of the language of books begin to use this same kind of language in their writing.

It took these children many months of writing before they assimilated the "storytelling mode," but their writing is a powerful argument which indicates how important it is to read to children every day if we want to help them become better writers and better readers.

# Teaching Written Composition as Process

JOHN HEENAN
*(New Zealand)*

Our school had long worshipped, on educational sabbaths, at the altar of individual differences, but had experienced difficulty in practising the faith when teaching written composition.

We were unyielding in our rejection of written language programmes that focused on the production of accurate but lifeless writing, programmes that taught skills in isolation and treated children as clones.

We espoused the concept of creativeness; we wanted children to learn the skills of writing while writing. We encouraged children to give expression to genuine ideas, to enjoy writing, to share their real world. We sought to develop confidence in the ability to write and to foster positive feelings of self-worth.

In short, we knew what we wanted to do. Yet we did not know how to turn our ideas to successful classroom practice. We knew where to go, but not how to get there. Then came Donald Murray (1972) and Donald Graves (1983) from the United States with their concept of teaching writing not as a product but as a process. Although our first attempts at setting up writing workshops and following the Graves model were tentative, children began to respond and teachers found a new energy and personal satisfaction in teaching writing. We were encouraged.

### What Is Process Writing?

Process writing is an individualized approach to teaching written composition and emphasizes personal discovery through language. It teaches children to follow the prewriting, writing, and rewriting sequence of the professional writer.

The time spent on each of these stages of the process depends upon the writer's personality, work habits, maturity as a writer, and interest in the topic. While it is not a rigid lock-step process, research shows that most writers most of the time pass through all these stages:

1. *Prewriting*—everything that takes place before the first draft is written.
2. *Writing*—the act of providing a first draft.
3. *Rewriting*—a period for reconsideration of topic, form, and audience.

### How Are Children Motivated to Write?

If children are going to work through the writing process (perhaps several times with the same piece of writing), there must be personal commitment to the writing. It must be writing that is valued.

The teacher's role has to change from instructor to a craftsman working alongside apprentice writers and placing upon them the responsibility for the discovery of topic, form, and audience. Implicit in such a role is the understanding that the teacher will resist the temptation to take over children's writing. The teacher's task is to listen and respond as reader and recipient of children's writing.

Among the implications of such an approach for the curriculum are:

- Children's own writing is the teaching resource.
- Children choose their own topic.
- Children use their own language.
- Children are given the opportunity to write all the drafts necessary to discover what they have to say.

- Children are encouraged to attempt any form of writing which may help them discover their message.
- Children learn the mechanics of writing while writing.
- Children are encouraged to discover their own truth.
- Teachers help children to maintain control over their own writing.
- Teachers help children discover their own voice as writers.

### What Are Writing Workshops?

Daily writing workshops, in which teachers work alongside children, replace the traditional, teacher-directed, written composition lessons. Workshops are centred upon individualized writing projects. In addition to writing with children, teachers hold discussions or conferences about individual children's writing. These conferences, which follow a counseling or effective listening model, may be individual, group, or whole class. Their purpose is to help children clarify ideas and gain greater control over their writing. As drafts are revised, the purpose of conferences changes from concern for clarity of ideas and topic to the organisation of the writing and finally the consideration of surface and mechanical faults.

### How Have Children Responded to Process Writing?

At our school, the children have responded to writing workshops with enthusiasm and commitment. They are stimulated to continue writing, not by teacher-centered motivation, but by publication and sharing. Publication has taken a variety of forms—booklets, bulletin board displays, individual and class magazines, and photocopied sets of booklets for use as reading material.

As children have developed an understanding of the writing process and become more competent writers, their attitude to *reading* has also changed. Gradually many have begun to read as writers and to demand of reading material the same clarity of meaning as the revision process and conferences have demanded of their own writing.

Undoubtedly the most exciting response to the writing workshops has been the fact that children's traditional reluctance to write has been replaced by enjoyment, commitment, and a growing sense of achievement.

### How Have Teachers Responded to Process Writing?

As the centre of energy for the teaching of written composition has shifted from teacher to children, teachers have found that they are teaching more effectively, that individual needs are being met, and that children are writing more genuinely. While acknowledging that the workshops are more demanding and require greater preparation, teachers are stimulated by the quality of the children's writing.

One young teacher summarised his experience thus: "When I teach other subjects I never know if the children are learning. In my writing workshops children learn before my eyes."

Teaching writing as a process has created in our school children who want to write and teachers who enjoy teaching written composition. Clearly, during the '80s and '90s many other schools will share our experience.

# Approaches to the Writing Process

NANCY J. JOHNSON
*(United States)*

My entire approach to the teaching of writing has changed remarkably since I first began teaching. Years ago, I felt compelled to teach composition as either expository or creative writing. I provided the topics; I set the form; I was in control of the process their writing "should be" taking—and too often that was a form accompanied by topic sentence and/or thesis statement, outline, and numerous drafts. I wasn't too enthused about the writing the kids were producing, and the kids were less than enthused about the whole thought of having to write.

Fortunately I became wiser. Encouraged by positive results from other colleagues and enlightened by the professional literature on writing instruction, I changed my writing curriculum from a teacher-directed to a student-centered approach. I gave the students more responsibility for topic selection and made their interests and their experiences an important part of what they wrote about. I provided more opportunities for students to explore a variety of discourse modes and often was surprised to discover these students had never considered writing in a form other than a story, a poem, or an exposition. I also found it was valuable for the students to have numerous and varied opportunities to write—not just writing on Fridays or when we came to the end of a unit and there were questions to be answered, but opportunities to keep journals, to respond and react to what we were reading or discussing, to write both informally and formally, incorporating writing naturally into more of the daily class activities; opportunities to write without worry about surface errors because not everything written would be graded.

I found value in having students keep writing portfolios to gather all their writing as they wrote, often surprising themselves at the end of the term to see how much they'd actually written. The portfolios became informative in parent-teacher conferences and provided an eye-opening progress report—far superior to any standardized test report. I also opened up more opportunities for all students to have a reason to write, and that reason centered on publication: not just for those few students who manage to have work selected for the annual school anthology, but all the kids, writing letters, small group dittoed booklets, end-of-term collections of "favorite pieces." And, I found the importance of actively writing myself. Writing with the kids and sharing what I've written made me more aware of the struggles they were experiencing and provided the model for what I'm professing as so important.

I believe that there is such a thing as a "process approach" to writing, but what often gets in the way are teachers trying to teach one set process. They package writing as a three-step maneuver: first you *prewrite*; then you *write*; then you *revise/rewrite*. Very simple, very cut and dried. But it isn't simple because many of us don't use the same process for our own writing. Often I spend a great deal of time prewriting on paper before ever getting a draft written. At other times I've mulled about what I wanted to write over and over long enough that the written prewriting is little, maybe even unnecessary, and I can get directly into the writing. Our students operate best when they've had a chance to explore different types of prewriting and idea-generating, different "processes" to approach their writing; then they can choose the "process" that works best for them for a particular piece of writing.

Student involvement in writing topics, actually *engaging* students in their writing from the very beginning, is crucial and leads to more lively, spirited, and honest writing. Means of assisting students with topic selection and helping them formulate something to write about can work when teachers:

1. *Provide writing interest inventories to assist students in developing lists of possible writing topics.* These inventories can be developed as simply a list of possible activities/subjects/experiences that apply to the individual writer, with spaces for students to indicate their own interests (or lack of interest). Not only can these inventories provide a rich supply of potential topics for writing, but they tap into the kids' own lives—involving the writers in their own writing through their own experiences. I've used interest inventories at the beginning of the year and have students staple them into their writing folders or notebooks as a ready reference for writing ideas during the year.

2. *Provide opportunities for students to keep journals, including an informal listing of ideas, personal thoughts and opinions, and responses to almost anything that affects their lives.* I've seen many journal entries used to trigger poems, narratives, and even drama written later in

the year. Sometimes I provide broad suggestions such as "sketches of significant people and places" for possible journal entries. I've also suggested they keep a running list of sensory impressions (smells they like, smells they hate; sounds they like, sounds they hate), and other times I've encouraged them to use their journals to explore different forms of discourse (ads, poems, letters, dialogue). Some groups of kids don't need or want any of my suggestions, and they relish the chance to write about whatever is foremost in their minds.

3. *Provide writing warmups, 10- to 15-minute writing explorations to serve as a springboard for topics and writing ideas.* Writing warmups can be as simple and unstructured as time to write in journals or more formal writing triggered from a list of categories or open-ended topics listed on the board or on a ditto.

4. *Allow writers to work together generating topics and writing ideas.* One way I do this is to hand out a ditto that has a box in the top center and nothing else but empty lines. Then I give the directions: "Pair up with someone else in class. Between the two of you find something you both know something about and have some interest in. It can be a place, person, ideas, anything. Then, once you've settled on your 'topic,' make a list of words and associations with that topic in mind." We usually "rehearse" together as a class first and come up with something like:

| FOOTBALL |
| --- |

Detroit Lions
1983 big win over Eastern High School
Coach Shannon
Practices and turn-outs
Getting cut from the team

After time is given for this idea generating, I offer the next set of instructions: "On your own now, use any, all, or even none of the words and ideas you and your partner generated and spend the next portion of time writing about your topic."

Peer editing can be effective and valuable to student writers if:

1. *Students are "taught" what's meant by editing; if they're given some direction (questions, areas to respond to) as they respond and react to a piece of writing.* Too many students edit by evaluating rather than responding and providing feedback. They play at being a teacher-evaluator rather than an audience. Years and years of having their own work evaluated as either right or wrong causes student editors to approach editing from an evaluative angle rather than the approach of "What 'worked' for me in this paper?" "What could/did the writer do to create that?"

2. *Teachers, as writers themselves, model and even "teach" response.*
One way to do that is have a colleague come into class and work
through the editing process with a piece of your own writing. Display
your writing on an overhead or provide copies for your students so
they can see how this one editor responds—both orally and in writing—
to your piece of writing.

3. *Student editors work in small groups of three to five.* These groups
work together throughout the term and establish a level of trust and
respect for each other as both writers and editors.

4. *Teachers provide numerous opportunities for students to act as
editors.* Too often teachers try peer editing once, and when it doesn't
"work" as planned, never try it again. Sometimes it takes patience from
the teacher; often students need reminding about what their responsibilities are; but it can work with exposure to editing and opportunities
for students to truly edit rather than be someone's proofreader.

5. *Teachers realize some classroom noise will occur during this process as writings are shared aloud and editors make honest responses and
reactions.* If a paper is humorous, it's natural for an audience to laugh.
Often that form of audience response is the best form of editing a student writer needs.

My own involvement exploring writing with fifth- to ninth-grade
writers, in Young Writers' Workshops and with college writers has
proven the importance of the writers' active involvement in their writing and that involvement includes making personal choices. I see the
teacher's role, then, as that of establishing an atmosphere conducive to,
and supportive of, writers in the process of writing, an atmosphere
where student writers' ideas, thoughts, and interests are valued, where
correctness matters but isn't the central focus of the writing program,
where the range of discourse forms is available and acceptable, where
writers have *real* reasons to write—beyond writing for the teacher—
where teachers write and rewrite, and write and struggle, and write and
revise, and write and publish along with their students.

# The Skeleton in the Cupboard

DEBBIE MYHILL

*(England)*

Poetry writing is the black sheep of the English syllabus. Few
elements are more reluctantly tackled, or thankfully put aside for another year—not even grammar and spelling work. Children themselves

rarely rate poetry writing highly, and many teachers approach it with undisguisedly gloved hands. So why, despite the popularity of teaching other people's poetry, should composition be relegated to so lowly a place? I suspect the answer is twofold: firstly, there is a basic ignorance, or at best haziness, of the way children write poetry, and secondly, there is at best only a vague conviction of the validity of teaching poetry at all. Perhaps also in our comprehensive society the idea prevails that poetry is for the elite, and elitism is not fashionable.

Justifying the inclusion of poetry writing in the syllabus should not be necessary. Poetry, like all creative activities, allows for a highly subjective and personal exploration of feelings and ideas, and as a medium it is particularly suited to concentrated, intense vignettes of expression. Through imaginative freedom children learn to make sense of their experiences and to cope, not only with fantasy, but with the real world. Much contemporary psychology insists upon the fertility and potential creativity of the subconscious and the value of poetry in tapping these reservoirs of unexpressed feeling (Kubie, 1957; Witkin, 1974). Directly related to the English classroom is the significant influence of writing for oneself. Children who themselves have encountered the thrill of success and the frustrations of failure in writing poetry will have developed a more refined and precise insight into the niceties of composition—of rhyme and rhythm, structure, and patterns of imagery. Reading and enjoying poetry is a natural complement of writing, and the two need not be rigidly divorced.

Perhaps most neglected, but most relevant of all, are the benefits of poetry writing which can be enjoyed by the less able. Traditionally these children rarely get the opportunity to write poems, composition being mysteriously categorised as fit only for the academically bright child (the elite once more?). Yet poetry can restore confidence to a child who senses failure in reading and prose writing, and whose efforts are dogged by stumblings, stutterings, and red ink. A poem can be very brief, yet succinct, and it is free from many of the constraints of grammar and punctuation which can cause problems for less able children. With encouragement, a child who can barely string together a passage of prose can write personally satisfying and expressive poetry. Here is the normal prose work of a bottom set eleven-year-old, followed by a poem written in class with no assistance other than the stimulus of silence:

> Once when I was waking home from schol we herd a noice behind us and it frighted me so I ran and ran we didn't no what had done the but I didn't home that way anymore.

>           Shuffling,
>           Scratching,
>           Rustling leaves,

Sighing,
Breathing,
Silence.

The latter is by no means classic poetry, but it is a significant achievement for someone painfully aware of her inadequacies.

The second barrier blocking attempts to teach poetry writing is the aura which surrounds the whole subject and the reluctance or inability of many teachers to get involved in barely understood mental processes. Torrance (1970) advocates that all training teachers should undergo a course on the creative process, including techniques of releasing creative potential, and an introduction to the many forces which can inhibit creativity. More recently, excellent work has been completed on the specific nature of the writing process (Smith, 1982), the creative impulse (Witkin, 1974), and how the teacher can become actively involved (Graves, 1983). Undoubtedly, poetry writing is one of the few disciplines in the school curriculum which is not principally rooted in conscious levels of cognition, and most teaching is preoccupied with learning at such conscious, logical levels. Preconscious or unconscious activities can be both daunting and threatening, obliging the teacher to abandon control of the learning and to concentrate instead upon initiating and stimulating patterns of thought and ideas over which the children themselves must ultimately take charge.

Yet fostering an enthusiasm in writing poetry need not be such a daunting prospect, and much can be done which is both positive and helpful. Opportunities to write should be given as regularly as possible as an integral part of the English syllabus, not every Wednesday afternoon, second lesson, but whenever poetry is an appropriate medium of expression arising out of classroom work. There is no need to pigeonhole poetry, and children will respect and value it more if it is not treated in isolation. The more children write, the less they will regard poetry as "special" or irrelevant. Poetry clubs or workshops provide a complementary opportunity for writing and sharing experiences and problems, especially if a working poet can be invited to join the group occasionally. Witnessing "professionals" writing and hearing about the difficulties they have may help to make poetry less remote. It is important, however, to make sure that an invited poet is able to communicate with children; someone who talks on a different level can overwhelm or discourage.

More specifically, it is unusual for children to be able to write poetry without some kind of warmup or stimulus, though with ample opportunity for writing, this work may become less necessary. The "stimulus" suffers as many fluctuations in popularity as the hemline, and is probably simultaneously underrated and overvalued. Michael Baldwin's (1976) vehement attack on the stimulus is a highly relevant warning of the dangers of initiating elaborate stimulus situations which serve only to entertain and have little value in stirring the creative imagination. The stimulus must not be treated in isolation from the response, and in using any stimulus one needs to be aware of precisely how it will lead into writing, rather than expecting the very presence of a lighted candle or the sound of a dripping tap to inspire 30 imaginations to fever pitch. The action of a stimulus may take two directions: one is to focus upon the essential qualities of the stimulus itself to perceive with the imaginative eye a wealth of qualities hitherto unperceived; the second is to trigger an outward movement into the experiences and memories of the child, often only remotely related to the initial stimulus. Obviously there are unlimited possibilities available for use, ranging from objects with particularly strong associations with one or more of the senses, to music, dance, and drama. There is no need for a stimulus to be elaborate or complicated—often talking and reading are quite sufficient to help the individual find something to say. And one of the best stimuli ever known to the writer is simply that of *writing!*

However the stimulus initiates ideas, it will not always sustain them, and it will certainly not be able to compensate for the frustrations of writing blocks or hunting for the right words. From the point of a germinal idea urging its way forward to its final resolution as a poem printed on the page, there are bursts of progress and slumps of inactivity. Witkin's (1974) concept of the "holding form" which traps and captures the kernel of the idea may be helpful, as it provides a base to which a frustrated imagination can return and rethink. It also has the advantage of maintaining the force of the original idea at the heart of the poem. There is always a danger that floundering in a pool of related images, the frustrated child can lose sight of the initial motivating thoughts and end up with a poem that is only a dilute, dissipated echo of the first ideas. The holding form can take the shape of a sketch, or just one word or image, or a series of jottings verbal or visual—indeed anything which will effectively help to crystallise the experience of the moment.

Another way of helping children write what they want to say without their being overcome by the problem of how to say it is to impose a particular form of poetry. An appropriate choice of form can channel a young writer towards a new perspective on language. Limericks, alliterative verse, haiku, ballads, sonnets, and a host of other forms can be used very successfully. Brian Powell's (1968) programme of poetry lessons is a notable example of how this technique can be used, and Barrie Wade (1975) similarly advocated the particular merits of the haiku in concentrating only on the most relevant and economic descriptions.

If writing poetry is at times problematic, then teaching and encouraging the writing of poetry is yet more of a challenge, not least because

of the general suspicion with which poetry is often regarded. Not only
does the subject echo with eccentric and "arty" associations, it is not
usually examinable and not obviously vocational. Yet it is a challenge
which can reward both teacher and pupil with a heightened awareness
of themselves, their consciousness, their language and their world.

# Successful Strategies in Teaching Composition

BRUCE HAMMONDS
*(New Zealand)*

It is a sad observation that as children pass through our education
system, the joy and spontaneity, the concern with intimate moments
of drama in their own lives, fall away. As this happens, a rich and meaningful source of real motivation for discussion, written language and
art is lost. Worse still, the child's own experiences are devalued and
the real world and schooling become isolated from each other, leaving
a number of disoriented children as a result. The topics, the studies,
and the activities that teachers introduce, even if they are of interest
to many, devalue the children's own thoughts and experiences. The
children who cannot cope with school learning, much of which research
has shown to be beyond their comprehension, must inevitably fail.

If teachers take note of recent research in a number of fields about
how children develop their own frameworks to make sense of their experiences, and how these frameworks are at odds with adult explanations, then there is a chance that teachers can help all learners and not
just those who can bridge the gap. Children bring their own meaning
to any experience. Their learning is affected by the attitudes they bring
to a task. The problem for teachers is to stop teaching and start listening to their pupils. All forms of language offer teachers an excellent
means to set up the necessary dialogue so that they can find out what
views children hold. This obviously applies to all subjects. With this
concept in mind, teachers can place the emphasis in all school work on
the individual's response, finding out what ideas the children bring to
any learning situation. This focus would do much to put children at
the centre of the learning process and make language, both written and
oral, a key investigatory tool for all teachers. There is a real need to per-
sonalise the learning process, to place the responsibility back on the
learner where it should always have been. Teachers are conditioned to
teach so this new role will not be an easy one to adopt, but once the

children realise that teachers are genuinely interested in their thoughts, this will dramatically alter the learning relationship.

Accepting the children's "voice" in the content areas would not be enough in itself. An equally important area is that of personal writing—writing about the children's own concerns, joys, fears, and interests. This is an area which, except for a few innovators (past and present), has been largely ignored. Through language, this personal world can be recognised and along with the other creative arts used as motivation for self-expression. This is not by any means a new idea, but up until now it has gained only a tenuous foothold in our classrooms. Pioneer teachers like Elwyn Richardson (1972) would be amused and a littled saddened that the ideas they developed so many years ago are only now being rediscovered in part by the work of Donald Graves (1983) and "his" process approach to writing.

Personal writing is a means of letting children feel that their own lives are significant and worth recording. By bringing their world into school, we are in a way legitimizing the children's unique existence and in a small way helping them come to terms with themselves and their experiences. We are also reinforcing the idea that small-scale events of one's own life are valid things to think about and express. Many children in our schools seem to mistrust their own way of thinking, finding security in the "right" answers that many teachers prefer.

There are a number of activities which can help children develop their own ability to express themselves, to recognise that they all have something of value to say and share. For children who have learnt to dislike writing (even early in the primary school), this will be no easy task at first and will require time. Teachers who contemplate introducing such a programme must appreciate that it will take a long time, even for the "competent" writers to share their innermost thoughts with a teacher. It will be up to the teacher to develop the right atmosphere and relationship so that the children will come to trust their ideas with him or her.

The first step is to establish personal writing, call it what you will, as a regular feature of the week's programme. One suggestion is to have a time allowance of 15 minutes a day—one piece of writing being forged through a process of revision for final copy at the end of the week. (Donald Graves, 1983, outlines this process in full.) This seems an excellent idea, but it must be remembered that it is the quality of the inspiration which is the most vital factor. A process of revision might be too much for a poor writer, and, in some situations (particularly early in the process), the teacher scribing the child's thoughts might be preferable. Elwyn Richardson (1984) has a number of valuable ideas to develop a total personal language arts programme.

Needless to say, the teacher's role is vital in the writing process, particularly in helping those whose confidence has not had a chance to develop. The teacher needs to listen to what the children are saying and to learn to recognise the potential in the ideas expressed. The sensitive teacher will help draw the pupils' attention to significant details and develop the children's insight. These ideas can be interpreted and refined by discussion. Up until now, the children's unique responses may have been ignored or worse still earned a reprimand, so it will be slow progress and there will be a long transition period. Teachers will need to learn how to recognise quality and growth in individual standards and give praise where necessary. As well, children who found success with teacher-assigned writing may find it hard to write their own thoughts with sincerity, and those who previously have had little success may, with encouragement, produce work of real worth. Personal language will allow development of self-realisation and give the teachers an opportunity to live the world of their pupils. When this happens, the classroom takes on the feel of a creative community— a community with language as a key element.

Two basic techniques developed by Elwyn Richardson are most valuable to teachers beginning a programme of personal writing. The first is "theme selection" and the second is "scribed writing." More recent work on the process approach to writing as developed by Donald Graves (1983) is readily available for all interested teachers.

Theme selection is an important idea because many children have great difficulty in focusing on the most important aspect of an experience from memory or from the here and now. Often language topics are chosen which are so broad in their canvas that little real intensive thought is possible. For example, an account of a day's visit starts from the moment the child wakes and continues with the excitement of a shopping list. To avoid this, ask children to quickly list all the things they remember about the trip (or happy event, or beginning school . . . ). From this initial list, the children then select one idea for development. In some cases, what is selected will need further refining. Skills of punctuation, spelling, and handwriting can be introduced after the ideas have been expressed and will be seen by children in perspective as necessary skills to help them in their final presentation or publication. Such lists cover a wealth of personal topics for further writing or art. With experience, their use of such a selection process will become automatic. All that is written will not necessarily be of high quality at first.

The second technique is known as scribed writing, and has been found most successful when used with infant classes and with older children who have lost confidence in their writing ability through repeated lack of success. Scribed writing is simply the children's language written down as it is spoken by them. This last point is vital if the teacher wishes to gain the confidence of the child. Scribed writing allows the children's thoughts to be recorded with immediacy. These thoughts can be used for the individual child's reading and can be kept on large charts to be referred to when necessary. Obviously, it is possible to work with only a small group of children. Others might well be busy at painting ideas they have developed. When the children have gained confidence, the teacher will need to ask them to focus on the most important thing they want to say, otherwise it becomes an impossible task. For older children, a discussion or question and response situation will be enough to encourage the children to write their own stories. Scribed writing can be based on a child's personal concern, a shared experience, or the recording of a science experiment. As they become more independent, they will want to write their own stories, but they will by then have developed their own unique way of saying things. Scribed writing recognises the very important link between talking, reading, writing, and visual expression. The emphasis must always be on the value of self-expression. Many infant teachers have subverted the idea and placed the emphasis on the reading process.

A number of other techniques can be utilised to help the children develop a belief in their own writing ability and their own personal style

- Personal writing related to the immediate environment of people, places, and things. What are the children's thoughts and feelings? What can they see that interests them?
- Awareness activities to develop a sensitivity to noticing things in their environment. Take advantage of dramatic seasonal or weather phenomena. Reawaken children's sensitivity and visual curiosity. Learning to look contributes to language development, adding to our storehouse of memories.
- Capitalise on any situation which might interest and gain a response from the children.
- Value their thoughts and views in all situations.
- Develop activities which slow down the pace of work and develop a more reflective atmosphere in the classroom. Slowing down the pace of work is vital in all fields to develop work of quality. In writing, the process of refining ideas through consultation and drafting, including the final handwritten and illustrated copy, is an ideal way of slowing the pace of work to develop this reflective atmosphere. With appropriate group organisation, this also allows the teacher the time to enter into dialogue with individual pupils.
- In the content areas, encourage the children to write interpretive language about how they would feel in specific situations in social studies, or what they see and think of science activities. This will contribute to the feeling that you value their thoughts as well as help them learn more efficiently. In this situation, the distinction between factual and imaginative writing is a false one. The situation

will determine the style, and even in a science record there is room for personal comment and in some cases a poetic thought.
- Read poems and literature to provide models to reinforce the total language programme.

All these activities contribute to the total creative classroom community where everything is focused on helping children express themselves in ways that best suit them. The teacher is a vital participant in this exciting adventure of self-realisation. With luck and good teaching, it will continue with the pupils into their adult lives.

# Essay Writing

MIKE MARSHALL
*(England)*

"Composition" now seems a curiously old-fashioned term, although it wasn't long ago that it was commonplace. I can remember from my own schooldays, in the '50s and '60s, receiving a weekly dose of the stuff from my English teachers. I soon came to believe that English homework existed to justify the setting of a "composition" at least once every week! As a pupil, I could rarely perceive any obvious connection between the compositions we were asked to write and the other preoccupations of our English lessons. Indeed, compositions seemed to be a product of at least one teacher's obsession with the sea and boats, as they always related in some way to this theme!

Today's English teachers in Great Britain talk about "essay" rather than "composition"; in doing so, they are possibly reflecting their concern for a variety of written forms, rather than simply one in which the imagination is given free rein. Teachers' "objective" concerns are with *audience, context* and *register*—the terminology of linguistics—rather than with discrete grammatical conventions. Essays are, of course, still often expressions of the creative imagination, but other types of writing have been identified and enshrined in the rubrics of the examination syllabus. These include essays which are *discursive, reflective,* and *instructional* in form and intention; each of these places particular sets of constraints upon writers, compelling them to choose a style and technique suited to the context of writing. Being able to recognise changing constraints and to adapt to them require a consciousness of context and purpose which few pupils—and, I suspect, teachers—would have possessed in the '50s and '60s. Nowadays, teachers talk to each other and to their pupils in a language which owes much to the field of linguistics.

Inevitably, the development of writing skills now appears a more conscious and considered art than it did even 20 years ago. However, the responsibility for transmitting and developing these skills still rests almost exclusively with English teachers, despite the pious hopes of the Bullock Report that responsibility would be shared by all "across the curriculum." This being the reality, English teachers require some coherent view of how they intend to influence the development of writing skills, whilst simultaneously stimulating the imagination. Clearly, teachers need to have their own understanding and—ideally—experience of "what it is to write": they need to have a conceptual "map" of the way writing skills develop and a clear idea of how this development can be influenced and supported by their own interventions.

My own fairly simple conceptual map is shown in the diagram.

The so-called objective framework and the stimuli are both located within a view of personal development. Thus any strategy which evolves is linked to a common-sense, empirical understanding of the personal and affective development of pupils.

My own conception of a personal development continuum is inevitably fairly simplistic. It owes a great deal to daily observation of pupil behaviour and little to a study of psychology or sociology. However, it has helped me to cross-reference my own teaching priorities and strategies with some view of personal growth.

---

**➤ Entry into secondary school ◄**

*Year 1, Age 11+–12*

Egocentric individuals and their experiences placed at the centre of talk, writing, and understanding; narrative and descriptive modes predominant.

*Year 2, Age 12+–13*

Some broadening of horizons; some capacity to place self elsewhere than at centre of activities; glimmering of social and moral perspectives; developing self-consciousness and "objective" awareness; intellectual growth.

*Year 3, Age 13+–14*

Self-consciousness more acute, more "troublesome"; potential conflict with established and conformist views; intellectual development affords greater objectivity—some capacity to evaluate/judge significance of experience, issues and facts. Variety of perspectives/empathies possible.

*Year 4, Age 14+–15*

Greater self-assurance as individuals come to terms with self-consciousness. Conflicts more acute; views more challenging and forceful; increasing sense of the "future" and thus the relevance of present activities; some further intellectual/cognitive development; skills more eagerly sought; growth in exam consciousness.

*Year 5, Age 15+–16*

Exams and future dominate consciousness; routine work can become dulling and tedious; views strengthen as ideologies form; passivity often assumed in learning situations.

**➤ End of compulsory schooling ◄**

---

Crude and simplistic? Of course. However, it does represent a picture of personal growth, in the classroom context, to which I suspect a lot of English teachers can relate. Furthermore, it can help the teacher to select and plan lessons, at least personally assured that they will both stimulate and stretch pupils' minds and feelings.

At this point, I would like to provide brief examples (in outline) to illustrate how this understanding of personal development, at key stages, can be translated into specific classroom activities:

*Year 11+*

A group of activities based on the theme, "Me, My Home, and The School." These can involve drawing and illustrations as well as talking and writing. The emphasis will be on personal experiences and impressions, on anecdote and narrative. Books such as *Danny, The Champion of The World* and *The Shrinking of Treehorn* can be used to extend and stimulate various expressions of personal experience. A structure for this work can be provided by a resource booklet in which illustration (from prose and poetry) and ideas are combined.

*Year 12+*

Here fiction can be more deliberately used to extend personal horizons and moral sensitivity. Relationships can be viewed problematically and some broader issues considered. What it is to be different can be explored through both role play and talk and writing: the latter can invite a measure of opinion within a predominantly narrative form. Additional poetry and prose can extend the impressions of both relationships and prejudices.

*Year 13+*

Once again, fiction can provide both stimulus and focus for personal and interpersonal awareness. Books such as *Walkabout* and *Summer of My German Soldier* can bring relationships and attitudes into sharp focus. Talking and writing can require a shifting perspective—a variety of viewpoints—so that both the characters and the pupil are seen from both different angles and through the eyes of others. "What picture do you have of yourself?" "What picture do you think others (parents, friends, teachers, etc.) have of you?" become stimulating questions. Very gradually, the complexity of appraisal and judgment can become apparent.

*Year 14+*

At this stage of development, problem-solving activities can prove both stimulating and relevant. A book like *Think It Out* can provide a thought-provoking set of scenarios where these are not easy to construct from available resources. Each scenario concerns some form of conflict where there is no obvious or easy resolution. The pupil is led through a carefully structured consideration of the evidence and the questions this begs. Perception, comprehension, discussion, and debate are all demanded at different times.

Eventually some kind of informed judgment is required for which some explicit justification has to be made.

This work lends itself to individual, small group, and whole-class activities; it can involve note making, character assessment and inventories, discursive essay writing and debate. The issues it raises can be further explored through fiction, newspaper reporting (and emotive language), television drama, and documentary.

Most English teachers, I am certain, would share a concern for the personal and affective development of their pupils, particularly within the context of their own subject. Given the daily encounters with significant fiction, and the personal experiences and issues it confronts, it appears difficult to either evade or reject this responsibility. In reading, talking, and writing about these experiences and issues, both the pupils' and teacher's levels of awareness and understanding will be raised. This, in turn, will sensibly inform the teacher's own approach to the teaching of the subject. Armed with these perceptions, the teacher can construct realistic and clear goals in all areas of English work, and prepare more consciously his or her own role and contribution in increasing both the awareness and skills of the pupils.

Thus, teaching pupils how to write essays becomes a deliberate and continuous process based on a perceived relationship between *activity, stimulus, objective framework,* and an *impressionistic view of the pupil's personal development*; the demands made are more realistic and relevant, promoting the personal involvement of the pupil and providing a keener sense of progress. Writing skills are seen as part of the broader maturation process—in which personal development and linguistic skills are inextricably linked—rather than as a set of instructions to be learnt or procedures to be followed. In this way, the value of these skills is set by the pupils' own sense of their relationship to both their needs and aspirations.

# The Experience of School as a Writing Topic

JEAN BLUNT
*(England)*

There is one well-used topic which seems to bring out the best writing and talking in 14-year-olds of all abilities: the experience of school provides young people with memories and hopes. Adolescents can look back and look forward; they can recreate, assess, and evaluate. They have direct experience and seem more than willing to talk about it and write about it.

I usually open the subject by talking about my own school days, recounting for them little episodes of rebellion, success, failure. I have a few old photographs, cuttings, and magazines which I sometimes share. At first, the talk is fairly informal and members of the class soon describe well-remembered moments from their own school days. Using those first-order experiences means that all members of the group have something to say. We read selections from *Cider with Rosie* and *A Kestrel for a Knave*. They see the humour in Laurie Lee's disappointing first day at school and the pathos in the predicament of Barry Hines being caned for bringing a message. Then we talk a lot more. They are asked to consider what they like and dislike, what they would include and exclude if they were the timetable makers. They then look back more particularly on incidents, minor or major, which they think will stay clearly in their minds for some time to come. How would they write these memories down? They have to focus very clearly on details which they scarcely knew they had in their heads.

I read my own attempts to put my memories down on paper—they become my audience. Then I read a handful of essays, collected over two or three years, which I think have been honestly, expressively, and vividly written, pieces which I have been privileged to read. These make up my own collection of "Memories of Schooldays," which I have had photocopied as source material. They are, I think, a lively supplement to the models of language provided by accepted literary works. I say this for several reasons.

Firstly, the writers are known to the listeners, sometimes as "swots," sometimes as "rogues," more often as ordinary, "just about average" associates. Secondly, these writings explore situations and locations the listeners have also known well. They can empathise readily. Thirdly, perhaps most importantly, I think they begin to sense that they can write something which others might like to listen to. Because I am reading out a collection of their friends' essays, they begin, perhaps, to see a purpose in writing. I hope I am giving them the feeling that I would like to read out their pieces too. They listen for snippets of humor and sadness, ways of expressing things well. They know which essays they like best and why. They know when the class is silent, amused, bored. They learn from being the audience.

I like to give teenagers this chance to write expressively. They seem to take to it with relief. Perhaps it provides a welcome respite from all the discursive, transactional writing they are asked to do. I always enjoy listening to and reading about their memories of school. Though they protest goodheartedly, they do like to have their pieces read out and I try to read an extract from the work of each member of the class. The latest batch of school stories has been as enlightening and entertaining (isn't that what writing should be?) as ever. One boy wrote about his turn in the "swing boat" when he was six years old.

I remember it well. The day Thatcher and me had our turn to use the swing boat. I distintly remember geting on and at first swinging slowly. But you no how when little kids get excited they work themselves up and forget about everything else but do what there doing.
We were just laugfing and laugfing until our stomachs turned over. We dident really realize how fast we were going. We were really belting along. The bars were creaking and suddenly the spot welding snaped. We went hurtling across the class room in mid air, under the table, strait into the raidiater with an allmighty clout and we were lying in it on its side, dust and chalk smoke filling the air and our lungs and there we were in fits of laugfter. That was the best laugf I can remember.

Another boy wrote about his "crush on a girl in my class" and the thoughtless betrayal by an insensitive teacher.

In my eyes she was great I couldn't take my eyes off her in class I just sat and stared at her but she never even looked in my direction. This made me miserable and I just moped around the schoolyard on my own and never spoke to anyone. One day in class I was just sat there not doing any work just sitting staring and dreaming about my girl when the teacher shouted something sarcastic about me staring at the red-headed girl whom I thought so much of. I did not catch all of it but it made me mad, I just saw red and said something that I later regretted. It landed me in the Headmasters office. . . .
I walked out into the yard worring more about what the Redhead was going to say to me after I had embarressed her in class that morning. I saw her coming towards me, She did not look very angry. This filled me with hope; she stood in front of me. I spoke.
"Hello," I said rather shakily my knees were a bit trembly in anticipation of what she was about to say.
"Get lost! and leave me alone," she bawled at me and with that she walked off with another boy, a boy! after all the staring and thinking about her I had done and there she was with another boy. All my hopes and dreams put in a car press and crushed to pulp. I was dumbstruck. . . .

Both these pieces have been written by less able adolescents producing their best through their own involvement. I shall add these to my inventory. The piece that follows is already in my collection. It has never failed to captivate each member of a class. It has an honest, unpretentious anecdotal quality about it; and it was written to be read. It is the schoolboy storyteller at his best.

The one lesson that sticks in my mind is the one related below. It was November the Fifth, Bonfire Night, and I felt really ill when I got up. Thinking it would wear off during the morning, I went to school. It was Monday and on Monday afternoon, all afternoon, we had Environmental Studies.

My mother had gone to work that day so I had to stay school dinners. I forced down a grey and cold beef stew and iron-hard dumplings. I felt much worse. The afternoon came and with it the infamous E.S. The other two classes came into our room because our teacher was giving a talk on dairy farming. I sat at the back near the windows with Mark Slater and two others on a table that still had drawers. With the additional people the room had about one hundred people in it and I felt sick. It was about three people to a chair and you had to work in a pattern to prevent blacking somebodies eye with your writing elbow.

The talk began and droned on like an angry wasp in my ear. At first, as I did every week, I took full notes which disintegrated into illegible abreviations which petered out into nothing. The talk went on, my stomach churned and my head ached. The bell went for three o'clock and I felt sick.

Suddenley I put my pen down, stood up and threw up. I never saw the people around me move so fast. Two hours worth of notes got drowned in stew, it dripped onto the floor, into the desk and over Slater. (He hasn't forgiven me for it yet). The silence was deafening, ninety-nine heads turned to look at me. The one clear thing I remember is a girl on the front row remarking, "Oh, look at the carrots in it."

There wasn't room to breath in that classroom but I got passage wide enough to drive a tank down to get out of the classroom.

I got four days off school and a weeks work to catch up on. Even now, when the bell goes around three o'clock I think of E.S., droning teachers and . . . carrots.

# History Through a Child's Voice

CORA FIVE
*(United States)*

### The Night the Revolution Began: The Boston Tea Party

*Prologue*

"What! This is preposterous! Who do they think they are saying 'No taxation without representation!'" shouted King George III. "After all we did for them during the French and Indian War, the least they can do is pay their taxes! I know what I'll do. I'll show them who has the power to make taxes. I'll put a tax on tea. They all love tea. From this day forward all American colonists must pay a tax on tea."

This and other unfair taxes brought on the Boston Tea Party on December 16, 1773.

### The Boston Tea Party

The night air was still as about 200 men and boys dressed as Mohawk Indians hurried down back alleys toward three ships waiting in Boston Harbor. . . .

*Jamie*

### The Time of Witch Hysteria: The Salem Witch Trials

Do you believe in witches? Back in the 1600s in Salem, Massachusetts, they did. They believed in voo-doo, spells, and the devil. They believed that the devil had a big, black book in which all the witches signed their names. In 1692 there was witch hysteria in Salem.

*Mindy*

These two samples of content writing, the leads to reports on the Boston Tea Party and the Salem Witch trials, differ markedly from the encyclopedia-copied reports I used to receive from my fifth graders three years ago. Since learning to use the process of writing, my students have written reports that sound like *themselves* rather than like the *World Book*.

Content writing in my classroom is an extension of the personal writing my students do throughout the year. From the beginning of the school year in September, they follow the writer's process. After

---

*Adapted from *Breaking Ground: Teachers Relate Reading and Writing in the Elementary School* by Jane Hansen, et al., 1985. Exeter, NH: Heinemann. Copyright 1985 by Heinemann. By permission.

brainstorming for topic choice, they draft, revise, edit, and prepare a final copy. Conferring is a crucial part of this approach and occurs often at each stage. Conferences provide response for the writer and help him clarify his ideas and improve the quality of his work.

I begin content writing in January after the students have written for several months and the writing process has become a part of their behavior. The content writing process can be organized into different stages, most of which are similar to the writing process: *research, rehearsal, drafting, revising, editing,* and *publishing and sharing.*

### Research

Before my students select topics, they spend weeks developing an extensive background in a general area, in this case, Colonial America. The class begins the study together with discussions and general textbook readings. During this time, I encourage my students to do as much background reading as possible in both school and public libraries. They read short, easy books first, and then move on to more difficult material (Calkins, 1980). Research occurs at the beginning and continues throughout the process.

As they finish reading books, they compile a rough bibliography in their journals. They write often in their journals while they read or after completing a book (Tchudi and Tchudi, 1983). They record interesting facts, opinions, feelings, and ideas resulting from their readings. For example, John wrote after reading about the colonial shoemaker: "I can't believe it, shoemakers pulled teeth! I didn't know that. I don't think I'd want to go to one." This fact became part of his lead when he wrote his report.

First, each student tries to acquire as much information as possible about the broad subject by reading both nonfiction and historical fiction for two or three weeks. They view filmstrips and films and listen to cassettes. Their ideas and findings are discussed with partners or in small groups. Then each student begins to focus on a specific topic that interests him the most—the colonial shoemaker, the Salem witch trials, the Boston Tea Party, school discipline—all having to do with Colonial America. For the next few weeks, they learn as much as possible about their particular topic.

### Rehearsal and Drafting

When my students become "experts" in their field of interest, they are ready to write. In conferences, they teach a partner everything they know about their topic. The room hums with accounts of the Boston Massacre, colonial school punishments, whaling, and shipbuilding.

After these brainstorming conferences, the children write everything they know about their subject, using only one side of the paper.

They record their information in any order and include questions they have and facts they need to know. If they can't think of words or dates, they leave blank spaces to be filled in at a later time. The purpose of this activity is to write everything they remember.

During the next writing session, they read their first drafts and look for two or three subtopics or chapters. These chapter headings are placed on separate sheets of paper. Then each child takes his or her original draft and cuts it up, taping all parts having to do with one chapter on the appropriate page in any order. They include any questions or facts they need to know. They read through their journals and place their thoughts, interesting facts, and opinions on the correct chapter page.

Once this activity has been completed, the class is ready for further research. Now they use encyclopedias to find the answers to specific questions, although they continue to read trade books as well. Their research is conducted independently in the school library, and they follow the rule established in the classroom: they cannot read and write at the same time (Calkins, 1980). Once they discover information, they read it, turn the book over, and write it under the proper chapter. The rule practically eliminates copying from a book or an encyclopedia. When they finish gathering the additional information they need, they are ready to write.

### Revising

My students take each chapter separately and treat it as a personal writing piece—*drafting, revising, editing,* automatically. Since the first draft of each chapter is very disorganized, their revision strategies are similar to those developed during the months of personal writing. After reordering information, they add supportive details, work on leads, and develop strong endings. John's journal entry about the colonial shoemaker as dentist appears in this lead to one chapter:

> The colonial shoemaker had to be a talented man, Not only did he make saddles and harnesses, he made his own tools and he pulled teeth!

The children are eager for response and confer with each other and me often. Because they are experts on their topics and frequently know more than I do, I have to be a listener. I ask questions when I truly do not understand. Conferences often take the form of discussions as the children explore their ideas about representation, authority, independence, and revolution. My respect for my students has increased as I have listened to and participated in their lively discussions. They have not only taught me about their topics, but also about their strategies for writing.

# What happened

The Boston tea party was
am act in ~~which~~ England
taxed the tea. ~~the C~~.

. 342 cases of tea were dumped
into ~~the~~ water

broke on board  3 ~~ships~~ ~~the S~~

hull. that had tea in their
~~They~~ broke ~~the~~ boxes and
cut through  the canvas and
~~dumped~~ the tea overboard
~~they~~ went into the water,
and found a problem ~~the~~

water was to shallow and
~~the~~ tea was ~~sticking up~~.
like hay. So ~~they~~
~~splashed~~ the ~~tea~~ around

Jamie's chapter on What Happened for his "Boston Tea Party" looked like this.

Many of the ideas expressed at these conferences appear in their reports. Jamie notes in his description of the Boston Tea Party:

> One thing I found interesting above all, was that not one ounce of tea was stolen. That way England could not call it robbery, but it could be called a demonstration.

Mindy expresses her feelings about the Salem Witch trials:

> Nineteen unlucky people got hanged. It was stupid and terrible what they did to these innocent people. Children were left home-less and many people died in jail of sickness and starvation. . . . Now you can imagine what a fix those girls were in. If they con-fessed the real reason—that they were pretending—they would get in so much trouble. If they lived in our days they would get grounded for five years. But, on the other hand, if they didn't confess, more people would get hanged and hurt.

### Editing, Publishing, and Sharing

When the students complete their revisions, in editing conferences, they search for vivid language and precise words to make their reports more interesting and lively.

They prepare the final copy with pride. After copying carefully in pen, they add a table of contents, illustrations, a cover, title page, and a full bibliography. Finally, they enjoy sharing their reports with their peers.

Report writing by this method takes more time than the tradi-tional approach. It takes time to read, to talk together, to revise. In the old days, my class would do five or six reports. Now they complete fewer, briefer reports. However, content writing in this manner offers many rewards for my students and me:

1. Real learning and thinking take place.
2. Reports are more focused, interesting pieces.
3. Students' writing improves.
4. Students, not the parents, write the reports. The child's voice, heard in conferences, comes through in the reports.
5. Students are more enthusiastic and involved.

As one student expressed it:

> I love doing reports this way. I know a lot about the Boston Tea Party. Last year my report on the Heart was 20 pages long. I copied it all from the *World Book* and *Encyclopoedia Britannica*—and I didn't learn a thing about the heart!

# Beyond Writing:
# Extending Revision Strategies

CORA FIVE
*(United States)*

As my fifth-grade students became more familiar with the stages of the writing process, I enjoyed listening to them talk to me and to each other about their writing. I came to realize the importance of a listener's response before real thinking and revising could occur. Questions and comments from others appeared to help writers clarify and expand their ideas, thus improving the quality of the students' work. Respect for student ideas was always present because the writer might or might not accept suggestions. The final decisions were his because ownership remained with him throughout the writing process.

Because I noticed revision based on response seemed to be part of my students' behavior in writing, a series of questions occurred that had implications for other areas of the curriculum. Would individual feedback or response bring better learning of other subjects, in addition to writing? Would brainstorming help students learn history, science, math? Could students improve their understanding of these subjects if they revised as they did with their writing?

## Revising Ideas About History

As our history unit, "Who Discovered America?" progressed, the class examined many kinds of historical evidence: artifacts from the Vikings, Columbus's journal, sea routes from China to North America, and pyramids found in Egypt and Mexico. They were encouraged to confer and revise their ideas. Initially, most were sure it was Columbus or the Indians who were the discoverers of America. A journal entry stated, "Columbus discovered America because my teacher told me last year." Another child wrote, "The Indians were here first because Columbus saw them when he came." Each new source produced discussion with partners or in small groups and also a change in thinking. Was it probable that the Vikings had arrived in North America? Was it possible that the Chinese and the Egyptians had come to our shores?

With each piece of evidence, I became aware of their revised ideas until, finally, as our unit came to an end, most journal entries centered around the generalization that America was discovered and rediscovered over time by many groups.

I could have provided them with this generalization easily and in less time, but how exciting to see it emerge from them as they revised their thinking with each new source of historical evidence.

## Revising Scientific Thinking

The process worked again in a science unit on bridges. The students first studied balancing through a variety of experiences. They brainstormed and conferred about the differences between mass and force, recording all their activities and ideas in their journals. The concepts they developed were then applied to bridge construction. Their project was to build a bridge using 50 plastic straws and as much tape and clay and as many straight pins as they required.

As they began the design and building of their bridges, I noticed they were going through a form of brainstorming. They did more talking than actual work as they discussed ideas and experimented with materials. Finally, when the actual building began, they tried many different ways of making a bridge that would not collapse. There was much conferring and sharing of ideas. They wanted response and were very accepting of suggestions as they revised their bridges by adding triangles and squares to make them stronger. They tore down and reconstructed their bridges many times. They conferred, researched, and revised again. And each time, the bridges improved.

The revision process was recorded in their journals.

1/18　I kept revising my bridge until I changed it 4 times!

1/20　Crash! Bang! Boom! My bridge has just fallen down for the eighty trillionth time. I'm going to make a new one. This time I'll add two towers, which will hold more weight.

*Mindy*

1/20　"Oh no!" I exclaimed as I stared at my ex-bridge. Straws were all over the place. My poor bridge had fallen apart. I took my straws and started to build Bridge, III. I put on triangles and attached straws and poked in pins.

1/25　"Now I will add on some trusses and supports," I decided firmly. "Good idea," said Emily, "because your bridge does not look very strong."

*Rebecca*

1/20　Bang! My crossbar fell apart. I made a better one by reinforcing my old one with millions of pieces of tape and new string. My teacher came over and said, "Now what will help make your bridge stronger?" I answered with an "Arch!" So I put an arch under my bridge. It looked DEMENTED but it is stronger.

*Emily*

Days later the same girl wrote:

1/31　It held 1,508 grams. It is probably the best structure I have ever built. Even though it looks like a mess it holds a lot.

After completing the bridges, the students solved math problems related to the unit. How long would your bridge have to be to hold you? Once again they went through the process. They brainstormed and experimented with different methods to find a solution. They conferred and revised their thinking until the problems were solved. The process had now extended into mathematics.

### Revision in Dance

I became convinced that this approach to learning had become part of my students' behavior when they were involved in an activity designed to increase their appreciation of dance. A teaching artist had come from Lincoln Center in New York City to work with my class. She and I had taught them the elements of dance. She left them with a very complicated assignment: to work in small groups and to create an original dance using definite movements and specific pathways.

It was now part of my teaching style to listen and look and let my students "own" their creations and be in charge of their learning. I gave them the time and the space, and I watched.

Once again they brainstormed for a topic or a theme for their dance. They planned their movements and use of space on paper as a first draft. In the following sessions, they revised their dances and performed them for the class. They wanted response. Which movements were clear? Could the pathways be seen? Did they focus on the topic? The response from their peers was invaluable. They returned to their groups, discussed possible changes, scribbled notes, and made revisions in their dances based on the feedback they had received from their peers.

Their process continued throughout the two-week assignment. When they finally performed their completed pieces for the teaching artist and their peers, they had produced outstanding dances.

What kept these 10-year-olds revising and perfecting their work? Why didn't they stop after their first attempt at building a bridge, solving a math problem, or creating a dance? Because they had attained success through revision in the past, they revised readily, looking forward to an improved product. Donald Graves (1983) says ". . . the force of revision, the energy for revision, is rooted in the child's voice, the urge to express." In order to revise, students need response to their ideas. Response helps them clarify their ideas and enables them to express in their own voice what they are thinking.

Revision based on response has now become part of my teaching and extends to all areas of the curriculum. My students know that revision eventually leads to an improved, completed project, piece, or idea. This understanding motivates them to expend "the energy for revision" that Graves (1983) believes "is not necessarily a natural act." By revising and refining ideas, my students take charge of their own learning and thereby gain greater mastery over the subject matter.

# Writing:
# From Motivation to Correction

JOCELYN TARRANT
(New Zealand)

Writing is a pain! Yesterday I read so much educational guff about how to teach kids to write that I was convinced I couldn't—at least not for teachers with their learned words, clever images, and fine twists to sentences. Well, if it is like this for me, how much worse is it for kids? Thank God for Donald Graves! His views have sparked the hearts and minds of concerned classroom teachers, revolutionizing writing.

I have been influenced by colleagues who loved kids, life, and literature, and had holistic approaches to teaching similar to the "organic" view of Sylvia Ashton-Warner. I have taken my perspective from sociolinguistic and anthropological scholars, and I view writing as one form of communication in relation to other expressive arts. I share with my pupils, not only in reading to appreciate the style of recognised past writers, but also towards realisation of the richness of culturally different expression in the writings of, for example, Achebe, James Baldwin, Naipal, and the collections and comments of Chris Searle, Witi Ihimaera, and Albert Wendt.

The adulation of the (outdoor, sporting, practical) "good keen man" (and woman) and the belief that modern technology is ending the need to read and write, produces a general lack of motivation among students to put pen to paper. When they do, they often show an inability to differentiate between appropriate use of colloquial and formal written modes. The oral orientation which continues into contemporary Maori and other Polynesian cultures and a definite antipathy among these minority group pupils towards learning English, also provide a challenge.

The first challenge is to motivate by providing immediate and real reasons for writing. Passing examinations and gaining employment can no longer be used as carrots. The desire to share and the love of learning are primary motivations which can be fostered by starting where each pupil is, by teacher enthusiasm for and participation in writing with pupils, by sharing in and vitalizing experiences with talk, and by capitalizing on special interests and individual knowledge. For there to be preparedness to bare the self on paper, there must be reciprocal trust and honesty between teachers and pupils. Without this, writing is "busy work," bland and boring., with the writers hiding behind meaningless fact or the fantasy of TV soaps and thrillers.

Writing should be exploring and often having fun with words.
There is a thrill in dictating to a competent scribe (usually the teacher)
and seeing your real thoughts in "print" even while your own writing
skills are still limited, in transforming words into music and art forms,
in shaping word/picture collage posters. There's the fun of "gyre and
gimballing" with words—their sounds with meanings, meanings with
shapes—of writing shape poems, and of summing up experience in a
haiku, a sentence, a single word. "Hot topics" (Graves) and "key
words" (Ashton-Warner) motivate and bring passion and liveliness.

We are fortunate in New Zealand in that our children write from
their first days at school when they dictate the stories in their drawings,
then proudly display them. The ground is well prepared by creative
approaches to reading and writing in primary schools where our children still shape their own words, scanning and analysing them as their
hands move. (Preserve us from sentence-makers!)

Yes, at times we write with our classes, show them our "roughs"
and those of recognised writers. We not only read our contemporary
literature but under a "Writers in Schools" scheme, have such as Barry
Crump, Patricia Grace (1975, 1978, 1980), Maurice Gee (1979a, 1979b,
1979c, 1979d), or the boilermaker poet, Hone Tuwhare (1964, 1970),
come to talk about their own work.

The second challenge is that of giving pupils confidence in their
own ability to write interestingly, appropriately and independently.
To do this they need to know what they are going to say, to have the
skills to say it simply, clearly and concisely (not wasting words), and
to be able to evaluate their work and that of others.

Most writing is preceded by talk in full class and/or small groups,
and in discussion and brainstorming sessions to sort ideas, build up
vocabulary, and reinforce certain structures. Skeleton outlines, sequence pictures, summary outlines (main topic/subtopic), incomplete
sentences and paragraphs, and substitution tables are built up in the
process as supports.

When doing writing, other than journal writing, pupils also need
models and patterns to extend, manipulate, or transform. There is need
to predict what language a topic will generate and to control or guide
if new language is to be learned. Too much free writing is leaving some
pupils floundering in a morass of words. Frequent class reading of all
sorts of prose and poetry, working on and discussing set readers or
extracts, displaying, and, whenever possible, publishing of successful
pieces of writing by their peers, setting aside time for sustained silent
reading—all of these build up language reservoirs as well as a store of
(vicarious) experiences. Themes, situations, and characters from poems,
prose, films, and plays are used to extend opportunities for writing in
appropriate registers and styles. Swarthout's *Bless the Beasts and Children* gives rise, for example, to letters to and from parents and camp

authorities, ads for the holiday camp, collage posters of word profiles and pictures (drawn or found) to represent each boy and his headgear, social worker's file cards for the boys, Cotton's death notice, the police report, thoughts of a boy looking back on events, and research notes on the buffalo or other threatened species. This writing is done over a period of three to four weeks, some as part of a group project and some as individual work.

With a class of poor and reluctant readers, I have read numbers of young children's books. I read some to them, they bring some to me, so that we can find the appropriate layout, size of print, illustrations, and language to make "big books" for infant class "shared reading." Each group which works on a book takes great pride in presenting and reading it to the children.

I can always honestly say that there is something interesting and worthy of comment in every piece of writing—in the experience, ideas, feelings, facts, and/or the way they are expressed—although sometimes my comment brings a wry smile from the writer. After conference with a pupil, if an "error" occurs again, I put a dot in the margin and underline awkward, inappropriate, or incorrect constructions. Pupils should be able to correct these previously taught items. When writing for formal and public purposes (including classroom display), their work should be "correct." To aid pupils in this, I use a cooperative approach, which also takes the loneliness out of writing. Pupils talk over what is going to be written in a group. Then, after going off to write independently and checking their work, they return to the group to read aloud or to have others proofread and discuss their scripts. Sometimes groups are asked to assess the scripts. When given guidelines, they do so very well.

The third and final challenge is hardest for pupils to face, for appropriate language is learned by living—by many exposures to a variety of situations real and vicarious. I find pupils who are being confused by being expected to write in a number of registers, dialects, and styles when the burning need is that they gain confidence in a simple, clear, concise style, basically appropriate for the formal writing which they will have to do and be judged by in the future. While expressive writing is important for all levels, we must make sure that pupils have practice in the high priority forms of transactional writing—letters, reports, minutes of meetings, notes, instructions, ads, etc.

We write letters to invite and thank visitors and to request information for English/social studies/science studies. Even the front row forwards were determined to be correct when they offered to reply to a girls' school. They had never received nor written a letter in their lives before!

The New Zealand national curriculum gives guidelines emphasising the importance of expressive writing, writing for various audiences and in appropriate register, dialect, and idiom according to purpose. There are no district curricula, and, in my last school, we were left free to meet the needs of pupils within the limits of time, materials, and public examinations. The school programme was coordinated by the Head of English mainly through frequent staff meetings and consultations with individual teachers.

Expressive writing was an integral part of our programme, although once pupils reached School Certificate (Form 5), transactional writing began to play a major role. By Form 6, expressive writing was largely limited to helping pupils come to grips with literature and language studies.

We made efforts to consult with other subject teachers, especially over format for summaries, letters, minutes, and study skills in general. There are always a number of subject teachers requesting help with general writing skills for pupils, but time and timetables militate against this being given to any great extent.

### A Footnote About Style

Teachers are constantly reminded that "errors" can be markers of nonprestigious dialects or variants. But have they become aware of subtleties of style as carriers of *cultural* as well as social values? Are "purple patches," the odd choice of metaphor, the use of present tense to refer to the long dead, and the unusual selection of detail and gaps in description, deficiencies or significant expressions of our pupils' cultures? I miss the unique style and freshness of my first Maori pupils' writing. Have we taught it out of them?

# Punctuation

PETER FORRESTAL
*(Australia)*

Our approach to the teaching and learning of punctuation must acknowledge the importance of careful punctuation in effective communication as well as taking into account what we know of the writing process and of students as writers.

There are times when students must concentrate on getting their ideas down on paper and clarifying what they want to say. This will be in the earlier stages of the writing process, such as working on a first draft. Once students have clarified their initial ideas to themselves, they are free to make their meaning clear to others. Through the drafting process, which involves revising, rewriting, editing, and proofing, writers struggle to clarify their meaning. It is at the later stages of editing and proofing that students need to focus on punctuation. At this juncture, we as teachers can do our most effective work—alongside writers striving to communicate their meanings, for we know some important traits of students as writers:

- Students, as do professional writers, find writing hard work.
- Students don't carefully edit their work because they haven't been given enough time or they didn't consider it important to produce correct writing.
- Students can't be compelled to care about writing.
- Students will write well when it matters to them.
- Students will improve as writers if they write often and if they acquire the habit of revising their writing.

All of these traits have relevance for what we as teachers do in the classroom to help students develop their writing abilities.

One of the great dilemmas we face in attempting to develop students' competence with the surface features of language is our concern with giving them assistance at the point of need and our desire for the security of a systematic approach. We need to provide students with information which sets out clearly *when* and *why* we use particular punctuation marks and gives examples of the way each is used. In this way, we can help them to understand when to use particular punctuation marks and by analogy, other features of "correct" writing.

The best time to do this is when they are editing their own writing. For example, when students are having problems using apostrophes, we should direct their attention to the rules for the use of apostrophes. After they have read this, they should review their own writing and correct it. This is teaching at the point of error at its best. What is different about it is that we are placing a focus on students understanding when and why punctuation is used. There is a good case to be made for this strategy being supplemented with a systematic approach covering all of the punctuation marks over a set time, possibly a term.

The approach centres around providing a technical focus for each extended student writing. This technical focus can be influenced by the kind of student writing completed. For example, direct speech can be the technical focus in any story and exclamation marks in a conversation which degenerates into argument. Other punctuation marks may be chosen in similar ways.

A brief explanation of the punctuation mark, with examples of its use before students commence their writing, draws to the attention of students the importance that teachers place on correct punctuation. By itself, however, this short input is unlikely to teach students the use of a particular punctuation mark. If teachers follow this up by allowing editing time where the primary focus is on looking at the particular punctuation mark under scrutiny, then students are likely to understand and use that punctuation with greater confidence and correctness.

Systematic teaching is both important and necessary, but is unlikely to be effective by itself. It will give teachers the security of knowing that they are covering punctuation systematically as well as ensuring that students are made aware of the range of punctuation marks on a regular basis. The key to the success of this approach lies in students understanding when and why punctuation is used. This is most likely to be achieved if teachers refer students to the rules on punctuation when they have a specific need.

# A Secondary Writing Programme

MARIAN HOBBS
*(New Zealand)*

I have been very heavily influenced by the seminars given by Donald Graves and John Dixon during their respective visits to New Zealand in 1982 and 1984. Prior to Donald Graves' teaching, I used to give topics and styles and expect essays to be completed in class. My judgment of what is good writing has not changed, but my method for achieving it has.

I am also lucky to have been a member of an English department whose head has encouraged us to experiment with different programmes to improve writing.

### Writing Programme for Forms 3 and 4 (13- and 14-Year-Olds)

Form 3 has three hour-long English classes in a week, and Form 4 has four. Students work with their writing for about one and a half hours every week. The time can be organised as either half an hour three times a week or one class for one hour's writing and a second class for half an hour. The three half-hour slots is preferable. It is important that the students know that they have a regular writing time to prepare themselves for what they want to write.

Each student has a writing folder. At the beginning of each year, I introduce my classes to their writing programme which includes setting out their folders. The most important task is making a list of topics they may want to write about. To elicit these topics, I use several headings:

1. What do I like doing?
2. What do I hate doing?
3. What would I like to do or to be?
4. What makes me angry or sad?

Should a student enjoy tramping, then I show that she could describe a tramp that she had done; she could base a murder story around a tramp; she could write a "mood piece" about waking up in the early morning from an outdoor sleep, or she could write clear instructions on how to cook an evening meal outdoors. What the student will be working at will be the expression, not the subject matter, because that is what she is familiar with.

The topic list inside the folder cover and the list of different styles and approaches provide a stimulus for those days when "I've got nothing to write about" is the prevalent mood.

Students quickly acquire a personal routine for the writing "periods." Some have one long piece of writing that is added to, others prefer short pieces, written on each day, and others have several pieces on the boil. I intervene by asking four or five students to bring their folders to me. We sit together and read and discuss what is in them. It takes a while to break the students' expectations that I am going to mark their stories.

If assessment is needed in junior school for reports to parents, I ask them to submit their three favourite pieces. But, again, grading these presents problems. A full written report to parents, showing their strengths and weaknesses in writing, is far more honest and helpful, even if time consuming.

A stimulation to others' writing and a social assessment or audience is provided by my reading aloud a student's work to the class or small group. Therefore, English rooms need to be *large*—they need space to think and write without distraction and space for quiet discussion.

## Writing Programme for Form 5 (15-Year-Olds)

The writing programme here is really threatened by time pressure. In my present school, fifth formers have five hours of English a week. We write for either one hour a week, or I have found it better to allocate a block of, say, 10 weeks in the second term to writing for three hours a week. It has had a marked effect on the students' writing skills, even for the kind of pressure writing needed in examinations.

Again, publication of the students' work provides a necessary audience and a purpose for writing. Typing classes practise deciphering scripts and layout and a bound volume of a term's best pieces makes a good publication.

## Writing Programme for Senior Classes

I haven't yet succeeded in providing a suitable senior writing programme. The examination pressure is worse than ever, and the demands of the university programmes are largely for expository and critical writing. Much of the creative joy leaves writing.

However, the study of writing, of literary works, and of language can be effectively interleaved. So although there is little time for block writing programmes, there is opportunity for developing a wide range of writing skills and styles for different registers.

Major problems face anyone attempting to establish an effective writing programme. In Forms 5, 6, and 7, examinations put a time limitation on what you can offer. In the junior school, the school structure works against a good programme. To enable students to dabble in a wide number of subjects, time for English is often cut back. Unfortunately, this is further compounded by the fact that in many subjects little sustained writing is done in the early secondary years. When the student reaches Forms 5 and 6, there is a sudden jump in writing demands, particularly for English, history, geography and economics.

Tertiary education demands clear writing in reports and essays. Many jobs demand writing skills—yet the student who leaves in Form 4 or 5 has done little writing.

The community envisages writing skills as being those of correct spelling, punctuation, and clear handwriting. They do not see the correlation with thinking and rethinking. Community expectations can actually work against the aims of my style of writing programme. Parents, therefore, should be shown how the programme works. They can see that punctuation is taught as the children see the need for it in order to express themselves more clearly—particularly when their classmates cannot understand what has been written.

We need time to write and need a pattern of set classes. We all need constant practice (as writing these articles has reminded me!). Perhaps we can persuade all subject teachers of the importance of writing as well as reading across the curriculum.

# Personal Involvement in Writing

CHARLOTTE JONES
*(United States)*

Renewed interest in teaching composition challenges teachers to develop practical strategies that are founded in current theory. For many years, English teachers have been trained to teach only the literature component of our curriculum. Now teacher-training institutions are preparing English teachers to guide students through the "writing process," so that essays speak with believable voices and students gain confidence in themselves as writers.

My composition students are actually encouraged to express themselves in their own language, calling upon their own experiences. I do not ask them to write on "What A Daffodil Thinks of Spring"; rather, I ask them to react to school, friends, contemporary issues, and themselves. I want them to become personally involved in their writing. I believe that when they are free to select their own topics, they have information, a voice, and an investment in their work. Their best writing presupposes focused and edited inner speech. Ownership and pride are critical considerations. In addition, I have found that students are more agreeable to revising their compositions if they have a personal investment in them. The purpose of writing is to carry ideas from the mind of one person to the mind of another. When we revise our writing, we better understand our own thinking.

Our first writing assignment for a college class focuses on autobiography or memoir. From this general topic my students choose to write on "My Trip over...," "A first in my life," or "A phase in my life." The second assignment focuses on people, places, and events. Possible topics here include: the most influential person in my life, a place of business (perhaps a possible career choice), and an evening at a pub. Students are encouraged to interview someone out in the "real" world who touches a corner of their lives. Through dialogue, these essays become lively and reflect students' own language patterns. Paper three focuses on opinion or persuasion. Here students examine troubling issues that face them. Some of these issues stem from their reading of *Time* magazine; others from local and school problems; still others spring from personal problems where students are working through difficult situations with parents, peer pressure, or dating. The fourth paper focuses on knowing and learning. Students use this paper to discover answers to questions they have about something personal. These papers include documentation and summaries. The final paper of the course is a series of survival writings. Included here are business letters, memos, letters of application, resumés, letters to the editor, the five-paragraph essay, and essay examination questions.

I spend approximately three weeks on each paper, working with the students through the actual steps of the writing process. I write along with them. Students gather their ideas in prewriting discussions and discovery drafts; then they submit their new pieces to a peer editing group of four other students. Sitting at a large circular composing table, a student reads her piece to the editing group. She hears her own words and becomes aware of her audience and the difficulties they encounter with her writing. By responding to one another, students learn that writing is not a mysterious act; it is a craft. The peer editing group tells the writer what they liked, what confused them, and then asks questions about future revisions.

After some reflecting time, a student revises her composition and gives me a cassette tape and the draft. This is the first time I have seen her writing, though I have visited editing groups to hear discussions and ask questions. On the tape, I read the composition to the student, stopping to talk about word choices, to ask for clarification, and to comment on her ideas. My students enthusiastically appreciate the tapes. Since I don't mark on the papers, taping requires very little time.

A student listens to the tape, revises the composition, and resubmits it to the peer editing group in carbon or xeroxed copies. This time the group closely examines the piece for misspelled words, fragments, run-on sentences, tense shifts, etc. In short, they are preparing the manuscript for publication. In addition, students may request a conference with me to work through any nagging problems.

The final draft is now typed for publication and given to me. I make two copies for each student; she keeps the original in her portfolio along with a page that records possible topics, works in progress, and personal writing that is not read by others (a journal).

We have created a community of writers by sharing our drafts in an environment that is saturated with writing. Classroom walls display quotations from writers on writing; effective pieces of student writing are taped to the walls and pinned on bulletin boards; raw manuscripts of master writers are exhibited; desk books and textbooks are available for reference; and materials which describe the current concerns in journals devoted to writing sit on bookshelves. An overhead projector is available to examine specific problems in sentences or paragraphs. Underlying this community of writers is a mutual trust that develops as we share our work with one another. Without my suggestion, students in peer groups exchange telephone numbers and meet outside of the classroom. Students learn to risk sharing their writing. Consequently, their compositions have a voice as they gain self-confidence.

Perhaps the success of this writing program, like Robert White's (1952) task of guiding children, can be represented by the metaphor of raising plants. White states that:

> This should be encouraging, because raising plants is one of mankind's most successful activities. Perhaps the success comes from the fact that the husbandman does not try to thrust impossible patterns on his plants. He respects their peculiarities, tries to provide suitable conditions, protects them from the more serious kinds of injury—but he lets the plants do the growing. He does not poke at the seed in order to make it sprout more quickly, nor does he seize the shoot when it breaks ground and try to pull open the first leaves by hand. Neither does he trim the leaves of different kinds of plants in order to have them all look alike.

The trustworthy composition teacher allows students to write confidently with their own voices.

# 4.
# Oral Language and Drama

Not every contributor to this part would agree with New Zealand's Jocelyn Tarrant that "there is now plenty of pupil interaction in our classrooms." In fact, one will read in the following pages a number of appeals to teachers to increase the amount of drama and oral English in their classrooms. However, virtually all the writers would agree with Tarrant that there are many unexamined assumptions in the drama/oral English pedagogy: "A widespread inference is that pupils who are talking are learning. . . . But learning what?" Here teachers describe a number of classroom teaching strategies which show that, in general, our profession is considerably more comfortable with oral English and drama than it was, say, 20 years ago. But, there is also a strong feeling that this is an area ready for deeper research—not *testing,* as Tarrant warns, but thorough investigation of what students experience and master as their teachers move away from the comparatively familiar domains of print literacy into oral language and drama.

# Learning Through Talking

CHRISTINE CHICK
*(England)*

When children first start formalised schooling, speech is the major asset they bring with them; yet it is equally true that children's talk is the asset least capitalised by teachers. *Why?*

Many British schools have spent months producing their own language policies; yet in the classroom, talk is still accorded low status— few teachers' voices are raised in its favour. *Why?*

Perhaps it is that teachers more often perceive their job as needing to curtail children's inherent talkativeness. Perhaps it is because "oracy" is still a relatively new area of the curriculum in its own right. Perhaps it is because, at the end of the day, talk is too elusive to be easily quantifiable; it is therefore difficult to evaluate—and it can't be saved for display.

In recent years, there have been many attempts to come up with some way of mapping oral development, but so far none of them has proved to be satisfactory. For simplicity and easy marking, innumerable checklists have been drawn up with little boxes to tick, cross, fill in, half-fill, or leave pathetically blank. But how can children's use of talk ever be checked off as though it were half done, completely done, or undone? If teachers acknowledge that verbalising is a lifelong process and not merely an accretion of skills, how can they ever perceive it as being finished?

Teaching and learning form a continuum of processes and it is important that teachers, pupils, and parents alike see them as such. Talk is just one strand in this continuum, but in my view as an infant teacher (and as a fully functioning adult), it is a crucial strand. How often, for instance, have you found yourself talking out loud when faced with a particularly knotty problem? Children in school are continually faced with knotty problems as learners; it follows, then, that we should encourage more talk and less silence. In this way, our pupils are helped to formulate their thoughts and feelings—and they also provide us with a verbal window into their thinking.

Perhaps it is more likely that infant teachers will accept the need for children to talk as it is so much second nature for young children to mediate all their experiences orally, whether they happen to be painting a picture, or experimenting at the water table, or responding to the pictures in a book. In kindergarten classrooms (before literacy has taken a firm hold), teachers have no option. To put it more positively, they cannot help acknowledging that talking is the outward and audible sign of the child's learning; that once experience is verbalised, it can take on a wider context to be shared, interpreted, and referred back to at some later stage. Learning doesn't end once we have "talked about" an experience, but it would be true to say that it often *pauses* there.

If talk then plays a natural part in the first classrooms that four- and five-year-olds enter, for me that raises two issues:

1. How can we help to develop children's use of their own mother tongue speech?
2. How can we ensure that space continues to be given for speech development in relation to all the other forms of learning that pupils are required to undertake as they move up through the primary school and on into the shadows of secondary education?

I have no answer to these questions, but I pose them because for me as a teacher and a talker they are important.

In my infant classroom, talk is given high status at all times. I encourage children to tell me about their personal experiences, to talk through their learning difficulties, and to communicate with each other and with other adults who may be visiting our classroom. I am keenly aware that as their teacher I need to be seen to be listening and responding positively so that a genuine dialogue, discussion, or conversation can take place. This aspect of my role is crucial because children learn all too quickly to switch off from such disinterested replies as, "Good, James, now go and do your writing," or reiterative responses which amount to nothing more than restating the child's formulation in a more adult way: "Look! My car wobbles when I switch the motor on." "Yes, your car is vibrating when you switch on isn't it?" In my view, neither of these examples is likely to encourage language development on the part of the child. Rather, the words the child utters should provide starting points for the development of further meaning drawn from the child and not from adult superiority.

If lack of expertise is one of the reasons why so little attention is paid to oral development—the more so as children move up the school—I would not wish this to be regarded as an insurmountable problem. My own interest in talk is based for the most part on my experiences in the classroom and increasingly upon my awareness of the importance of different language uses. This means that in listening to a conversation with children, I can quickly and easily discern their varying purposes for using talk. I can sense the extent to which a child can develop her thinking to reasonable and/or logical conclusions, how far she is content to make a simple statement or to speculate scientifically or imaginatively. From these observations, I am more able to provide appropriate experiences to extend the child's thinking through talking whether in response to verbal or concrete experiences.

The expertise which is required on my part is, in many respects, similar to the expertise of a caring parent: I need the ability to listen attentively, to respond in a way the child understands and appreciates, and the imagination to provide a variety of contexts that will enrich and extend speech and thinking through speech.

Schools need to provide Basil Bernstein's "enabling environments" with powerful models of language for children to experience, both actively and passively. Talk is our major form of communication. It does not need a formalised teaching programme for its development, but it does need the kind of classroom in which children's expressive voices can be brought at all times to the learning which confronts them, alongside teachers who are prepared, at the same time, to raise their own awareness of how talk provides the chief mode of shaping and reshaping meaning.

# Classroom Drama —
# Another Approach

NOEL PRICE
*(New Zealand)*

I teach in a school where 90 percent of the students are Polynesian (Maoris or Pacific Islanders) in a country where the dominant culture is European. Whereas in other schools I have found it relatively easy to run a discussion-based classroom, I now find this very difficult. I have run up against numerous barriers. I recognise some of these: cultural mores which discourage children from expressing their opinions; cross-cultural barriers and misinterpretations which hinder the mutual flow of meaning between the class and me; minority ethnic status which undermines the pupils' self-image, their belief in the value of their own culture and ideas; widespread unemployment which produces feelings of disaffection and powerlessness; working-class experience which tends to downplay facility with spoken words and discussion generally; and a consumer society which emphasises fun, speed, noise, gratification, and a general passivity. There will be many other causes.

Dorothy Heathcote (1980) pointed the way to a different approach, that of involving pupils in various dramatic activities. These offer an alternative to discussion work. Worthwhile role play demands real thought and language. The issues and ideas that form the substance of the role play must be worked through and turned into speech. The process is perhaps less conscious and structured, less abstract and objective, and this may be why it has greater appeal for my pupils. Yet the process may be even more complex because the ideas must be examined within the framework of an assumed role.

Unfortunately, "taking drama" is normally seen as a specialist skill; English teachers attend drama courses in droves, but few of them use drama in their own classrooms. The simple truth is that the majority believe it to be beyond their pedagogic and management capabilities.

For this reason, people have been trying to develop an approach to classroom drama that can be used by ordinary teachers in their own classrooms, that doesn't require special equipment or training, and that will work also with pupils who are normally uninterested or lack the confidence to speak out in a standard classroom discussion.

What follows is a step-by-step procedure that has been developed, together with a real example from my own teaching.

### Stage 1—Input

This is the most important stage, but not one requiring any expertise in drama. A "story" of some kind is needed. It could be a poem, a short story, a film drama, an incident from a longer story or film, an issue or event from a newspaper, or something you make up yourself.

This story must involve issues that are of interest and significance to the pupils. The issues raised should be likely to bring out different, conflicting attitudes in different people and different groups in society. Finally, the situation should allow for several possible decisions/developments/courses of action.

### *Example*

Here, in bare outline, is a story I made up and told the class. (It was more detailed, and put into language that they could understand.)

"When I was on supervision patrol at lunchtime I found a group of 16-year-olds who had, contrary to the rules, gained entry to a locked classroom. When I entered the room I found that they were drinking (or sniffing glue, smoking marijuana, etc.), and some of the group were noticeably under the influence."

### Stage 2—Giving the Example

This step requires a teacher to be the first to take a role. You can do it yourself, or rope in a colleague. Prepare the class by asking which character(s) they would like to talk to, and, especially, what questions they would like to ask. Then bring in your colleague and introduce him or her as the appropriate character. Or, if you are doing it yourself, leave the room, change your jacket, and come back into the room in role.

The initial response is normally laughter, but this stops as soon as the first answer begins. The intensity with which pupils believe this transparent fiction is often astonishing—and exciting—especially if the character is unpleasant.

#### *Example*

I followed the suggested procedure, waiting till I had several recommendations so I could choose the ones I thought most workable. I began by taking my own role as the teacher who had discovered the goings-on. I was able to embellish my story and describe some of those involved.

Later, I introduced a colleague (who had been prepared and told the story) as one of the pupils.

Depending on the story and the class, this stage can be repeated with several characters. It may even be possible to persuade one of the pupils to take a role. Knowing the class well is important.

### Stage 3—Putting the Pupils in Role

The class is divided into groups of three to five, each group collectively representing one person or group in the drama. They have three or four minutes to discuss the situation, and to talk about how the person or group will react to the situation. The teacher has become the teacher again, and moves around the groups, asking questions, making suggestions, trying to ensure that they are ready to be publicly questioned.

One person from each group is then elected or selected to speak in role, say what should happen, and answer questions that you or others may ask. Knowing your class well will help ensure that your first speakers will perform this task satisfactorily.

*Example*

The groups were chosen to represent the students, the duty teacher, other teachers who taught the students, and the principal. One person from each group then spoke about what should happen next and why. I asked other questions such as: "Should I tell your parents?" "Where did you get the drink?" "Whose ideas was it?"

*Note:* It is important to emphasise listening at all stages. Anything said by anyone in role becomes part of the story. Thus, the class collectively creates the story of the drama as it goes along.

This stage may be repeated more than once simply by changing the situations and characters as the story develops. For each new situation, a new spokesperson is chosen, but you may wish to use the same groups.

*Example*

The school principal wishes to talk to some or all of the students, their parents, other pupils, other parents, members of the staff, the guidance counsellor before deciding what to do. Or the situation could involve a doctor, a local minister, a Maori warden, a community worker, the school's governors.

**Stage 4—Elaborating the Role Play**

At some stage during the phase described, two further activities can be added.

The first is for the teacher to assume a role and ask questions, ask for opinions, etc. in that role. If the role is that of an authority figure, it may be possible to handle discipline in that role.

*Example*

The teacher acts as principal, or school governor, or as an official investigator from the Department of Education. This makes it easier to ask questions, to ask for corroboration or disagreement.

The second development is to put groups or individuals into new roles by asking questions which assign roles at the same time.

*Example*

Typical questions might include: "I know you were in the same class as _____. What was he like in class? Did he have many friends? Do you know anything about his family?" Or, "Mary, you've taught/lived next door to _____. How would you describe her? Were you surprised at what happened? How do you think the problem could be solved?"

All of the activities described so far can be done without the pupils leaving their desks. They require no properties, no acting area, no acting even (apart from the requirement that pupils speak in role). Thus it is much easier for shy pupils to participate. And they do. Most pupils enjoy playing games, and they see these activities as a game. Indeed, when I begin, I say that we're going to play a game. It's only later that I explain that what we are doing is creating a drama.

### Further Developments

The activities described are likely to occupy three or more teaching periods. The activities described are interesting and worthwhile in their own right. But they can easily be extended by introducing other language activities, such as writing, reading, and listening.

*Example*

- Pretend that you are a pupil/parent/principal/social worker. Write a letter/report explaining . . .
- Research: finding information on the problem/on the legalities involved. There may be books on the subject that could be recommended.
- Create a poster which warns . . .
- Invite a speaker to address the class.

The activities can also lead to further drama work. A group of (selected) students can be brought out to the front, put into role, and given a situation.

*Example*

I used a group of four—a miscreant plus her parents being interviewed by the principal. Note that situations involving meetings, discussions, or interviews are most useful.

Thereafter, the steps might include having the whole class involved in similar group role plays. In other words, the class (and teacher) can now move into a more conventional classroom drama programme. The role plays can be performed for the whole class, or taped, or filmed. Performance drama now becomes possible.

I believe the approach outlined here is within the capability of most ordinary teachers. The activities are valuable in themselves, but also lead to more sophisticated drama work. They give virtually all pupils an enjoyable experience and a growing sense of personal competence, and the class gets a sense of achievement from having created its own play. Finally, the programme has included a good deal of thinking and languaging.

# Dramatization: One Modality for Oral Language

CORA FIVE

*(United States)*

Drama takes place often in my fifth-grade classroom. It occurs informally as my students write. When questioning John to better understand the picture he had in mind, Jennifer asks: "How did you fall when you went over the ski jump? You didn't show us." Since I have encouraged my students to act out events that appear in their drafts but are not clear, John demonstrates the action or event. He "falls" in slow motion, landing on the floor, saying: "Oh, I remember. My skis were crossed and my poles were behind me in the snow. I had a terrible time getting up. This is the way I had to do it." In such writing conferences, my students use drama to help them add rich detail to their writing pieces.

Drama also occurs in various subject areas throughout the day in simulations, storytelling, skits, and plays. My fifth graders learn about American history through simulations. The boys become delegates at the Consitutional Convention. The girls sit in the back of the room listening intently, angry at being excluded because of their sex. When the simulation is over, the girls express their feelings. "How could they leave women out of the Convention when the colonists were so upset when they weren't represented when King George started taxing them?"

At other times, the students act as members of a town meeting, discussing the problems of future planning for their small community. Or they become part of a wagon train heading west and set up specific rules for their safety and survival during the long trip. They participate in a game where most of the class is treated unfairly for days by a small group given special power to rule. They become totally involved in the experience to the point of yelling in rage and frustration, and finally refusing to play the game or obey the rules. They well understand the feelings of the colonists toward England!

Opportunities for the continued development of oral language and listening skills through drama occur through storytelling. Last year, in order to learn the art of storytelling, my fifth graders selected a story to tell and rehearsed it with a partner. During this time, a professional storyteller visited the school and performed at an assembly, combining pantomime with storytelling. Later in the day, she worked with my students in the classroom, telling stories, explaining the importance of different tones of voice, and the use of pantomime. My students then revised their particular storytelling techniques and told their stories with pantomime to first through fourth graders.

Storytelling leads into the formal aspect of drama. The Scarsdale schools participate in a program with Lincoln Center in New York City designed to increase the children's appreciation of the performing arts, specifically dance, music, and drama. It involves a joint teaching venture with Lincoln Center teaching artists and Scarsdale teachers who have studied at Lincoln Center during summers. Students go through many activities to prepare for a particular Lincoln Center production, most recently *Wind in the Willows* and *The Lion, the Witch, and the Wardrobe.* In both instances, our Lincoln Center teaching artists were real-life directors.

To prepare for *The Lion, the Witch, and the Wardrobe,* the teaching artist and I created a "magic circle." Anyone outside the circle was always a narrator; anyone inside, an actor. Storytelling was once again put to use as the narrator told parts of a fairy tale outside the circle while an "actor" acted it out inside the circle. Eventually the narrator stepped into the "magic circle" and became one of the characters before returning to the outside to continue his narration.

Following the storytelling, the children were introduced to the use of props. They were encouraged to bring a prop to school to use in their actions within the circle. They brought umbrellas, phones, a cane, a ball. After acting with these props, each child selected an animal and researched it to find out how it moves, what it eats, what noises it makes, and what kind of personality it has. The children spent a week "being" that animal. They even learned to talk like the animal. The "sloth's" actions and speech were very slow. The "cow" *moo*-ved in a cumbersome manner, while the "puppy" yapped at her owner's heels.

In class, the students learned about characterization as they focused on their animal. After they had seen *The Lion, the Witch, and the Wardrobe,* they selected props that seemed appropriate to their own animal's behavior—a cloak, a glove, eyeglasses, a purse, fabric. A "panda" wore eyeglasses slightly askew and the "sloth" wrapped fabric around her body to achieve a special effect. The "cow" wore a bell and the "kitten" became tangled in a ball of yarn. They experimented with these props in small groups and with the whole class. Eventually, they formed groups of two to five, and either rehearsed a scene from the play, or developed their own original skits to perform for the class and the teaching artist.

Opportunities for drama abound in social studies, reading, and writing throughout the year. The development of oral language extends into all areas of the curriculum at various times. Drama is part of an integrated language experience which is central to everything my students do. They learn through language.

# Oral Language Literacy

NANCY J. JOHNSON
*(United States)*

Oral language literacy, termed "oracy" by Andrew Wilkinson, is the general ability to use the oral skills of speaking and listening. My experiences teaching in U.S. secondary schools have shown little oral language teaching and exploration, with the exception of speech units isolated from the other languaging processes. Students are often expected to master the "how to" speech in the ninth grade, the explanatory speech in the tenth grade, and the persuasive speech in the eleventh grade. Sometimes a drama unit is offered, but this is usually in the form of drama as literature rather than performance. Those classes dealing with dramatic performance again deal with oral language only in the formal mode.

I believe teachers need to create more informal opportunities for students to explore both speaking and listening. These opportunities can include speech situations with an audience, but need not. Placing students in small groups to discuss themes, conflicts, characters, responses, and reactions to novels, short stories, poems, or films can result in more student participation discussions rather than the all-too-familiar, teacher-directed, question-answer discussions where a small minority of students dominates the entire discussion. Opportunities for students to talk about the books they're reading, the music they're listening to, and the movies they've seen lately often involves more students when groups are arranged by interest.

Here are some oral language explorations I've found successful:

1. *"Fractured Fairy Tales."* Students work in small groups and select and familiarize themselves with a fairy tale. Then they rewrite it either with new characters, a new setting, a different time period, or a different premise, somehow taking the familiar story line and "fracturing" it. Many of may students have seen Saturday morning TV cartoons with Bullwinkle's "Fractured Fairy Tales" and find it easy to work through this project. No lines need to be memorized, but I do find many students conjuring up rough costumes to help create an atmosphere when they "perform" for the rest of the class. One of the funniest fractured fairy tales was a rendition of "The Princess and the Pea," retitled "The Valley Girl and the Credit Card."

2. *Storytelling.* I "teach" storytelling first by having students tell stories about their own lives. I pass out a ditto entitled "Ideas to Trigger Some Great Stories" with ideas such as relating an embarrassing

moment from their past, or retelling the time they discovered there was no Santa Claus, or a particularly frightening experience. From personal stories, we move to an exploration of children's books, fairy tales, myths, legends, and tall tales. I bring in a variety of short literature, and students read until they discover a story they'd like to work into an oral retelling. Then they read and reread that story—to themselves, peers, siblings, parents, to anyone who'll listen. They read until they're so familiar with the story and the characters and the flavor of the story that they don't need to rely on the text anymore. I discourage memorizing and stress a more informal "tell-us-a-story" approach. Kids then share stories with two or three other students, finally sharing with the entire class or with senior citizens or elementary school kids or even on videotape so the stories can be accessible to other classes, libraries, and elementary schools.

3. *"Three-Card Draw."* Students divide into groups of three (number varies, depending on what you want). Each group is given a pink, blue, and green slip of paper. On the pink piece they write an occupation, on the blue paper they write a setting or location, and on the green paper they write a brief conflict (e.g., the toilet overflowed while you were using the bathroom at your date's house). I then collect all pieces of paper, mix them up, and have each group draw one from each of the color piles. The groups are then to attempt to create some kind of oral presentation (one-act play, radio show, dialogue) somehow using all three ideas on the papers they drew. Results have been varied, some quite humorous, and others quite serious. The key here is allowing for a wide variety of possibilities. Your students may need help exploring the options available. "Performances" are given for the entire class, followed or preceded by each group announcing the three ideas they were given to work from. The audience is often more anxious than the performers, as they're curious to see how their occupation, setting, or conflict fit into the oral presentation.

4. *"Response to Literature."* Again students work in groups (size can vary) and select how they want to present a novel, short story, play, or poem to the rest of the class. I prefer to leave the final decision of the presentation form wide open for groups and find the results varied and often top quality when the students have had a say not only in what they present but how they present it. The following are examples that college teacher education students created for oral presentations for particular young adult novels (as they wrote the scenarios themselves):

for *After the First Death* by Robert Cormier:

Rewrite the ending. As a group, pick one scene, rewrite the dialogue, and act it out. Act out the phone call between Ben and

Nettie, changing it to our own personal liking. Write a scenario in which one class member, cast as a media representative, interviews several of the main characters (i.e., Miro, Kate, Ben, etc.) as to their reactions and roles in the drama. If possible, have the reporter draw conclusions or editorialize on some aspect at the program's conclusion. Along the same lines, pretend that it's 10 years later. Interview any surviving members of the incident. (We can decide who's living at this point.) This may include teenagers who were preschoolers on the bus.

### for *Killing Mr. Griffin* by Lois Duncan:

Act out a trial that includes all the characters involved in the crime.

Make a videotape blurb for a movie of the book, advertising the movie by showing several brief scenes.

Make a radio play by selecting certain chapters and rewriting them into shorter scenes. Tape record it and add advertisements.

### for *Tiger Eyes* by Judy Blume:

Choose an important scene from the book and perform it as a one-act play.

In groups of five, debate a two-sided question. Is it better to die suddenly, as Davey's father did, or to be forewarned like Wolf's father was? Or, did Davey handle Jane's drinking problem the right way?

Each student group listed many possibilities for an oral presentation and then selected the one they most wanted to work on. One group had even tape-recorded music to play in the background and added taped sound effects to enhance their presentation. The key in the success of these has to do with student choice. They created the "project" they wanted to work on and present. My staying out of their way during the narrowing and selection process seemed to be an advantage.

# A Secondary Oral
# English Programme

SHAUNA O'CONNOR
*(Australia)*

At Woodridge State High School. oral activities take a variety of forms. At least 30 percent of the English curriculum from Year 8 through Year 12 is devoted to the study and practice of spoken English. This is common practice in most high schools throughout Queensland. As a result, the students at Woodridge have come to perform significantly better in oral English than they do in written English.

The programme is developmental, and the framework can be described as follows:

In Year 8, there is a concentration on helping the students develop the personal confidence to be able to express themselves in front of their peers. These activities are all handled in nonthreatening situations, and students are encouraged to talk about things with which they are familiar.

For Year 9, the emphasis is on public language and the unit titles for this particular year reflect this: *Magazines, Television, Newspapers, Radio, Film* and *Public Speaking.* Each unit deals in some degree of detail, with reading, writing, listening, speaking, and viewing. Students experience the different types of language that are appropriate for each medium, and produce and perform a radio play and a quiz game for television.

*Work Man* and *Leisure Man* provide the focus for Year 10, with emphasis on talks. For Years 11 and 12, students present some of the literature they study in seminar form to class groups, with the literature emerging through such thematic topics as "Australian Identity" (11) and "Romance & Reason" (12).

In recent years, the Year 12 students have been involved in the production and performance of a play that carries significant weight toward semester assessment. It should be noted that the school does have a separate drama department, but this only caters to the relatively few students who wish to study speech and drama as separate subjects.

The Year 12 drama project that students were involved in this year was unique and quite complex. The school was approached by the local community arts officer to participate in a joint community arts production with Kingston High School. The major reason for the project was the lack of entertainment and creative outlets for young people locally. (The project was funded largely by the Australia Council Youth Arts

Incentive Scheme, with assistance from the Queensland Directorate of Cultural Activities, and through special fund-raising events.)

The project consisted of a major community theater residency at Woodridge and Kingston High Schools. A team of community artists—some local and some from interstate—worked with the two schools over 10 weeks. The team included a director, writer, musical artist, composer, administrator, production manager, workshop leader, and two actors.

The students were involved in all stages of the production, including writing, working with the encouragement and guidance of the theater team. As well as this, some of the team and the teaching staff actually took part in the production which focused on community issues and was presented at the Woodridge Shopping Centre. The students benefitted enormously from the whole process of writing, producing, and staging a show. The end of the project coincided with a series of interviews at which Year 12 English teachers discussed with students their feelings on the semester's work. Students were almost unanimous in their high praise for the program. Their self-esteem was clearly higher after the project, and their work was a great credit and source of pride to the community.

# Teaching Oral English and Drama

JOCELYN TARRANT
*(New Zealand)*

A widespread inference is that pupils who are talking are learning (Stubbs, 1976, pp. 113–114). But learning what? There is now plenty of pupil interaction in our classrooms, but more planning and guiding are necessary to ensure that pupils *are* gaining communication skills, and above all, have something worth saying.

Fortunately, our new national curricula link production and reception of language in exploring and developing communicative competence. Teachers who focus on the learner's needs will not go far wrong here. I am concerned, however, that with a growing emphasis on oral language there is also growing pressure on teachers to test pupil performance—even when we know the inhibiting effects of the school on minority group pupils and those others whose home language is not that of the school.

Only recently has attention been given to cross-cultural communication in teacher training programmes. On the whole, we are not well equipped to interpret strategies, let alone teach them. The culturally specific nature of silence, for instance, is little understood. In oral programmes, there is extra pressure on the silent pupil. On the other hand, sensitive use of strategies to create social ease (Labov, 1974) and to take into account ethnically different attitudes and values can open floodgates of fluent speech (Dumont, 1972; Philips, 1972).

Our new English curricula require pupils to be introduced to a "rich diversity of dialects, registers, and idioms" in various formal and informal situations. Plenty of attention is given to what is said, and it is fashionable to talk about body language; but little is done about the prosodic elements—those "contextualization conventions" (Gumperz, 1977) which carry *cultural* messages so frequently misinterpreted and therefore giving rise to ill feeling.

To help rectify this, I have come, among other things, to place importance on story*telling*. It is an enjoyable means of sharing traditions and personal experiences. Powerful "expressive motivation" (Pride, 1978) results in unexpected fluency when conditions are right (Labov, 1972).

Here is an opportunity to show respect for the languages and backgrounds of our pupils, for them to show their skill, and for members of their communities to tell anecdotes, reminiscences, and traditional stories which bring the local area alive. Pupils become aware of the artistry of the skilled storyteller, of cultural as well as social differences in style, and of the richness and validity of orally transmitted material.

When a storyteller is not available, I use tapings (with permission) which I can replay to senior classes for analysis of styles and the structure of oral narrative (Labov, 1974). I have taken lessons which start by pupils listening to a short version of a story in the language of origin. Only *after* listening is a text or translation made available. Pupils are reliant on body language and prosodic "cues" to guess at meaning, or, for a taping, on the prosodic element alone. In giving reasons, for example, as to whether a Maori or European is telling or reading, attitudes to Maoris and their language are revealed and knowledge of prosodic elements is divulged. Few pupils, even at Form 6 (16-year-olds), mention anything more than pronunciation and "tone of voice." In a fast-moving world, pupils need help in coping with the speakers of languages they do not understand. At the moment they are ill-equipped.

If we are to cater for social, cultural, and individual differences, there must be a variety of approaches, methods, and materials. Group activities now play a bigger part in our secondary schools. Pupil-led, small-group discussion promotes talk and hypothetical thinking (Barnes, 1973, 1975), but requires teacher support. I found that 11- to 15-year-olds in a mixed-ability, multi-ethnic class required redirection after five to seven minutes. I make sure that pupils have access to written questions, instructions, and high-priority phrases and vocabulary. I also keep group composition fluid and sometimes refuse free choice in favour of pupils learning to work with personalities and language styles they might not find easy.

In a mixed-ability class, there are always pupils who need more control and guidance than free discussion allows. I use cloze procedures and dictation in a variety of ways, e.g., for testing and for listening as well as written comprehension. Within the usual activities associated with mass media, visiting performers and speakers, role playing, taping, interviews, etc., I now incorporate such things as barrier games and combining and classifying activities which use content material from the various subject areas. These activities give repetitive practice and other reinforcement in interesting ways (Nation, 1976).

The "strip story" (Gibson, 1975) enables pupils of all abilities to operate together in an enjoyable, oral sequencing exercise. An anecdote, for instance, is cut into strips, one sentence per strip. After memorising his or her sentence each pupil repeats it to the others in the group until they arrive at the best sequence. The story is then told to the class, pupil sentence by pupil sentence. Sometimes I have pupils dictate their sentences to each other to provide the bare narrative element as a starter for writing. I have used the "strip story" to revise plots, historical events, and instructions and processes across the curriculum.

While most English classes would have, perhaps, two out of five lessons weekly which are totally or chiefly oral, it is difficult to assess the time given, as oral activity is so much part of most lessons, and all oral lessons have some reading and writing involved. A good part of our oral work springs from class readers, films, etc. Role play, values clarification exercises, and simulation games are quite common in teaching humanities.

In New Zealand, teachers go to considerable trouble to make sure that pupils are exposed to formal standard English by using it for formal parts of teaching; reading to pupils; recording and studying radio and TV news and interviews; taping office, shop and school assembly language, etc.; and inviting visiting speakers.

The encouragement to "talk posh" is mainly through role play, formally run class and school council meetings, and reporting to the class, or on occasions, to the full school assembly. Pupils take turns in welcoming, thanking, and farewelling visitors.

There are usually annual public speaking competitions in which it is expected that all pupils will take part at class level. Among the best, who speak before the whole school and visitors, there are always one or two nonconformist, nonstandard speaking characters.

The success of all oral activities depends on good classroom relationships and a relaxed, accepting atmosphere. It is the teacher's job to provide a variety of models and experiences and support for pupils to make good use of them.

# Living Theatre

ROBERT SQUIRES
*(United States)*

When I was on leave in England in 1973, I read with considerable interest and chagrin that over 50 percent of Americans have never attended a live play, either professional or amateur. Determined that that could not be said of the students in my school, I persuaded the English department to include a live play as part of the curriculum. With the somewhat skeptical support of the administration, we began in the spring of 1974 with *A Midsummer Night's Dream*. The original intention was to operate on a three-year cycle of British, American, and world classics, but we have had to relax that rule because of the difficulty of finding suitable plays for our available talent.

From the beginning, we adopted an extremely broad definition of "classic." Any play that has proven to be enduringly appealing to audiences (even some quite recent ones) or which has some significance in the history of theatre fits our definition. The list of plays at the end of this essay will, I think, demonstrate the breadth of our definition of "classic." We also give a great deal of consideration to our student audience which is, after all, required to attend and is responsible to know the play's content for writing assignments and classroom discussion. That means, of course, that the play must be entertaining enough for a captive audience, easy enough for ninth graders, and challenging enough for twelfth graders. To date we have not done a totally serious play, but *The Diary of Anne Frank* is under consideration. We believe it will be a "safe" choice because all ninth graders study the play and the film, and all students will bring that background to a performance.

The play is usually scheduled for early May. Most of our productions have taken slightly more than three periods. We schedule half of the play during the two periods before lunch and the remainder for the first two periods after lunch. The students attend without charge. One or two evening performances for the community are scheduled to pay production costs. Since this is educational theatre in the best sense, we try to make the project break even. Only twice has the show lost money, and those losses were made up by the modest profits from other years.

The study of plays is, of course, part of our literature curriculum at all levels, but we believe Oneonta High School is unusual in making the study of a play in performance a curriculum project. We are, we hope, training students to study and to appreciate plays as their authors meant them to be appreciated, but we are also training students in critical skills and in audience etiquette.

Because they have all seen the play, students who have managed to get through class discussions of literature without having read the books suddenly begin to contribute opinions and critical comments, making discussions livelier and not the exclusive property of the brightest and most industrious. Most students are also assigned by their English teachers to adopt the role of the theatre critic and write reviews as though for publication. I am always pleased by the intelligent and open way in which my ninth graders lavish praise and offer criticism. And they seldom agree among themselves, which means that discussions before they write are great fun for me because I rarely have to prod or ask leading questions. They are eager to persuade each other.

Besides our major objectives, we are continually discovering curriculum possibilities. Students who ordinarily shun theatre, both as participants and as audience, have become involved in "safe" activities like designing posters and program covers. Once we took all English classes to the stage so that they could see how the intricate set change and special effects for *The Madwoman of Chaillot* were managed. Sometimes we are able to get students in the building trades curriculum to work on scenery, especially when we are able to make plausible the excuse that we have an insoluble problem.

A minor benefit is shared by a relatively small number of students. Unlike the two wholly student-performed plays each year, casting for the English department play is done to age, resulting in a cast that is composed of students in youthful roles and adults in maturer roles. In 11 years we have cast members of the English, history, foreign language, physical education, music, and administrative departments, and several adults from the community. The student actors and theatre technicians, as well as the student audience, benefit from seeing their teachers in roles in which the students are often more expert.

I hesitate to append a list of the plays we have done and of those we are considering, partly because some are questionable "classics," but also because, if anyone considers adding such a project to the curriculum, I would hate to think that our list might become *the* list. Every school must consider several factors, among them production costs, limitations of the facilities, available talent, and, probably most important, the sophistication of a captive and possibly hostile audience.

However, the plays we have produced are *A Midsummer Night's Dream; R.U.R.; The Matchmaker; Pygmalion; The Madwoman of Chaillot; The Odd Couple; Harvey; Count Dracula; Blithe Spirit; Bye, Bye, Birdie;* and *Happily Ever After?* (our collective title for three one-act plays on the theme of marriage: "The Ugly Duckling," "Cinderella Married," and "Sorry, Wrong Number"). Plays we are considering for the future include *Much Ado About Nothing, The Diary of Anne Frank, Twelfth Night, The Fantastics, Barefoot in the Park, The Miracle Worker, Tartuffe,* and three one-act plays by Chekhov.

# Drama and the New Media

SUE IRVING
*(England)*

In common with many English teachers, I believe that children learn about language by using it in realistic ways, not just by studying it as an object. At first, I chose to study the media with my 10- and 11-year-old pupils because it seemed to offer many dramatic opportunities to develop their language abilities. With careful planning, it was clear that I could use a study of the media to enable pupils to develop an awareness of the different functions of language. Opportunities would arise when the children would be able to use all four language modes (talking, listening, reading, writing) for realistic purposes, in an interrelated way.

The middle school where I teach is in one of the many semirural areas in Worcestershire. The catchment area for the 9- to 12-year-olds includes some farming villages, but most of the children's parents are commuters. There are approximately 150 children in the school, who, wherever possible, are taught by subject specialists. Generally, the children are fairly articulate and do not have any major reading or writing problems, although there are inevitably some students with specific difficulties. They are biddable and quite gentle, and fierce arguments are rare. For this reason we did not have any qualms about embarking on projects that would at times seem like organised chaos and involve expensive equipment. The children are quick to forgive and fairly uncritical; they are able to sustain interest in one topic for a long time. However, their work rate is quite slow, and they do not seem to be influenced by the pressures of time. For these reasons, they are both a delight and at times a frustration to teach.

At the time when this first media study was undertaken, the 10- to 11-year-old age group consisted of two classes of 20 pupils each. The teacher of the class parallel to mine, although not a specialist English teacher, was keen to learn from others and willing to undertake much team teaching. With only 40 children, it was most often like teaching one class with two teachers, each contributing their own particular strengths. An ability to set up audio-visual aids and adapt electrical equipment quickly, was my colleague's invaluable contribution. We were both keen to carry out some form of media study with the pupils. This was further enhanced when we realised that due to pupil and staff absences on a field course, there would be one week during the spring term in which we would be forced to abandon the usual timetable and follow our own improvised programme. This carrot, commonplace to most primary school teachers, spurred us on and was to prove a priceless stimulus. We decided to use that week as a "Video Week" in which the pupils would be able to use a video camera, making their own video, but, now that this seemed possible, we wanted them primarily to become aware of the artifactual nature of the visual media.

These aims did not appear to be incompatible with the development of language skills, which were the original reasons for such a study. Study of the media can provide opportunities for drafting, proofreading, reviewing, extending, and expanding oral, dramatic, and written work. Purposeful talk can arise from small group work and opportunities given to expand these utterances to a wider audience. Creating an environment in which the pupils felt able to learn from each other and to communicate what they had learnt was an important element in this study. We were at times taken over by our own enthusiasm and tried to do too much. We were also sometimes brought down to size by a child complaining that someone had pinched his or her idea.

The children's first look at the media was through a study of advertising. This began with a straightforward, anecdotal class discussion about which adverts on TV they liked and which they did not. Lists of these revealed the audience being aimed at; and further discussion centered on how these audiences were appealed to by the advertisers. With the conclusions to these discussions in mind, some pupils invented new products and tried to aim a written advert at a specific market. Others made adverts for existing products for unlikely markets; for example, *Smarties* for adults. Although until now these children had not accepted the claims of adverts as gospel, they became more critical of the claims and more aware of how language can and must be manipulated in order to communicate messages effectively.

The children then looked into the language of questionnaires and the differences between open and closed questions. For fun and interest, they produced their own personality questionnaires. Interviewing was a natural follow-up to this study of questions, and the children made audio tapes of interviews that they made themselves. These were played and future improvements suggested. Making these tapes introduced the pressures of time to the children, which prepared them for the next project.

Each class was now working well in their small mixed-ability groups and now were able to produce a "live" radio broadcast to each other's classroom. The children worked in their groups at specified assignments, usually chosen by them, to an immovable deadline. Some parts of the broadcasts were live, others taped. The broadcasts included adverts, interviews, quizzes, news, jokes, limericks, and competitions. For the first time, the children really seemed to react to the pressures of working to a deadline and managed to work quite quickly.

The children were now able to cope quite well with taking on responsibility for their own learning and final productions. Much planning went into the "Video Week," including consultations with the local television companies' education sections, the enlistment of parental help, and the production of suitable work cards. One classroom was converted into a studio using hired video cameras and recording machines, several borrowed black-and-white monitors, and a school set of spotlights. The children were divided into groups and timetabled into the "studio." When they were not in the studio, they were either planning their use of the camera with a teacher, or working with parents on a variety of work cards. These were concerned mainly with how TV works, how studios work, and the power of image and language, for example, seeing how different captions affected the interpretation of a picture.

The filming sessions were quite difficult, and we had been warned that the children might be disappointed with the results. However, we had explained to them the technical limitations and the fact that we had little time and limited expertise. For this reason, the children were in fact pleased with their results. They knew how hard they had had to work to achieve a final result. The two- to three-minute videos were varied: an interview with the headmaster, an advert, a minidocumentary of the school meals service, a breakfast TV slot, a games lesson, a news section, and a quiz. The final tape was sent to a school in Australia with which a language exchange was underway.

At many stages of their media study, the pupils commented, "It is not what it seems." They were becoming aware that media messages were not solid fact, but controllable and artifactual, requiring understanding of how language works. They had had to use all four language modes for realistic purposes, and, within the limitations of their age and understanding, had arrived, through active involvement, at a fairly critical evaluation of the media.

# Writing in Role

NOEL PRICE
*(New Zealand)*

Writing in role is a variation of role play, with the student asked to assume the identity of a character from a play, story, or film, then to do some kind of writing in that role. An example is:

Pretend that you are Jem in Harper Lee's *To Kill a Mockingbird.*
Write a letter to your cousin explaining what happened during

and after the trial of Tom Robinson, and describe how it affected you and your sister Scout.

A writing task such as this is complex because a number of different operations are involved:

- Clearly, it requires a thorough familiarity with the text.
- It demands a good understanding of the character, for the writer needs to write about feelings and ideas that are never explicit in the book itself.
- It may well necessitate interpretation: the story may have been told from a different point of view from that required in the writing task. In the example, the story was told "about" Jem by Scout, but the writer has to try to see events as Jem would have seen them.

There is much to be said for encouraging an "expressive" style for writing of this kind. I use the term here in the sense that it is used by James Britton (1970). To begin with, allowing for an approach that is more tentative and exploratory helps the writer to feel her way into the character and situation. It also is closer to the way real people might write about such things. Further, it is a personal task when handled in this way, not a process requiring objective, analytical thinking.

I admit freely that I have made no effort to make any kind of formal evaluation of writing in role as a component of response to literature. I am, however, fully convinced by my subjective impressions that it does offer a great deal. It seems to engender a much greater willingness on the pupils' part to carry out the written task: they appear to find the activity interesting. I have been impressed by the depth and perception in the responses of many students who are ordinarily unable to handle standard analytical statements about the work. Students seem to be much more at ease when they are on the inside of the work. It is clear to me that the different nature of the mental processes involved in role writing allows the students to find and reveal meaning much more easily.

Asking suitable questions to launch writing in role is something that needs to be given thought and care. For younger students, the questions will probably be intended mainly to elicit information about people, places, and events, but there is still scope for including an imaginative or creative element. Thus, rather than asking the putative Tom Sawyer to tell someone what happened when he and Becky got lost in the cave, it might be better to ask, "What were the main things that you were worried about when you and Becky were . . . ?"

As students mature, they should be better able to handle questions that encouarge them to deal with the ideas in the work. Kino (in *The Pearl*) might be asked why he was so eager to "buy" an education for Coyotito when he had sold the pearl.

On occasions, especially for more advanced students, it may be possible to introduce further complications. Asking Banquo to write a letter of advice to the incoming President of the Republic is not being tricky for the sake of being difficult; rather it urges the students to engage with some of the central issues of the play and articulate them. It also helps them to see that literature is about the real world we all live in, even historical literature.

Some other typical questions at different levels are:

- Jim Hawkins is asked to describe those features of Treasure Island that would make it a suitable place for a holiday.
- Santiago's obituary is written by the boy who wants to describe the old man's main qualities and values.
- A descendent of Sir Thomas More writes to the Church of Rome to argue the case for his canonisation.

We know of the benefits of dramatic role play in the response to literature programmes. Writing in role capitalises on some of those benefits, but it doesn't require the pupils to leave their seats or do any performing. Thus, even the very shy can enjoy some experience of role play. It is also worth mentioning that writing in role demands familiarity with the text. Requiring this kind of work encourages close and repeated reading.

Finally, given that the tasks are devised with sufficient thought, writing in role involves students using their own imaginations. In this way they become more fully involved in their classroom work.

# 5.
# Language and
# Learning

The essays in this part begin with classroom practices designed to help children learn to use language better, with emphasis on language taught through actual use in reading, writing, listening, and speaking. In this respect, *language* can be seen as a unifying concept in the five countries, providing the rationale for integrating traditionally separated parts of the curriculum such as composition and literature. However, the reader will quickly discern that the contributors see more to language learning than mere adroitness with words. As Australia's Jo-Anne Everingham observes, "every teacher is a teacher of aesthetic and social values and political ideology." English teachers are increasingly conscious of the role that language plays in shaping and transmitting values. Teachers are concerned with having students study language choices in the media, sexist language in literature and the classroom, and the role of language in sustaining national identity and promoting understanding of other cultures. Jonathan Swift of the United States observes, "It is not surprising that the first line of St. John's Gospel should be 'In the beginning was the word.'" Language and learning, he explains, "are at the basis of human relations."

# Language and Learning

JOCELYN TARRANT

*(New Zealand)*

Education may be defined as the cultivation of modes of expression. . . . The aim of education is, therefore, the creation of artists, of people efficient in various modes of expression.

*Herbert Read*

Read's view of education includes, but also takes up beyond survival skills, the joy of self-expression and communication with others, living and dead, from various backgrounds, and in the real and imaginary worlds.

Language is learned by living, by being exposed to it, and by having opportunities to use it in different situations and for different audiences—not by talking about it, analysing it, or teaching it. Pupils learn by wanting to know something which requires observation (or viewing), listening and reading; and by knowing something they want to share with others through speech, writing, movement, and shaping (e.g., illustration, diagram, and film). Language and learning involve total communication, both receptive and productive.

Language is best taught or learned in context—words in sentences, sentences in discourse (text and speech), and in a variety of *real* (as opposed to classroom) situations involving a variety of audiences. Language is best learnt not by focusing on it, but on the message.

My desk is always tucked away in a corner at the back of the room, for the teacher is not the controller nor the source of knowledge but a contributor, advisor, facilitator, listener, and observer. At certain times, the teacher learns alongside and from her or his pupils and allows them some choice in the programme through consensus as well as majority decision making. Above all, the committed language teacher is a constant juggler, attempting to cater to individual, social, and cultural differences, and maintaining a balance between, for example:

- transmission-type lessons and shared learning
- class forums and small, pupil-led group discussions
- cooperative and individual efforts
- formal and informal situations
- spontaneous, impromptu, and prepared responses
- the oral and the written
- standard English and home language(s)
- free and controlled and guided language practices
- transactional and expressive (including poetic) writing
- shared reading (set books and being read to) and sustained silent reading
- instructional and recreational reading
- national and British and other literatures
- mass media and real-life experiences

In creating conditions for ease of interaction, we should also consider reasons why a pupil remains silent (the "how" and "when" of speech), especially for those who are from cultural minorities. The testing of oral language appalls me. We should also consider the paralinguistic elements of communication, our own as well as that of others, and the unintentional microaggression and ill will and friction which can arise from misinterpretation.

Pupils of other backgrounds might have little inclination to be like, or to speak like us. This can be countered by such things as pupil-led group activities, e.g., not just discussions, but barrier games and other activities where there must be interaction in order to find or complete information; team teaching, especially with teachers of other ethnic/cultural/language backgrounds; and by taking pupils out into the community and having members of the pupils' communities come into the classroom (not just visit the school). A pupil's language is not usually the cause of underachievement. A pupil's self-image and motivation can be affected by factors over which we have no control. We can at least attempt to enrich the social and physical environment at school.

Secondary school classrooms are still mainly "square and brown like all the other rooms" (Anonymous, 1972). Notices in different styles, variants, and languages, displays of work from various subjects, self-made and "pop" posters, begged and borrowed magazines and newspapers, and even an old armchair have been used by pupils to transform *their* room. We have decorated and put multilanguage greetings on the door, and greeted each other and visitors in our various languages. Having the same class for integrated English/social studies and/or other subjects makes this easier. With the new secondary English syllabus in New Zealand, teachers have more opportunity and facilities for classroom displays which pupils and teachers from other classes also enjoy.

A "thought for the week," prominently displayed, exposes pupils to aphorisms, epigrams, proverbs, and quotations from various sources and sometimes in other languages. If pupils want to know about them, they must ask.

Let's start with the pupils and what they have to offer. We can play on superlatives to get lively talk, writing and impromptu acting from: "The most frightening thing . . . ," "My greatest embarrassment was when . . . ," "The longest night I remember was . . . ." "I am the greatest/most intelligent/best looking/dumbest/etc. person because . . ."

A project on "Our Traditions" had pupils talking to parents and grandparents about migration here (by jet or ancestral canoe) and to local identities and Maori elders for stories behind local place names. It had them reading traditional stories from ancestral lands, and each others' projects in voluntary sharing when their work was finished. They acted out myths and legends, illustrated them (even on the classroom windows), and began on poetic writing by listening to mood music. Then, they went on to make up their own myths for explanations of something in their world. Some pupils came to terms with death by doing this. Other benefits:

- Listening to two skilled storytellers gave opportunity to observe and hear *culturally* different styles of English. The interrelationship between oral and written literature began to be apparent and respect was increased for the former.
- The use of myth and legend, especially the *telling* of these stories, reveals values, attitudes, and customs of the people they belong to; they spark the imagination, show our shared humanity as well as cultural differences, and give opportunity to bring together various disciplines.
- Entertaining parents and friends at the end of a unit of work gives real reason to use social language, write letters and invitations.

We live with the myth that "every teacher is a teacher of English," but there are few occasions when we can cooperate with other subject teachers on this matter. A supervised study period each week means that materials on study techniques, how to tackle a textbook and to make summaries, etc. are used by most staff.

Those teachers more concerned with communication than "correct" English are excited by our new curricula (Department of Education, 1972, 1973) and the guidance given by Janet Holmes (1982). The approaches are strongly sociolinguistic and direct teachers to relate all language modes such as "Watching and Moving" and "Viewing and Shaping." Reference to "language" rather than "English" encourages acceptance of all dialects and variants as well as maintenance of tongues other than English.

I have been used to the freedom of meeting the needs of pupils within the confines of these curricula and the dictates of public examinations. The Head of English coordinates programmes by means of regular fortnightly meetings to share and discuss problems, materials, and methods.

Our teaching of grammar is incidental and arises from pupil performances, particularly their formal writing. Teachers home in on grammatical structures and misuse of conventions of spelling and pronunciation as they affect clear communication. Vocabulary is our centre of concern, the word in sentence, and the sentence sequenced in discourse. The work of Chomsky and Co. has destroyed teachers' confidence so that pupils are often at a loss for words to refer to grammatical structure. On the other hand, some are weighed down with sociolinguistic jargon.

Accepting our pupils' language is too often interpreted wrongly as "She'll be right." While providing opportunities for pupils to be exposed to and to use various styles, registers, and particularly their own dialects, and variants, there are some of us who believe it is our duty as teachers to see that they are familiar with the standard, formal English necessary for success at school and in later life. Where else do they have this opportunity? We must prepare pupils for the expectations and judgments made in society. They should realise the advantages of code and style switching in speech, and should be given encouragement and opportunities to read and write in a simple, clear, formal standard style, and be aware of the manipulations of language and audience when people deviate from this. English, in its various standard forms, is not just prestigious. It has a tremendously important function as a neutral unifying code nationally and as an international form of communication. All pupils should know this.

# "Good" Language

LESLEY PASQUIN

*(Canada)*

Having taught "language arts" at both the elementary and junior high school levels, I came to realize that year after year the same "grammar" was on the curriculum and the students did not remember subject, predicate, or descriptive phrase no matter how often they were taught. Nor did any of the grammar skills taught carry over to their writing. Obviously, formal instruction was inefficient. A more successful method would be to examine our language and how it is used and to expand the language of the students to better serve their communicative needs (Smith, Goodman, and Meredith, 1976). Language could be best taught and learned by beginning with the written and spoken words of the user. "If a child has something to say he will want to write and he will want to share his writing and thus need to know about forms that will make his written thought most effective" (Smith, Goodman, and Meredith, 1976, p. 255).

Recently, I was conferencing a Grade 2 student about a story he had written. There was a lot of dialogue in the story. I asked him if he knew what to do when someone was speaking in a piece of written work. He replied that you put "sixty-sixes and ninety-nines" and he knew which was which. However, the knowledge of this punctuation rule had not carried over into his work. Yet he could tell me who was speaking each time and read the story aloud with the appropriate punctuation. We then took different coloured markers and we wrote over the different lines of dialogue so that they stood out on the page. In doing the final draft, the student had no difficulty putting in his "sixty-sixes and ninety-nines."

Another suggestion for helping students to use quotation marks is to have them transpose the dialogue from a play into a story or take the dialogue from a novel and change it into a play. This latter exercise is particularly successful with junior high school students who turn their favourite part of a novel into a "screenplay."

A typical punctuation problem young writers have is ending the sentence appropriately. Very often, they do not know what a sentence is (Smith, Goodman, and Meredith, 1976). Yet in rereading their story aloud, they pause correctly. The tape recorder can be a useful tool here. The student writes his story, then reads it into the tape recorder, and then edits his work using his own language. Then he can prepare his final draft.

The student's own writing can be further useful in learning sentence patterns and order. Once the writer and an editor (who can be the teacher or another student) have put the work into a final draft, it can be cut into strips for the student to reassemble. The reader must observe the rules of syntax in order to make sense of the story again, and, because it is his own story, it will be easier and more meaningful.

A second important aspect of syntax is word classes and functions. Some linguists still use the traditional terms: *noun, verb, adjective,* and *adverb* (Smith, Goodman, and Meredith, 1976, p. 179). We need to help students look at the function of words. One suggestion is an exercise to come up with the longest or funniest sentence. The class is divided into groups and each group is given a circular cutout with a spinner in the center which points to section marked "person," "place," "thing," "helping word," "doing word," and "describing word." This way, they take turns and see which group can come up with the most interesting, the most descriptive, or the funniest sentence.

Group work can be used to teach adjectives and descriptive phrases as well. Each group is given a photograph of an object, say an old tree, large sheets of blank paper, and a coloured marker. They are asked to brainstorm as many words as possible to describe the tree. Careful guidance will help the group put words together into descriptive phrases. When the class reconvenes, each group adds a word or a group of words to the sentence: "A tree stood." This way the concept may be better understood.

To be aware of and use the "rules" of grammar, student writers must be encouraged to prepare a final draft. There should be a purpose to the task. In our small writing group, all the works are typed by the teachers and put on the bulletin board for others to read. However, the work will not be accepted for typing unless it is in a form which can be easily read by the typists. This is an incentive for the writers. In the writing conference that comes before the final draft, the story should be read aloud. This oral reading is important ". . . to hear the flow or lack of it and to help raise questions of how to deal with problems of communication" (Smith, Goodman, and Meredith, 1976, p. 259). A self-checking card on the student's desk is also valuable. It can ask such questions as: "Do I have complete sentences? Is my spelling correct? Have I left out any words? Have I used good punctuation?"

Once again, the question of using good language seems to be one of learning by doing. Allowing students to write as often as possible, encouraging good editing, and giving a purpose for communicating with our language appear to be effective tools for both teaching and learning language.

# Opening Doors Through Language

MARIAN HOBBS
*(New Zealand)*

In all my social interactions, I demonstrate different values. Many of these interactions are in the classroom. But I do not intend that all or any of my students should adopt *my* value system.

It has been my experience that we learn values and apply them to ourselves from actual situations, rather than through being told to do something. For example, several students marched every weekend during the 1981 Springbok (National Rugby Team) Tour of New Zealand. Through those actual experiences, they learned the value of working together, of self-control, of discretion, of commitment far more than if I had lectured about those values in a classroom.

However, within the classroom community, I expect certain behaviours to be learned and applied. Students must learn to respect others' opinions and therefore to listen and to argue constuctively. Students must acknowledge the existence of other ideas and value systems. The tone in the room should be a supportive one—where everyone is encouraged to express views, ideas and standpoints, without fear or ridicule or aggression.

When a student takes a strong stand that may be diametrically opposite to ours, then we must listen and allow for discussion and argument. The difficulty for us arises when we are unsure as to whether we should chair the discussion or enter the argument as an opponent. That decision is made on a basis of the age and strength of the student. But if we oppose, we must never smash. Within class arguments, we must always control the comments which hurt any member of the class. As we don't know all that may hurt another student, we must set guidelines. There should be no jokes or comments that belittle racial groups or women, or which poke fun at mental and physical handicaps.

In my classroom, I try to counteract sexism in our society by using feminine pronouns in sample sentences. I set up wall displays that feature women and make use of the women's calendars and diaries. I point out appropriate slogans to bolster the self-worth of my women students. I read stories, poems, and plays that explore the difficult facets of a woman's life.

To counteract the racism that is so much part of our formal school structure, I try within my classroom to place a positive value on things Maori. I try to instill in all my students a respect for Maori language, by pronouncing Maori with care and attention. All classes get the lessons I learned in my first few lessons on Maori pronunciation. No child gets away with the mumble or nonattempt. I try to demonstrate a knowledge, respect, and love for Maori literature. I do this by using Maori writers who write in English, such as Witi Ihimaera, Keri Hulme, Hone Tuwhare, and Patricia Grace. I am also beginning to study translations of Waiata and other Maori songs, so I can use these in the classroom.

I would never read to the class any writing that I considered racist or sexist, but I would promote the discussion of these attitudes.

I see our role as English teachers is to offer a wide range of different opinions through films, poetry, short stories, articles, essays, and novels. We don't have to promote what we abhor, such as a racist novel.

Within the school community, you become known for the standards in your room, and students begin to behave according to those standards, at least in your presence. However, it is too hopeful to expect that these will translate to their behaviour outside your orbit. By making those stands, you do, however, extend a hand of support to those groups within the school community that are most put down.

The role of the state school is not a revolutionary one. We are used to produce the next generation of workers. The teacher will not lead any revolution, nor will she cause a revolution. But through language, the teacher can open other doors, thereby allowing students a chance to view their society from another perspective. Whether the students choose to walk through those doors is not the choice nor the task of the teacher.

# Teaching the Language of Media

JO-ANNE EVERINGHAM
(Australia)

Notions of the hidden curriculum are no longer new, and we should have faced the fact that every teacher is a teacher of aesthetic and social values and political ideology. English teachers tend to perpetuate and uphold a particular ideology and class structure. I believe we should be using our classrooms to make this ideology explicit and explore alternatives to it. The media provide ideal textual material for analysis of prevailing ideological messages, since it is the implicit values and messages of many popular television programs to which English teachers object.

Students' social and political development will grow from an understanding of the societal conditions which closely and concretely affect them; an ability to see society's structures as the works of man rather than as unchangeable natural phenomena; an ability to see alternatives to a particular reality. This is the essence of the content of media studies: to perceive the values and prevailing social messages of media.

Since politics, in the narrower sense of the word, is such an important part of the explicit content of the media (particularly news and current affairs media), study of the media inevitably involves, at some point, discussion and clarification of a wide range of political concepts and issues. At this level, we can develop in our students skills like translation of political doublespeak and detection of bias in interviews. However, we can proceed beyond this to the implicit political messages of the mass media and develop in students growing awareness of the ideological frameworks which are inherent in the media. "When pupils move from seeing programs as 'the way the world is' to seeing them as 'the way the world has been constructed or interpreted' they have taken a profound political step" (Masterman, 1980). Masterman goes on to point out that "the most pertinent ideological questions are not: 'Is this well argued?' 'Has he falsified the issues?' 'Who got the better of the debate?' but 'Who says these are the issues?' 'Within what assumptions and frameworks are the arguments presented?' and 'What other possible agendas might be set?'"

I find high school students very willing to critically study the language of newspapers, news broadcasts, and television current affairs programs. These are not "their" media experiences; they don't particularly enjoy or choose to read, to listen to, or to watch them, and so don't see classroom study as threatening to undermine their enjoyment or to criticise them through their personal tastes. Since these media items have explicit political subjects, they are excellent starting points for developing student awareness of other dimensions of ideological content of the media through the subtle influences of technique (especially the deliberate processes of selection and presentation), production and ownership constraints, and audience perceptions of media credibility. A wealth of learning can come out of a comparison of two newspapers on the same day; comparison of the XYZ's radio and TV bulletins (often the same script . . . what effect do the visuals, if any, have?); or interpretation of the observations about a television news bulletin.

Political and social education is also about changing students' awareness and views of not only their own place in society but also that of other groups who make up our society, and the representation of them by the media. Media representations are very pervasive and persuasive, and issues like sexism, racism, and stereotyping cannot be fully tackled in the classroom without confronting relevant media "definitions" of women, and ethnic and other social groups. Some students grasp the distortion of media perceptions best from their own experience and resentment of media representations of youth. Others find this too close to home as a starting point and the dispassionate approach of content analysis may be a more revealing way to discover the distorted picture of reality represented on television. For instance, in considering the portrayals of sex roles on television, a simple counting exercise can be analysed to show the contrast revealed by Pingree and Hawkins (1980):

| *Real World* | *Television World* |
| --- | --- |
| Fifty percent of people are male. | Seventy percent of major characters are male. |
| Most adults are or have been married. | Two-thirds of women are married, were married, or are engaged; most men are unmarried and always have been. |
| Fifty percent of women aged 16–65 work. | Most women are housewives, not employed. |
| Average life expectancy for women is greater than for men. | Fifty percent of TV women are under 30; twenty percent of TV men are under 30. |

In these times, when Australia's multicultural nature is being emphasised and teachers are encouraged to reflect this in our classrooms, I regard a study of the representation of ethnic groups in the media especially important in my students' social development. With respect to television, we explore such questions as: "Are ethnic groups represented at all?" "Can we list characters, characteristics, and origins?" "Is their ethnic background the essence of their role portrayal, or are they depicted as persons in their own right?" These studies of representation and of the prevailing world view can be extended to investigate questions of cultural domination and media imperialism, particularly of our television offerings. We watch segments of a number of programs and decide whether they are Australian, American, English, or otherwise. Then we determine what it was about the programs that showed where they came from. Some suggestions have been: people's accents, houses, weather, cars and buildings, money, place names, and dress. If programs are classified according to genre or type, analysis is possible along the lines: "Where does most TV comedy come from?" "Which country do the commercial stations import most from?" "What category do most Australian produced programs belong to?"

While they may argue about the necessity or morality of being involved in values education, English teachers generally agree that they are involved in developing aesthetic values. Many teachers hail media education as yet another way to teach "discrimination" and cultural heritage. This seems to me dangerous ground, which implies that teachers can *teach* students what is good, and what is bad; that teachers have the right to change what students are viewing so that they conform to an established idea of culture; that students and their preferences, responses, and language are unworthy, while teachers are experts.

Masterman (1980) has given many warnings on this front and points out, "The aesthetic experience which changes us . . . is the experience whose validity we accept yet which forces us to ask questions of our own attitudes and beliefs because it points to contradictions and inconsistencies within them." Yet the media, particularly television, *can* play a vital role in aesthetic education. Television "texts" are ones which speak directly to students and to which they respond personally. Such a response is the necessary first step towards independent aesthetic appreciation. Presently, schools neglect or criticise the television experience of students. If students find no personal contact with a text (as has so often been the case in literature studies), they become reliant on second-hand, plagiarised responses of others—usually the teacher or the literary critic. Students have been known to write (and pass) even university papers entirely from critical sources without reading the text at all! This is not the aesthetic development we want for English students today. We want them to develop habits of exploring the *text* to clarify their own responses to it. As in exploring their own writing, this can often be facilitated by discussion in the peer group. We need to abandon old practices of teachers asking questions about the text and put the responsibility for asking questions on the students. I believe we can use television studies to develop these skills.

# From the Barricades

HELEN WATSON
*(New Zealand)*

Although I am committed to a feminist philosophy and would dearly like to teach in a nonsexist way, promoting the concerns of females and males equally, I have found it impossible in a coeducational school. I do my best, but the sexist nature of New Zealand society, the entrenched sexism of the pupils, the sexism of the English language and much valued literature work against me.

A teacher cannot break down the deeply held beliefs and practices of a society in four hours of class contact a week. All she or he can do is try to inject a few doubts, show by example that there is an alternative view of the world, and support those who try to think things out for themselves.

I believe that girls are better off in girls-only groups in the present state of society. Because as things are now, any teacher faced with a mixed class and the task of keeping both sexes interested and occupied inevitably gives more attention to the dominant group and nine times out of ten that group will be male. Research on what happens in classrooms and who gets most of the teacher's attention shows boys get more attention, and, if the teacher attempts to favour girls or even treat girls and boys equally, boys demand their greater share by behaving in such a way that the teacher must attend to them (Dale Spender, 1982, and Womens Research and Resources Centre Publication, 1981). I have found this true myself. Test how many times a boy answers when you ask a girl a question. Last year, I had a Form 5 class with five girls and twenty boys—poor class organisation, but then who cares about five girls!—and I did my best to give those girls the attention they deserved. The boys refused to let me. If I tried to talk to the girls, a certain number of boys became noisy, banged furniture, and called out to me. If I asked a girl a question, a boy answered. The girls coped by silent, self-effacing behaviour.

This year, I have the top-stream, Form 5 English class (15-year-olds). There are three very poorly behaved boys in it, one especially who is loud and argumentative and does not hesitate to challenge my choice of activities. Another boy is friendly and talkative, always engages me in conversation as he arrives, speaking to me in a slightly patronising manner. He is perfectly happy to articulate blatantly sexist attitudes. The girls in this class are bright, hardworking, and, with a few exceptions, very quiet.

I have also found that attempts to challenge sexist language, attitudes in literature, or to discuss social issues, are often met with denial and outright hostility by both girls and boys. I do not raise these matters constantly, as I am well aware of my reputation as an extreme "Women's Libber" (in fact, I would class myself as a reasonable reformist, and if I were really radical, I couldn't bear to be in the education system at all). I have been told objections to sexist language are a lot of nonsense, have been told by girls that they are quite happy with language the way it is, and have had writing bemoaning the fact that all they hear about is women and racial prejudice. All this from a class which had just studied *To Kill a Mockingbird* and had been given the opportunity to write about any sort of prejudice they felt strongly about. The literature studied by this class during the year included *Lord of the Flies, Unman, Wittering and Zigo, Animal Farm,* and *Arms and the Man,* all good male-oriented stuff.

Which brings me to another major problem—source material and literature. American texts, such as those published by Scott, Foresman, tend to be excellent in their choice of material for sexual and racial balance. As I understand it, writers are given guidelines on how to eliminate sexist use of language. I have seen those put out by McGraw-Hill and consider them first class. But American texts are very expensive for us and not used very much. An examination of what is used in New Zealand schools would demonstrate that most is male biased in authors used, characters depicted, and photos used (Lesley Taylor, 1980). Female writers, books, poems, and plays with interesting female characters take a minor place. Examiners reports for university entrance and bursary give the names of the most commonly used literature—most of it male. Why is this? Well, English teaching in our universities validates this bias as does the whole English literary critical tradition. But also it is true that boys are more difficult to interest in English, and are more reluctant to read so that teachers look for texts to study and reading material to interest them—and very few boys are interested in literature about girls, relationships, or emotions. Girls will read literature about males. Therefore, teachers opt for what will appeal to boys. This bias can be modified by more individual reading and assignment work, easy for prose fiction. But, it is harder to find poetry and plays which are written for women.

Another difficulty in attracting boys' interest is that the only reading material which does interest them is usually terribly sexist. I have just been reading *The Outsiders* by S. E. Hinton with a reluctant Form 4 class (14-year-olds). They like it, but I am horrified at its emphasis on male violence and toughness. Is it an advance if I get boys to read but what they read is about war, violence, or science fiction? And what about the girls who adore romances in *The Heartlines* and *Wildfire* format?

Of course, you can attempt to get pupils to analyse the treatment of women in male literature. I have just attempted this with Arthur Miller's *The Crucible,* pointing out his distortion of the historical facts in changing Abigail from a girl of 12 to one of 17, creating a relationship between her and Proctor, and putting the blame for the whole witchcraft episode onto her. My 16-year-olds said Abigail was a slut and more to blame than John Proctor for his adultery because she knew he was married and married men "are like that" and therefore not as much to blame.

However, bloodied but unbowed I keep on and do have some successes, mostly on an individual basis with responses to books and poems, and reports from other teachers on challenges made by some of my former pupils to sexist practices. I also feel that a refusal to allow male sexist behaviour and remarks in the classroom and valiant attempts to support and encourage girls must help some girls. I am passionately committed to the value of literature in stimulating thought and analysis, in providing comfort and excitement, and promote books as much as I can. I try to develop awareness of sexist language, especially in

Form 6. As Head of Department, I do not buy source books which are not balanced; if I buy 10 copies of a book of interest to boys (e.g., *Survival* by Russell Evans), I balance it with *Island of the Blue Dolphins* by Scott O'Dell. I search for books which show women in a strong positive light. The struggle against sexism is a long and arduous one, but no group of teachers is better placed than English teachers to undertake it, and, as promoters of individual worth and development, it is our duty to do it, however difficult the task.

# Teaching a National Language

BERNARD GADD

*(New Zealand)*

The teaching of a national language must surely be one of the most politically sensitive areas of curriculum. So it is with the teaching of English in New Zealand. The subject has become a ground of conflict between those who seek change within our society and those who prefer their world as it is. The contemporary conflict has two major forms.

The first concerns especially the one-fifth of our nation's youngsters who are of the indigenous peoples, the Maori. The discussion here concerns how far it is possible for our schools and for our classroom teaching to admit into them Maori ethnicity and Maori forms of English, and how far teachers and administrators are willing to try to do so. The Maori, after the land ownership wars of the 1860s, had been pushed to the periphery of national life and of its educational systems. The Maori language, as a consequence, poised on the very brink of extinction. Modern Maori, however, are city dwellers, highly visible, and possessed of leaders skilled in the political use of ethnicity.

Maori have recently established their own early childhood schools to foster their language and culture. The first bilingual state schools to be inaugurated this century have been a direct result. Soon hundreds of bilingual Maori students will reach high school throughout New Zealand. Their parents will be wanting schools to affirm their children's Maori identity, even wanting English to be taught as a foreign language or as a second language. The parents will be demanding of teachers a cessation of cultural assimilation or denigration as the price of schooling. They will be seeking a genuine equality of educational opportunity for Maori children.

English teachers were and are ill-prepared for this relatively swift development. Few English teachers know Maori language. Few know much about Maori ethnicity. Few have given sufficient thought to the place of variants of English within the classroom. Official papers from the education department reveal a painfully inadequate conception of culture and its relation to language. Few teachers know much about even the Maori writers in English; few commercial publishers will print works in Maori, and even fewer will print works that speak the authentic voice of the Maori and Polynesian working people; few teachers grasp how very thoroughly schools must alter if they are to accommodate Maori aspirations, and few realise how determined Maori are, and how much impact on schools with falling rolls the withdrawal of even some Maori students would have.

The second arena of conflict in English teaching is to do with the growth-centred style of English teaching that has been the official policy for a decade. The deeper animating hopes of this style of teaching have been that the individual student might become more aware of and more in control of her language and its development, and therefore more in charge of her life.

The challenge to teachers has been to open young minds rather than to close them or to shape them to inhabit particular cages. The continuing and often covert conflict has been whether to teach more in the spirit of a Blake or of a Dr. Johnson. The conflict's nature and reality have been muted by the absence of an adequate body of homegrown language theory upon which to build arguments for the "new" English and its teaching practices.

These two new directions have become the twin battlefields for all the ongoing strife between educational and social "conservationists" and "developers." Into these two turbulent—and interconnected—currents run the tributaries of quarrels between those who want a single national language and culture, and those who advocate recognition and affirmation of diversity; those who want the common person's fingers on the keys of the electronic media, and those who prefer entrepreneurial control; those who want more democracy in schools and elsewhere, and those who do not; those who seek that students should emulate the privileged, and those who seek to dethrone privilege; those who look to the past and those who anticipate the dawning of a new century; those who want to foster the imaginative ability to think beyond one's own life and experience, and those who want imagination to reflect upon the orthodoxies of the middle-class world that dominate our society.

I teach at a school which is almost a model of a school torn by precisely those fundamental conflicts. As Head of the English Department and—almost by definition—a Pakeha (European) middle-class male, I direct our programmes for out 90+ percent Maori and Polynesian and 100 percent working class students toward the more radical directions—towards growth and multicultural oriented teaching. I do this because I see the prime role of the English teacher as being not to mould the language of students, nor even to promote its growth (since maturing itself is doing that far more effectively than a few hours a week of schooling can), but rather to foster a sensitive imagination. And, with that, to promote a courage to speak out and to act when the individual perceives wrong and can sense what the suffering of the victims is, and how the inflicting of the injustice is affecting those who do it.

And I do so also because I see the need to offer students a greater opportunity to grow in confidence and in self-respect as well as in their language(s), and also because I see these directions as going some way to meet the impatience of Maori parents and students with the present system.

The top in-school administrators, the controlling board, and the education department provide a conservative framework that effectively offers constant challenge to existing reforms, makes fresh reform hugely difficult, and encourages some of my teachers to stay with conventional thinking and teaching, offering their black and working-class students paternalistically what teacher considers to be good for young people.

Our school, then, is one in which the battles are fought each day. That at least has the merit of forcing everyone to think not merely tactically and day by day, but also strategically and long term, and to reflect upon how a school portrays its society at large so accurately.

The two conflicts outlined above fundamentally are about whether or not New Zealand people can become more open, more tolerant, more aware of the riches inherent in our society's diversity.

# International Perspectives on Language Learning

JONATHAN SWIFT
*(United States)*

It is not surprising that the first line of St. John's Gospel should be, "In the beginning was the Word." Speech and what it conveys are at the basis of human relations.

It is for this reason that language assumes so great a humanizing, empathizing, and predicting role in multicultural education. The cornerstone of multiculturalism is the ability to question, discuss, communicate, collaborate, and respond to others. It is, in fact, the expectation of the "group" or community of interdependent humans. J. W. Patrick

Creber (1965) says that, in a curricular setting, young people's needs *and* the knowledge of the academic discipline must coincide. If they do not, then the needs of the young people are paramount and the curriculum must be reshaped. This does not suggest weakening of content, but rather a selection of experiences (as in Dewey) which will be more meaningful to the young and which will also meet the goals of such an education. Creber's terms "sense" and "sensitivity" are especially fitting to the global goal of making students more sensitive to other cultures as revealed in their language and in their questioning. Developing an inquiry model in language rests on several suppositions about the way students learn, beginning with a belief that the most important learning to take place is a reaction to the image of the instructor and the way the lesson is taught. Postman and Weingartner (1969) explain that McLuhan's "the medium is the message" implies that the invention of a dichotomy between content and method is both naive and dangerous because this suggests that the critical content of any learning experience is the method or process through which the learning occurs. For this reason, language preparation for a multicultural world must stem from the student's own experiences, choices, perceptions of need—as incorporated, for example, in simulations of "real" life.

In U.S. schools, some of us have become involved in teaching what is called "global education," using the classroom language experience to constitute a more global, multicultural view of the world for our students.

We have used in our classrooms short descriptions of multicultural incidents to stimulate role playing with a class analysis on what follows from the point of language, body language, attitudes, and cultural interpretation. As a result, a student can become aware of the power of language to heal and hurt. There are implied value judgments in our use of words—colors such as *black, yellow*, etc. Just the mention of words such as *Communist, Jew*, or *Democrat* will send some people into a panic of fear or frenzy or anger In his seminal work, Gordon Allport (1979) addresses the burden borne by language. To liberate a student from ethnic or political prejudice, it is necessary first to make him aware of what language carries and then free him from word fetishism. Any multicultural program, then, must contain an element of semantic therapy to repair all damage which might already have been done to the student. This suggests that we *do* have an element of control over our language and lives. If the role of language in a global education is central to the very description of the curriculum, it is because language has the power to liberate us. Yet we must also consider what that language *carries.* Everything that happens in a language arts curriculum, whether it be inside or outside the classroom, is culture laden. The task is to increase student awareness of the power of language to build as well as destroy, to initiate as well as to terminate communication, to liberate as well as to shackle. A more recent consideration, of course, is the global spread and use of English as a *lingua franca.*

Larry G. Smith (of the East-West Center's Culture Learning Institute, Hawaii, in the Summer 1981 *Perspectives*) states that English as an *international* language is on the rise while English as a *national* language is on the decline as a result of national desires to reaffirm indigenous cultural identities. This says a great deal to global educators. For one thing, it tells us that though others speak English, we *cannot* assume they (or we) are familiar with the national culture, or that they will understand our way of thinking, feeling, and behaving. A Japanese doesn't need an appreciation of the British life style in order to use English in his business dealings with a Malaysian. It is crucial to note here, however, the use of the term *business dealings.* In the *school,* our concern is not business dealings but social, interpersonal relationships. It is the awareness of these relationships and the skill in building them that will prepare students in a multicultural society for tomorrow.

The language arts curriculum for the last 15 years of this millennium will probably emphasize the positive, human contributions of our global cultures. We tend now to eschew our past preoccupation with the more esoteric and bizarre aspects of various cultures. Two current concepts for teachers are that the reality of the world is neither perceived nor communicated universally in the same way, and that within a given social group, the members have different access to knowledge, relative to their positions in the social structure. In order to determine more accurately which *students* get which particular kinds of knowledge and capacities, however, researchers need also to do *classroom* research to see the kind of interaction that occurs there.

Our shared existence as a community rests on our ability to talk. Certainly, this is as true of global education as of all education. Our attempt in a global education curriculum is to make young people more sensitive to their own world—from the neighborhood to the other side of the world. One of the most significant learning experiences for our students can be their contacts with exchange students. We simply don't get the number of exchange students we would like—neither from schools in the area nor from abroad. The sharing of values, feelings, language, hopes and disappointments in the past has been the content for more compositions and class discussions than can be counted. Couple this with the reading of authors who, besides being gifted, are also black, Chicano, Oriental, African, or European, and we approach a global perspective.

Any global education is first and foremost an attempt to bring forth in students of today's multicultural society a certain perspective. This perspective is a *weltanschaung,* a view of the world—with its assets, problems, needs, and deficiencies. It is a perspective which should lead to a certain kind of world-aware behavior. To achieve this perspective, a teacher may choose from a number of contents and methodologies. Some teachers put the emphasis on global issues, others on intercultural awareness and understanding, and still others on global systems. Many teachers, myself included, tend to be eclectic. The dispute often seems to be over content rather than perspective, which may be a case of "missing the forest." Anyone who reads the literature on the subject can see to where all the apparent divergence leads. Yet no matter what we call the curriculum, language arts teachers deal with values and enculturation. This is one reason why in our curriculum literary works and simulations are done as comparisons. If a student reads Stephen Crane's *The Red Badge of Courage*, then he must read a comparable war novel by a non-American author and contrast the two. If, in a model United Nations, one student role plays the U.S., another role plays the U.S.S.R., or the People's Republic of China, or an African nation, and so on.

If these attitudinal and educational changes are to be effected, will they occur in the school or in the community? Ivan Illich (1970) argues that we need to "deschool" society and effect our changes beyond the walls. Perhaps the answer as suggested in a global context and as explained by Stephen Judy (1980) will be found in a cooperative *community* both inside and outside the school walls. It is possible for the teacher to select activities which will enrich the language experience and sensitivity of students by having them perform reading and writing activities based out in the community. With some imagination, the "community" can become the World (as in some American city school projects, notably Indianapolis). However, most of the organizing, talking, planning, showing, and telling can take place inside the school. Thus, through language arts, students are introduced to various disciplines, various bodies of knowledge. We must remind ourselves, however, that the "body of knowledge" in a curriculum guide simply *represents* the hopes of what our students will discover, grasp, and build on as discussion develops language experiences. There is no package—only a guide.

# 6.
# Multicultural
# Education

Multicultural education increasingly provides both challenge and opportunity to teachers around the globe. Here are descriptions of teachers of English struggling to teach students whose first language is not English and whose culture is not Anglo: New Zealanders teaching Maori, British teaching Jamaicans, Canadians teaching Mohawk and Cree Indians, Americans teaching Japanese, Libyans, Puerto Ricans, and Eskimos. In many respects, the pedagogy described in the earlier parts of this book applies to teaching in multilingual/multicultural settings. English teachers today have deep respect for the cultures of the students they are teaching; they are reluctant to impose their language and dialect on those students; they want to make connections with their student' lives through language and literature. The profession has provided teaching methods and even electronic devices to put to the task: barrier games, language experience, journal writing, computer-assisted instruction, and networking. However, one writer in particular, Malcolm Reed of London's Hackney Downs School, raises serious concerns about what might be called the deep structure beneath this pedagogy. Teaching is a matter of politics, he observes, and despite strong statements from our professional leaders favoring respect for the language and culture of non-native English speakers, he finds discrepancies between intent and practice. "Free the writer and free the writing," he says. "Would that it were that easy." Reed observes that in schools, especially those with a multicultural mix, neither the writers nor their writings actually exist in the kind of freedom which promotes the language use many of us would teach. With increasing numbers of second-language speakers enrolling in the schools of all five countries represented in this volume, it is clear that multicultural/multilingual education is an area that deserves concerted efforts on the part of English teachers, not simply in exploring pedagogy, but in discussing and debating the politics which underlie all of education.

# English and Multicultural Education in New Zealand

TREVOR WILLIAMS, PART I
JOCELYN TARRANT, PART II
BERNARD GADD, PART III
*(New Zealand)*

## Part I

It is difficult to say what is the "typical" multicultural/multi-ethnic mix in New Zealand schools. New Zealand has three major types of secondary schools—the state secondary, the private secondary, and the integrated school. The last named is a relatively recent hybrid—once a private school which has now come under the state umbrella in exchange for increased financial support and the guarantee of protection for its "special character." Within this range, you will find private and integrated schools that are almost exclusively Polynesian, and you will also find state schools that are largely, in some cases 90+ percent, Polynesian. On the other hand, examples exist of all types of schools where the population is almost entirely European.

In my school, the largest cultural group after the European is the Maori (the indigenous people of New Zealand). There are other Pacific Island groups represented (Samoans, Cook Islanders, Tongans) and the combined Polynesian population varies between 15–20 percent of the total school roll, depending on the year. In the first year of secondary schooling (Form 3), the Polynesian intake is 25 percent and sometimes a little higher. I will explain the discrepancy in these percentages later. Other ethnic groups represented in the school—Chinese, Indians, Vietnamese, Dutch, Greek, where English may not be the native tongue—are small in number.

We have an ESL department, and students whose English is not functional because it is not native are taught in separate groups. They are not necessarily timetabled out of normal English classes. The school tries to reflect a bicultural nature at least. Visiting groups are welcomed to the school in the traditional Maori way; there is a strong Polynesian club that travels and performs, and a major investment in a school *marae,* or meeting place, is nearing completion. (Strictly speaking, a *marae* is a courtyard of a Maori meeting house, although the word has come to mean the building itself.)

The success of the Polynesian students scholastically causes concern. As you can see, there is a discrepancy in the percentages mentioned earlier, which is largely explained by the high dropout rate after two or three years at secondary school. This is not a local issue; it is a national disgrace and the cause of much soul-searching in educational circles.

We are presently trying an experiment with a group of Polynesian students. We have created one class at the Form 3 level, which is predominantly Polynesian (20 out of 30 pupils). The pupils were selected in consultation with their previous school on the criterion of potential leadership or strength of character. The word in Maori is *mana*. We wanted to see if we could improve scholastic achievement by first enhancing the self-esteem of the pupils. If we could foster success in a variety of high-profile activities in the school, we hoped we could also influence the way these pupils regarded their performance in the classroom. We wanted to create the expectation of success as a natural part of a pupil's self-esteem. Perhaps we thought, too, that the promotion of expectation on the part of teachers might be an interesting byproduct.

The experiment is still in its infancy. It was not intended to be a one-year wonder but to continue over two to three years, although there will be a major review at the end of each year. There are difficulties: the class is unstreamed academically, as are all classes except one, and some pupils have no habits of work. Much of our initial effort has gone into creating routines. Mana is not necessarily dependent on academic ability; in fact, among pupils it can quite often stem from the complete opposite, a disdain for scholastic achievement, and therefore we have tried to find the right keys to modify behaviour.

I take this class for English and it may be natural to assume that literature by Polynesian writers would form the basis of our reading. Several interesting writers are available, although much of their work is reserved for study at other levels in the school. (Literature by Witi Ihimaera, Hone Tuwhare, Albert Wendt, and Patricia Grace, in particular is quite commonly used in English classes from Form 4 upward.) I decided to try a different approach and work through concepts, not simply resource material; I try to identify ideas in English literature and see if there is a common experience in great stories that is cross-cultural.

I started the year by having the pupils compose an autobiography. This, however, took the shape of a sacred box (the Maori concept is *wakahuia*) in which is sealed the truth of you, your most prized possessions, the essence and spirit of you—written, of course. There was much discussion beforehand of anecdotes and presentation by me and the pupils of objects that contain a sense of the sacred in them. I, for instance, showed them my silver pendant of the Welsh dragon especially made for me and a piece of mosaic tile from a Roman bath excavated at Caerleon. In this connection, there is an interesting New Zealand story, Joan de Hamel's *Take the Long Path*, which concerns a young

Maori boy in modern times searching for the sacred *patu,* or club, lost by his family last century.

From this initial unit, we branched out to look at the greatest myth in English literature, the Arthurian cycle. In these stories are two powerful sacred objects, sword and grail, symbols of rightful kingship, of honour, unity, and health. John Boorman's magnificent film, *Excalibur,* enthralled the class; writing exercises were set from it where pupils tried to identify with a character at crucial moments of decision. (What an opportunity *Excalibur* provides from which to package an educational kit. Why doesn't someone approach Boorman for permission?)

In *Excalibur,* Merlin had a dream of how Britain could be. His dream caught up other characters, so they too had their personal dreams. In some—like Arthur, Percival, Lancelot, and Uriens—Merlin's vision touched their lives and engrandised them. In others—like Morgan and Mordred—the dreams became corrupted by personal ambition. Boorman showed the transformation from clod to king, from butcher to champion, in those who tried to find and live by the best in themselves. It lived in the capacity to dream.

The film *Excalibur* was supplemented with the class reading Rosemary Sutcliff's *Sword and the Circle,* and her *Light Beyond the Forest* was also available for those who finished the first title.

The Maori concept of *Whakamaori moemoea* (the believing, interpreting, living of dreams) provided the link between Merlin's vision and the Maori visionary Te Whiti. In the 1880s, Te Whiti conceived the tactic of nonviolent resistance (long before Gandhi made it famous) and used it when a force of 1600 militia and armed constabulary were sent against the village of Parihaka in Taranaki. This force was met by singing women and children wielding white feathers. The white feather (*raukura*) became his symbol. His story can be found in Dick Scott's *Ask That Mountain.*

Two men and two traditions—Celtic and Maori—were thus linked by their imaginative power. It is through the appeal of these concepts that I have tried to work with the class and am still doing so. The unit we are studying at the moment is based on the concept of *turangawae-wae* (a place to stand [in the sun] ), but the set reader for the unit is Mildred Taylor's *Roll of Thunder Hear My Cry,* which concerns a black American family in the Mississippi of the 1930s. However, that's another unit and another thousand words.

### Part II

The greatest threat to the world's future may not be a nuclear holocaust but a Tower of Babel. We are only at the beginning of learning to live with people of other cultures and languages in a crowding world. In peaceful neighbourliness can we retain identity, cherish inheritances, but value and share elements with and from others? This is the real and exciting challenge of our times.

By the year 2000, it is predicted that the school population of Auckland will be 50 percent Polynesian (New Zealand Maori included). So while there is some (rather haphazard) provision for all nonnative speakers of English, and special arrangements for Southeast Asian refugees, it is with the Maori and other Polynesians that we are most concerned. Very few Maori children are now Maori speaking, although there are strong moves for maintenance and revival. New Zealand-born Pacific Islanders are also losing their languages. Little recognition is given to how much of their culture is being conveyed in the English they use. Lack of school success is still frequently blamed on their variant of English, as well as on "laziness," "dumbness," and lack of parental interest. Teachers are beginning to be aware that culturally different child-rearing patterns and learning strategies need to be taken into account. Most often, however, prescribed treatments are remedial withdrawal lessons and placement in slow learner classes. In many schools, this is also the lot of non-English speaking immigrant children.

New secondary prescriptions and the proposed, new primary English syllabus have broad approaches allowing for a variety of learning strategies—allowing for cultural as well as linguistic differences—which could result in more equitable opportunities for all. However, a change of government and subsequent ministerial emphasis on "back to basics," as well as pressures of public examinations and past inadequate teacher training in attitudes to language militate against this.

Most of my teaching has been in schools with a quarter to a half Maori pupils, some others speaking Polynesian languages, a scattering of Croatian and Dutch, and isolated other European, Chinese, and Indian language speakers. Until the 1970s, we plugged away as best we could in the normal mixed-ability classroom with no particular expertise in teaching English as a second language. There were few chances to take pupils on out-of-school visits, but we tried such things as pattern sentences, vocabulary building, "daily dashes" (a type of journal writing), writing to music, emotive topics, telling yarns, charades, teaching courteous exchanges before sports trips, and formal greetings, thanks, etc., for visitors. It wasn't all *Plain Sailing* (a basic text in secondary schools in the '50s and '60s). Yet there was laughter in the classroom; teachers worked together to try to meet the needs of pupils; and there was good group feeling and pupils learned.

In later years, we found there were interesting ways of short-circuiting second-language learning by controlling and reinforcing high-frequency, high-priority language, and promoting pupil talk by using substitution tables, sentence combining, extending and sequencing, and by barrier games, combining and classifying activities and controlled and guided role play.

Hard but rewarding days for me were spent running a class in inner-city Auckland for 15–25 (mainly Pacific Island) newly immigrant pupils of seven to fourteen years. It was a pioneer effort, similar in some ways to those classes described by Margaret Rogers (1971) and Rachel Scott (1971) in England.

The day started with greetings in our several languages followed by controlled exchanges. In the welter of English coming at the learner, there is need, at every level, for controlled, guided, repeated practice of utterances and written forms. These were embedded into the day's activities. Language was learned through school subjects, and in practical and *real* situations. Oral language usually preceded reading and writing, but sometimes only marginally. We explored the local area and went on day trips for "centre of interest" studies. We read each other books excitedly selected from the weekly library van.

Speaking with strangers in the host community and entering their homes for the first time are traumatic experiences. So we built up a group of people, our friends, from various walks of life, invited them to class parties, wrote (or drew) to them, and sometimes spent a day in their homes, finding out about food, furniture, and friendliness. I aimed to provide pleasant experiences and personal confidence as supports for future interaction with members of the host community.

Today, some fortunate nonnative speakers of English have English as a second language specialists working with them in withdrawal groups, usually on a part-time basis. Sometimes ESL specialists also work alongside teachers in the classroom, act as resource people in the school, and supervise teams of voluntary helpers—students for peer tutoring or parents who can spare time to assist a pupil an hour or two a week. ESL pupils in schools away from main centres are catered to as best they can be, by reading teachers taking withdrawal groups. ESL is being used to label pupils, especially the physically conspicuous Polynesian (including New Zealand Maori) and Southeast Asian, who speak an interlanguage but also nonstandard variants of English.

My feeling is that ESL specialists, while necessary for teaching older, newly immigrant pupils, should be advisors and resource people for schools. They cannot substitute for teachers equipped with skills to successfully accommodate our growing numbers of pupils from culturally and linguistically diverse backgrounds. When preparing ESL materials, I have tried to create those which could be used in the normal unstreamed classroom. I have produced units on the use of strip story and composition teaching techniques, barrier game activities in several subject areas, and the use of myth and legend and storytelling.

Traditional storytelling gives opportunities to use pupils and to bring in members of their communities as resource people, the repositories of treasured oral material. Tellings in the language of origin support language maintenance and development of strategies for coping with unknown languages. Cambodian tales have been compared with Aesop's Fables; the various Maori and Pacific Island versions of the Moon myth have had pupils realise that Polynesians share traditions. Studies on a theme, e.g., "Fire" (McKay and Smart, 1972), link Prometheus, the great fire of London, Hersey's *Hiroshima*, Southall's *Ash Road,* and other extracts to which I add the Maui myth.

To draw attention to the *culturally* significant use of English, I have used a tape and transcript of a Maori and Pakeha telling a Maori legend. While pupils guess and discuss which is which, many attitudes as well as linguistic revelations are made. It can be a particularly valuable study in the senior language programme.

In my last school, freedom was given staff to use the materials and methods they thought fit. There was a wide selection of class readers and other literature available in the English department by New Zealand (including Yugoslav and Maori), Samoan, Black American, a Russian, and various British and American writers. A well-stocked library and a national request service were used for studies which included race relations, immigration, South Africa, and land questions. When dealing with the latter, some staff found it advisable to divert strong feelings and to clarify thinking by using Dee Brown's *Bury My Heart at Wounded Knee. The Cay* by Theodore Taylor was popular as part of a unit on survival. The race relations message in it spoke for itself. As a counter to the message of *Lord of the Flies,* my senior students also discussed the true account of survival through corporate effort by six Tongan teenagers.

Because I'm tired of monocultural shortsightedness, apathy, and tokenism and their sad results, I also want to tell you about the Cross-cultural Community Involvement (Arts) Programme (CCCIP), in which I was involved as language advisor. (Further information about CCCIP is available through the District Senior Inspector, Department of Education, Auckland, N.Z.)

The CCCIP started in 1975 under the direction of Arnold Manaaki Wilson, an eminent art advisor and sculptor, for the New Zealand Department of Education. It builds on the 1954 project of Gordon Tovey, which used integrated arts, Maori and European, successfully to infuse life into language programmes, social studies, science, and even mathematics, in rural primary schools in the far north of New Zealand.

As a step towards multiculturalism, the CCCIP aims at *bi*cultural understanding. It uses as a base the Polynesian inheritance unique to this land, i.e., Maori culture. It attempts to bring about a deeper appreciation of the essence of Maori beliefs, attitudes, and values which underlie surface forms—to go "beyond recognition of difference, beyond respect for diversity, even beyond tolerance"—in keeping with the McCombs Report (1976), to create something culturally unique and a feeling for what it means to be a New Zealander.

For each workshop/*hui,* six to eight groups of 15 to 20 secondary pupils, representing a cross-section of their schools from Forms 3 to 7, accompanied by their Maori language, art, and English teacher, spend three days at a *marae,* community centre, or church hall, or sometimes sleep in at their school, while they paint, weave, and carve murals depicting local Maori legends. These they have had to seek out from the Maori community. Maori elders who have recounted the stories, parents, and other local peole with special skills in visual and expressive arts, traditional Maori crafts, modern dance, and recording, live and sleep communally in the *aroha* (love) and *whanaungatanga* (family feeling) which prevail at Maori *hui* (gatherings). There is respect for elders, specialists and their knowledge; time is clockless and young people are free to work as and when they will, learning by listening, by observing and by "doing" rather than by book learning, and guided and supported rather than directed. The delinquent, the shy, the gifted, teacher and pupil, old and young, find new roles in cooperative effort, consensus decision making, and the general social levelling of a *hui.* The past and the present are brought together as "tradition is cut with a jigsaw," sometimes well into the night and past mealtimes.

Stimulus is given to language learning in various formal and informal registers, variants, and styles of Maori as well as English because this is a *real,* highly motivating situation. Other languages of pupils are also encouraged. Unexpected pupils are found taking notes, keeping diaries, and writing poems—once, even during a disco!

Back at school, while the mural is being finished for presentation as a *koha* (gift) to the people who hosted the workshop/*hui,* other people become involved. In this way, further impact is made on people and on the school.

Two months later, the schools present their murals with due ceremony, involving such things as decorative coverings, masks, *whaikorero* (and speeches in other languages), poetry reading, storytelling, *haka, siva,* guitar, *tamburitsa* and other instrumental music, *waiata* and song, drama and mime, according to pupil strengths and interests. Written outlines of the legends, booklets of illustrations and writings sparked by the story or to share experiences, and thoughts and feelings associated with the mural making are collected for copying and distribution.

People change, schools become more aware, pupils and teachers find creative energy and a stronger desire to understand. Maori hearts are uplifted and halls are renovated in respect for the work of "our children, now always welcome here." No longer can the forms of expression be said to be Maori or European. They are a fusion of both in modern materials and words, worked by young people with their own vision.

Two of these pupils wrote of their feelings. The Maori girl had been a gang member. She wept when her poem was selected for publication:

Pride in representing school and subtribe
Past becomes the present
Before, there was no caring
Sadness in modern day Maoritanga
Nga Tupuna° fading away
Maori children looking in darkness
for fine knowledge
The world of the ancestors GONE!
Without it there is no longer
Te Aotearoa°.

Tears flow inside a
Pakeha° shell, but I
can't let them out.
Softly
touching my naked skin
I feel
blood, flesh, bone
and a tiny bruised dream.

In a way still sad . . .
Maori culture for Maori alone?
But Pakehas° here
All looking.
Called upon to be New Zealanders
All seek and share Maori culture.

°Nga Tupuna: ancestors
°Aotearoa: ancestral name for New Zealand
°Pakeha: native-born, European New Zealander

## Part III

The 1980 Sydney International Conference of English teachers produced a paper (Parker and Gadd, 1980) which, so far as I know, has never been published. The paper noted that education for a multicultural society "may be better thought of as a perspective than as a package of techniques," and that the issues involved in such educating "relate to all teachers of the curriculum, to school organisation, to administration, to teacher education, and to school-community relations at all levels of education." It ends by noting, "The English teacher's role is a crucial one in this move towards recognition of the nature and implications of multiculturalism in society."

I want to mention some of the ways the English teachers at the school where I teach have attempted over many years to put that kind of thinking into practice.

It is a decade since we made the first moves to abolish English as an independent subject in the core curriculum for Forms 3 and 4 (Grades 8 and 9). English is, like the arts, a contentless subject for junior students in that the learning is done by the doing—the growth in language itself is both the subject and the object of the course. But, for many of our students, if the language itself becomes too much an object under study, too much a set of examples of other people's language growth, too much a collection of variables to be labeled, then impetus to personal development can be entirely lost. But an integration with social studies offers the opportunity for teachers to provide students with studies or projects of potentially great intrinsic interest, and, therefore, with the chance to use and to develop their English in the many ways required in the course of their work. Such amalgamation of school subjects also affords time during the week for students to investigate topics in some depth and to complete their work to their and their teacher's satisfaction. Fewer timetabled periods per day and longer periods enhance this effect. More importantly, this subject integration cuts down severe distractions to our students—the moving from learning environment to learning environment, from teacher to teacher, or place to place, and the chopping up of a single topic, such as "Local Environment," among several school subjects. We also have instigated a "double English" option at Form 5 (Grade 10) to allow this integration of subjects to continue another year for some students. We see that in time the entire compulsory curriculum core can be amalgamated into a single broad subject whose content will in fact be the needs and interests and concerns of the students. Already the integrated subject is embracing Maori studies, art, crafts, basic science, and maths.

We have tried to make use of the strong Polynesian family feeling. Every student and every teacher in the school is now a member of a *Whanau* (Maori for "extended family"). Students of the same family are enrolled in the same Whanau. Although teaching is as yet usually done in independent classes, the Whanau regularly brings students together, teachers together in planning meetings. Thus moves toward cooperative teaching and mutual teacher support are made more feasible than in other kinds of school organisation that we have had. The structure also allows for students to come together from different age or class levels. This again reflects a deep Polynesian family pattern called *tuakana/teina* (Maori for "elder/younger" sibling).

Within classrooms, we encourage teaching that is according to what we have discovered through our experience and according to what we have derived from the scanty research literature congenial to Polynesian forms of living and working together, and of learning and experiencing together. The stress is less upon individual competitive learning and more upon joint cooperative learning. It is less upon everyone doing the same thing within the same time, and more upon options within the same topic. At all times, content is related to the students' lives and knowledge. For instance, Macbeth can be related to a self-seeking ambitious candidate for a title within a Samoan *a'iga* or Polynesian tribe.

Print and other resources that relate authentically to our students' lives have been sought. And, since not enough are available, we have written and published reading and literature materials.

I ask teachers not to attempt to mould the students' English into middle-class English. (It is not so very different anyway. Failures of cross-ethnic communication in our country stem less from diction and syntax and more from the extra- or para-linguistic aspects of expression.) I point out that their English expresses our students' selves and lives, relates them to their families and community. To reject the one is to reject the whole. Of course, we help those young people who wish to move from their backgrounds just as we help the growth of those who do not. But teachers are counseled not to assume that social climbing and ethnic boundary hopping are, or ought to be, the norm for our students any more than they are for us teachers. These are concepts too radical for some teachers to accept. Nevertheless, we have an across-the-curriculum language policy which stresses the need to foster the home languages and the home English, to help build up student self-esteem and ethnic identity, and to foster respect for others. We also have our own Grade 10/Form 5 evaluation of English as an alternative to the public examination. It is endorsed by the education department. It is a prose statement of the students' competencies in English and other languages, and meets employers' requirements.

We try ways of bringing school and community together. Members of the community are continually in the school and classrooms, and students are often in the community. From time to time, we talk education with students and community members. At the earliest stage of its development, the school was the community *marae* (Maori centre for meeting, community building, and the performance of various traditional rituals). Later, the students helped the community raise funds for its major recreational facility. Currently two staff members (one a teacher of integrated studies) represent the community on the city council.

A few of our English teachers have adopted a role of advocating to the public and to teachers in general the kind of multicultural vision embodied in our own only too partial reforms and innovations.

None of these things has been accomplished without struggle with school administrators (and recently the school board has selected a conservative principal to try to swing the school away from our conception of multiculturalism), and with educational authorities beyond the school. Nor have community leaders always been unanimous in their support of us. Yet, the multicultural ideal has remained our animating hope and our compass in charting ways to serve our local community and our society at large.

# Sound and System

MALCOLM REED
*(England)*

car zero zero one one nine
car Yellowman mek yu feel so fine
me chat out me lyrics me chat em inna rhyme
*Yellowman*—Zungguzungguguzungguzeng!

Maybe you haven't heard of these poets: U Roy, Big Youth, I Roy, Yellowman, and Eek-A-Mouse. They don't tend to be anthologised; in fact, their lyrics are rarely written down. They are the talking artists, famous in reggae music for their deejaying or toasting which they will perform "living an' direct" over a record, discoursing with the lyrics already recorded, or, "dub," talking out over a prerecorded piece of instrumental music full of electronic wizardry. They originate from the sound systems of Jamaica, where the toastmaster calls the tune and his chat fuses with the succession of singers.

The sound systems have traveled wherever reggae music is cherished. They are important businesses, to be protected, rooted for, and set up in competition in the halls and clubs of inner-city Britain. In the area where I live and teach, they are as important as the football clubs, more to some, and their names bedeck the billboards and walls: Jah Warrior, Jah Shaka, Jah Tubby, Unity, Saxon, and Casanova. When they play, the youth come to skank and shout and whistle in a thunder of drum and bass, pulse and echo. Like youth everywhere, they have fashioned their own style, reflecting their significance as misunderstood and unemployed in an adult world—Hooligan stylee.

Maybe you have heard and used the poetry of Linton Kwesi Johnson, Michael Smith, Valerie Bloom, and Oku Onuora. These are some of the "dialect and dub poets" becoming popular in schools where poetry does not stop at Heaney and Hughes, but has made the anti-colonialist step to Langston Hughes, Derek Walcott, Edward Brathwaite and beyond into Africa and South America.

Yet Michael Smith is violently dead and this weekend Prince Far-I is gunned down, and maybe the papers will suffer a few lines of cautious distance to condemn these vile murders. We are left with their words and the continuation of their struggle to fashion words—until the words

are taken away. We are being cautioned by our government to leave
the politics out of our teaching—so where shall I begin to censor my
own teaching of poetry and language?

I am what is known as a "multicultural English teacher" and my
teacher training was conducted in the inner-city borough of Hackney.
I have taught in two boys' comprehensives in this area. I hope that I
am the last of my kind to be trained out of ignorance and into power,
out of my elitist grammar school and university background which
fulfils the standard requirements needed to teach, but ignores the experience and knowledge of discrimination needed to teach for change.
I realise that for a multicultural English teacher I know very little about
Islamic culture, for I have just learnt to distinguish between a Moslem
and a Sikh by looking at their names. If someone was to tell me the
name of the greatest Urdu writer, I would still look at them dumbly. I
wonder incessantly about the distinctions between black, working class
life in England and what is circulated as West Indian culture by the
*books* with which I have been partially trained. I learn most from the
adolescents who take time and patience to answer my questions whilst
I attempt to answer theirs, and from friends who have lived in this area
longer than I and more properly belong to it.

I am the servant of Babylon, however unwilling. I am in the process of being integrated, ghettoised, and estranged. I don't think that a
cultural polymath is a confusion but a step forward, so I stand by
C. L. R. James. I'll try to think in terms of race and class and gender,
which in practice are not distinct, so I stand by Amrit Wilson, Chris
Searle, and Sivanandan.

I would like us to keep these disturbing thoughts in mind when
we read the example of my pupil's work which follows. We will see it
disembedded, isolated, and deconstructed. We will see it on the path
to finding a voice which is acceptable to the examiners these children
face, whilst coming from a powerfully political, modern, oral culture
which is left mainly unconsidered as the bedrock of literacy. We should
see the trappings and experience of a modern communication technology which we barely possess in schools, but which has structured the
performance of lyrics beyond our classical notions of rhetoric and grammar. We should be noting the effect of the recording media on the creation of poetic language.

If you've got a poet's hat, put it on. Let's think about foreground-
ing, versification, and ambiguity; about keeping your listener enthralled
up to the moment. Think about stepping off the printed page to the
last time that someone stood up and their words sang.

If you've got a teacher's hat, look hard. Is it still our school bon-
net frayed at the edges? Let's think about Curtis, who has been taught
and taught to make those prose sentences conform with the rules of
prose; who has swallowed many words of advice and still gets it wrong

at our first glance; who leaves his writing in the dark, in a scrumpled ball; who will write only rarely; who rides daily the nightmare of correction. Let's think about Curtis, whose rhetoric will make you fray at the edges; who once gave me a tape he had deejayed over at a time I didn't understand as seminal to us both; who I left to survive with another teacher last year.

## Prince Charles meets The Alien

Prince charles meet The Alien that come from Space The Alien dont Fit in with the human Face. The Alien have Three fingers on it hand and That is what I dont understand because it come From venus bam bam bam didle didle It come from venus an unknown land but I dont know Where The Space Ship land it could oF land in a park Some where in the dark but it come from venus it come from Venus. when morning come The Alien run a hunter come with him Shupd gun him shoot up di Alien Jest for fun Then di parents come to collect di son when tay see it dead Them squash di man head and that was The last oF The Aliens.

A cursory glance at Curtis's text makes me describe it as unpunctuated prose. I call it prose because that is how Curtis has been taught to record his language. It is this method of recording that he would understand as the proper lesson of English in school, and, no doubt, he has an ideal towards which he is aiming which is similar to what the teacher wants. It is also the lesson he undertakes most unwillingly, since he knows that he fails in the teachers' eyes and goes for extra tuition to the Special Needs Department. If they can catch him.

How and why was this topic set as a writing task? The film *ET* was about to have its English premiere, to which Prince Charles and Lady Diana were invited. The papers were full of this important piece of news and I wanted to cash in on the interest that was being sparked off among my third-year pupils. The proposed plot for newspaper story-writing was that ET also attends the premiere in secret, and, by chance, is sat next to the royal couple.

Now Curtis wasn't going to attempt this task in this form, so I had to change the rules. Since I knew that he could toast, I asked him

to write a toast out for me using the headline as a title. What you have
read is a first draft—live from his head.

Curtis is trying, with some success, to adapt and record the complexities of an oral form to writing. He has no experience of poetry
writing. The writer who can convert from prose into a metrical line
without being shown is forward indeed. Yet Curtis is conscious of
metre and rhyme and uses a roughly two-beat line and rhyming coup-
lets. So, this unpunctuated prose is full of significant information
about the foetal poem. By redrafting into lines rather than sentences,
we witness the emergent knowledge of form that Curtis possesses.

*prince charles meets The Alien*

prince charles meet The Alien
that come from space
The Alien dont fit in
with the human race.

The Alien have Three fingers
on its hand
and That is what
I dont understand
because it come from Venus
bam bam bam didle didle
it come from Venus
an unknown land
but I dont know
Where The Space Ship land
it could of land in a park
somewhere in the dark
but it come from Venus
it come from Venus.

When morning come
The Alien run
a hunter come
with him stupid gun
him shoot up di Alien
Just for fun
Then di parents come
to collect di son
when they see it dead
Them squash di man head
and that was the last of the Aliens.

In this form, we can understand and appreciate Curtis's skill as a poet. His punctuation fits and he is beginning to make line starts with capitals. If he could see this new draft, he would be able to extend the content, for there are narrative branches in this poem which are already asking to be followed: the question-and-answer routine that self-consciously exposes the toaster in the second stanza; the moral tone of inditement against hunters in the third stanza. Here is a rhetoric to be built on.

I have left out a discussion of what toasters do with the form. It would take another essay. Curtis is a novice when it comes to writing it down, but he won't need to write it if he comes to take the mike when a sound system plays. My present fifth year tell me that it is dangerous to write your lyrics down. Someone might nick them. I remember that Homer was a poet trained in a rhetorical tradition that works by memory, and that many cultures retain their bards and griots who can recite the night long in unwritten verse.

We can't ignore the skill with which Curtis has distinguished and phonetically recorded a grammar which is not taught in British schools.

We can't ignore his opposition to the dominating standard English dialect (sic).

So where does all this lead? In the realm of English teaching, are we skirting the border roads, unsure of our credentials? Pass forward. It is written clearly in the Bullock Report (1974a):

> No child should be expected to cast off the language and culture
> of the home as he crosses the school threshold, nor to live and
> act as though school and home represent two totally separate and
> different cultures which have to be kept firmly apart.

What does Bullock mean here? How far will we carry these implications in English teaching?

The barriers that have been erected, of *race* and *class* and *gender* (look again at the "overseas boy-child" of that last quotation), permeate our institutions—they are the oft-spoken laws of prejudice, ignorance, and intolerance, which rise throughout this realm in which we teach. We should be conscious of just what has been left unanswered in the past, fully expectant of misunderstanding, wise in the wiles of the lawmakers, uncowed. The politics of literacy are not so simple. Consider Bullock (1974b) writing about writing.

> Children reach a point where they need new techniques, having
> run through the satisfaction of their spontaneous performances.
> If the climate is one which is discouraging to such a concern there
> is obviously stagnation. The solution lies in a recognition on the
> part of the teachers that a writer's intention is prior to his need
> for techniques. The teacher who aims to extend the pupil's power

as a writer must therefore work first upon his intentions, and *then* upon the techniques appropriate to them.

Would that it were that easy. Free the writer and free the writing. Yet neither the writer nor the writing exists in the freedom Bullock offers. Our struggle and stand is to note carefully the writer's intention and support the politically complex portrayal of the land, which is often this land, that surrounds us.

# A Reading Centre for the Kahnawake Survival School

NANCY EDDIS and BEVERLY PYKE

*(Canada)*

Kahnawake is a Mohawk community, located on the south shore banks of the St. Lawrence River, across from the city of Montreal, Canada. The Mohawk, one of the nations of the Iroquois, are the eastern doorkeepers. Traditionally, the education of the young Mohawk was done in the home with parents, grandparents, aunts and uncles all taking an active role.

In the early seventeenth century, one treaty entered into with the Dutch was the Two Row Wampum Treaty, supporting mutual respect and parallel development. With respect to education, this meant that the Mohawk would travel in their canoe, and the Dutch would travel in their own vessel, each having their own beliefs, rights, and powers. Unfortunately, the ideals of the Two Row Wampum Treaty were upheld only by the Mohawk, who have not tried to convince their neighbors to become Indian, not by the non-native procession of French, English, American, and Canadian peoples, who have attempted to control the Mohawk, culturally and politically, through control of native education.

The most recent violation of the Two Row Wampum occurred when the Parti Quebecois came to power in Quebec and legislated Bill 101, the Charter of the French language. With the bill as law, native children attending school away from the reserve were treated as immigrants to Canada and required to apply for an eligibility certificate to obtain education in the English language. Attempts to remove this restriction for native students met with denial. By signing the license to obtain education in English, the Mohawk felt that they would be recognizing the right of the provincial government to legislate culture and education for native people. Hence, on September 6, 1978, the

Mohawk students enrolled at Howard S. Billings High School marched from Chateauguay to Kahnawake with about 800 supporters carrying signs reading "Human rights, not language, is the issue." This historic occasion marked the beginning of a new school for the Mohawk community.

The name Kahnawake Survival School was chosen for the new school, which was designed and built to fill the needs of and for the survival of the Mohawk people. Classes for Grades 7 through 11 began on September 11, 1978. Volunteers from the Mohawk community, as well as many qualified teachers from outside the community, offered their services to organize and staff the school. Classrooms were initially set up in various churches, schools, and private homes within the Mohawk community. After operating with volunteers for approximately two months, the school received funding from the federal government.

In May 1979, the end of the first year, we two women, a white anglo and a Mohawk, were hired to create a reading centre by September. During three busy summer months, we agreed upon the basic philosophy of the reading centre and designed the physical setting. Our basic philosophy, established with the input from students, a school committee (local board), teachers, and outside professionals, included eight points:

1. Reading is for everyone and is everywhere. Everyone can learn to read better.
2. Reading, writing, speaking, and listening should be included in a reading centre program.
3. A positive, student self-concept should be engendered.
4. The reading centre is neither a clinic nor library but a place where all may learn more about the reading process and the pleasure of reading.
5. Student groups should be small—six to eight students.
6. Rules should be few and kept.
7. Mohawks should educate Mohawks.
8. Equal time should be given for recreational, functional, and instructional reading.

During our first year in the reading centre, the school was housed in prefab bungalow buildings, about 40 by 80 feet, divided into two sections. Six of these buildings were perched within a stone's throw of the encroaching St. Lawrence Seaway and its huge ships. The shores of the seaway had formerly been an area for Mohawk homes and farms with clean water, family swimming, and canoeing readily available. Small wonder, then, that the students were wont to throw rocks at the enormous vessels churning by.

One bungalow building housed the reading centre in one half and the library in the other half. We created a comfortable area where everyone was made to feel welcome. We divided the centre into six different sectors for six different activities. The first sector had carpeting, comfortable chairs and a sofa, a fancy light, plants, and lots of different kinds of books. Here, people sat and read for pleasure. Staff and school committee meetings were frequently held here. This made it easy to establish a positive rapport with people as well as to enforce our rules of no eating, drinking, or smoking in the centre. These rules were for everyone, not just students. This place also became a social centre for students. Our official work hours that first year were 8:30 a.m. to 5:00 p.m., often stretching to 6:00. Our second sector was a group teaching area with a chalk board, chairs and trapezoidal tables which could be used in rectangular or circular formation. Here, more formal teaching lessons, group discussions, or projects took place. A third sector, where several students could work individually, had study carrels, a tape recorder and listening stations ready for use. The following year, we set aside a fourth sector, a small conference area in a separate room for testing and for private conferences with staff and students. A fifth sector was stocked with books, periodicals, and information related to the reading process for use by the staff as a teacher reference area. Lastly, we created a sector with desks, student files, and catalogues for the reading centre staff. These six sectors have been maintained, although the reading centre itself has had three different moves.

Books and materials were categorized as pleasure reading (hundreds of books with a variety of topics and reading difficulty), reference (many dictionaries and thesauri), comprehension (books on autos, child development, carpentry, agriculture, science, and math). It took us almost a full year to establish and communicate our philosophical requirement for a reading *centre* rather than a reading *clinic.*

Notable events the first year we worked with our 100 students included student participations in a province-wide, "I Love to Read" celebration, with winners receiving book awards from McGill University, and involvement of staff, administration, and school committee members in reading activities in the area. We joined the Montreal Reading Council, attended the national language arts conference, became members of the International Reading Association, the Canadian Council of Teachers of English, and the Association of Teachers of English in Quebec. We also arranged our own reading conference for the whole Mohawk community: five schools in Kahnawake received invitations and attended the conference held at our centre.

That first year never had a dull moment: A horse tried to come into the reading centre, and there was the dog mascot, who slept outside with her red kerchief around her neck, while we all waited for the birth of her puppies. Being right in the middle of the community, we had visitors dropping by frequently. As we wearily reached the end of

that first year, we had to overextend ourselves, since the entire school
was moved, buildings and all, to a new site. This was away from town
in a country setting, ideal for the farm and agriculture program, but
with the inconvenience of having no running water for some time. All
our books and resources were packed into boxes and we took a few
happy weeks of warm summer rest and relaxation.

We returned the second year, once again facing the task of physically arranging the centre in a new building and coping with the physical realities of no indoor plumbing or running water. Drinking water
was trucked in daily to make tea and coffee. In winter, heaters were
placed in these small buildings to combat Quebec's snow and cold.

We developed a feeling of continuity, tradition, and stability in
this native setting. The ensuing five years led to many accomplishments.
A book fair celebrating literacy is now an annual community event
(1,100 books were sold the first year). A formal evaluation of the reading centre by an external evaluator resulted in a highly positive report.
We created an elective program for Grades 10 and 11; a multi-age read-
ect involved Grades 7–9 students reading to four-year-old day care
children. We made presentations to the Quebec Reading Association;
we also collaborated in a microworkshop (at the International Reading
Association Annual Conference in Chicago) with a native woman, who
was president of The Native American Educational Services. Also note-
worthy were the student-created reference books of ads, haiku, and a
hex sign project that involved students creating their own designs and
writing their own meanings.

It must be pointed out that the native dimension of the reading
centre was always uppermost in our minds. Much contributed to that
dimension. For example, reading materials purchased contained much
native content. In choosing these books and other materials, we took
the advice and recommendations of native persons as well as using our
knowledge of the students and their culture. Many materials have ster-
eotypical views of native peoples and these were discarded. The reading
centre was festooned with Mohawk student artwork as well as native
content posters from various sources. The book fair we had at the
school involved the entire Mohawk community. In the multiage reading project, older Mohawk students were serving as Mohawk models to
the younger children. In the hex and advertising projects, many students used native designs by looking in native art books and by creating their own.

One incident in particular makes clear our emphasis on respect for
this native dimension. One of our students, a Grade 9 male, came to
chat with us in our comfortable Mohawk atmosphere (i.e., soft chairs,
time to talk and listen, interest in people, a feeling of welcome, such
as is found in many Mohawk homes). This student didn't really enjoy
reading, but earlier we had worked with him to fulfill a reading project.

Since he was interested in carving, we encouraged him to read a section of the Foxfire book on carving. He finally finished his project and it was added to the dozens of other projects which we housed for student reference in the reading centre. Since this student was respected by other younger students, when they saw his reading card and knew that he had read some of the Foxfire book, they began to do likewise. This student was able to express his rage constructively at being belittled by a particular subject teacher. He not only passed that year, but two years later, we were thrilled to see him graduate from Grade 11, proudly wearing his ribbon shirt and accompanied by his girlfriend, resplendent in buckskin beaded mocassins, black beaded and colourfully ribboned skirt, and her long hair decorated with leather, beads, and coloured feathers. His family surrounded him, beaming approval.

These, then, were some ingredients we found to be essential for success in a native reading centre: a pride in one's culture, a need for survival as a people, a community spirit, and, most important, Indian control of Indian education.

# Education in Alaska: Innovation or a Star Wars Approach?

ELAINE SNOWDEN

*(United States)*

Teaching literacy to Alaskans in the 1980s is a challenge with a twofold problem: on the one hand, there are the Alaskan natives from the village schools who speak a nonstandard English that reflects the native language of their homes and culture, and on the other, there are approximately 204 different non-English speaking minorities in a district like Anchorage.

The Alaskan natives are both Eskimos and Indians. They speak a dialect called "village English," which is, of course, as effective and as understandable as any dialect, but creates problems when these native students attend school. Lack of knowledge of standard English makes reading difficult. Further, there are extreme cultural differences. For example, students can remember stories about their own culture, but have trouble remembering those from another culture.

Some other problems that arise are also cultural. The University of Alaska Fairbanks Cross-Cultural Department observes that there is a high rate of ear trouble among native children from eighteen months to two years of age—this, of course, is during their early language development stage. As well, native culture emphasizes "right brain" dominance, which affects the students because they don't work well in our "logical," sequential method of lesson instruction.

As a result, a major problem in the village schools is in reading. The students usually don't like to read because their vocabulary doesn't match the vocabulary encountered in most published textbooks. To counter these problems, the Department of Education has embarked on an ambitious program to teach literacy to Alaska's native students. A major component of this program is the mass use of computer assisted instruction.

An example of the wide use of computers is a project called APEL (Apple[Computers] for Proficiency in the English Language). By their definition, "APEL is a bilingual microcomputer project of the Yukon-Koyukuk School District. Funded for three years as a Title VII Basic Project by the United States Department of Education . . . The primary aim of the project is to improve the English language proficiency of the bilingual students in their school district through the use of computer assisted instruction." A real plus for this project is that its creators have developed four pilot lessons on computer disk which are relevant to the culture and language of the students.

Another pilot project, developed for the Alaskan bush country, is called QUILL, a microcomputer system for teaching writing and reading. QUILL is being used in eight different sites in Alaska, ranging from small, rural Eskimo and Indian communities to large, urban, multiethnic areas. Integral to the development of the QUILL project in Alaska has been the development of a computer network which links QUILL teachers with one another and with program developers in Cambridge, Massachusetts.

Because the sites are so far apart and because the success of the program depends upon exchanging information and calling on resource people, the sites are equipped with modems connected to THE SOURCE or the University of Alaska Computer Network (UACN) databases.

A teacher in this program, Ernie Manzie of Chevak, Alaska, explains that his students use the computers to exchange pen pal letters and information about whales with students in San Diego, California.

Another component of teaching literacy to Alaskan natives involved establishing a statewide television network for the distribution of instructional television to rural Alaskans via satellite. This network is jointly managed by the University of Alaska and the Department of Education. It is called "Learn Alaska," and it has two separate networks—instructional television and audio conferencing. This network now reaches over 240 communities in the state. It currently broadcasts 18 hours a day and provides programs for a variety of audiences. These audiences include students enrolled in K–12 and in higher education, adults, and preschoolers. For example, more than 150 series are broadcast for the K–12 audience and more than a dozen university courses are broadcast each semester.

The Learn Alaska audio conferencing network handles more conferences per month than any other facility in the world. This network can be accessed by telephone anywhere. Calls are bridged together and the system can link up to 80 sites in a single audio conference. At present, this audio conferencing network is mainly used by professional organizations and administrative groups. The majority of use is for university and continuing educational purposes. However, the instructional benefits for students are there—an example is a project called Dial-An-Author, which has allowed elementary students throughout the state to talk directly with some of their favorite authors.

The other challenge Alaska faces is in its city schools with multiethnic students. To meet this problem, Alaska has a state-supported bilingual program which provides monies to school systems to assist foreign speaking students in learning to speak English. These students are mainstreamed into regular English classrooms and are tutored by bilingual tutors until such time as they become proficient enough in English to remain full-time in their regular assigned classrooms.

In addition to the bilingual program, the Anchorage School District has set up a Multicultural Education Program. The philosophy underlying this program is to assist teachers in developing and adapting materials to reflect the ethnic compositions of their classrooms.

An example of a lesson developed by the MEP department, using the interdisciplinary approach is as follows:

*Title:* Kites.

*Suggested instructional goals:* To illustrate that people bring their arts and crafts with them when they immigrate from other countries.

*Grade level:* Fourth.

*Subject matter:* Social studies/art.

*Material:* Books: *Dragonwings* by Lawrence Yep, *High Flying Kites* by Don Dwiggins, and other books from the library on kites. Film: *Kite Flying.*

Procedure:

1. Introduce the topic by showing the film *Kite Flying.*
2. Ask students if they know where kites came from. Suggest that they may decide one of the sources when they listen to the introduction to the book *Dragonwings.*

3. Have as many books about kites in the room as the library has available. Tell the students that they will be making kites the next day; before they start making them, the students need to know other places kites came from and what makes kites fly.
4. On the second day, plan enough time for oral reports, actually making the kites, and time to go out and fly them.

A follow-up activity the next week can be, "What did the Chinese contribute to our way of life?"

In addition to these activities, Anchorage's bilingual students, their parents, and teachers also use the Learn Alaska network for bilingual audio conferences. For example, a group of Vietnamese students has held a series of audio conferences with other Vietnamese students from Nome to Juneau. These participants learned more about their own culture, formed support groups, and shared information on bilingual education.

Alaska is spending much time, energy, and vast amounts of money to teach literacy to its citizens. With the advent of all this expensive equipment and technology the inevitable question arises: Is this method of trying to achieve quality education in Alaska an innovation or a Star Wars approach?

# Linguistic Diversity in a U.S. College English Class

### CHARLOTTE JONES
*(United States)*

This fall, I read the following paragraphs from diagnostic essays for my freshman composition classes:

> I like Kyoto in Japan. I think that most of Japanese people love Kyoto, because Kyoto can calm ourself. There will be lovely place in America. But I don't know yet. If you have it, I want to go there soon.
>
> *Chieko*

> In Libya my studing in jouner and senier High school was successful I learn a lot from many subjects special English but just simple gramer and How to read, and I was not good in math because it was hard, not like here and I couldn't understoud until my last two years in senire I start to understand the math and I can like it.
>
> *Safia*

I think that the Puerto Rico's education is good, but the English class is the exeption. One of the big problem is the subject is that the majority of the classes are fifty minutes, and when you go outside you only speaks Spanish, and you can't practice How to speak English and the most import what the teacher teaches in the class.

*Mara*

Chieko, Safia, and Mara present special opportunities for me. Their pieces illustrate the linguistic diversity in my classroom. Each year since 1968, when I returned from the Peace Corps in Thailand, I have worked with nonnative speakers or English as a second language students. I do not claim that this mix is typical of all schools in North Carolina, but we do have a diverse population in the central part near the Research Triangle Park.

Because I was trained as a teacher of English as a foreign language to work in Thai schools as a Peace Corps volunteer, I have been asked to work with our international students in my composition classes. Last semester, our class included four students from Japan, one from Puerto Rico, one from Panama, one from Argentina, one from China, one from Korea, one from Iran, and one from Venezuela, as well as native speakers of English. The ESL students are automatically placed in our English 20 course, designed for a student who scores 370 or below on the verbal section of the SAT and whose diagnostic writing sample shows that she "consistently lacks 'sentence sense': her sentences predominantly include mixed constructions, contorted syntax, or lapses in sentence logic" (Rubric for English Department Diagnostic Writing Sample).

These English 20 students obviously need a special curriculum, for they have faced failure frequently. They long to hear praise, to believe in themselves, and to express their thoughts with clarity. Nevertheless, defeat plagues their efforts. Over the years, the omnipresent red pen has convinced them that writing is a painful and unrewarding requirement for graduation. They have been told they can't write or have little worth saying. Their experiences give them mixed messages. On the one hand, they have been persuaded that they cannot learn to write, and on the other hand they have been told that they *must*.

In order to reach the international students and the "defeated" students, I have incorporated a number of activities to establish a supportive classroom climate where we can respond to one another with respect and appreciation as we develop competence in composing essays through the process approach.

Our course consists of five major compositions and a portfolio of many short ones. In addition, students are required to write in their journals three times each week. Their journal entries must be at least one page in length. They must respond to something they read in *Time* in one entry. Usually the ESL students search for news from their native land. As the semester evolves, other students search for articles that relate to their peers' countries. The other two entries are free writing, and frequently, the ESL entries reveal frustrations and loneliness. One-page entries quickly develop into two and three pages. The journal writing is confidential, graded for quantity, not quality. Journals help students to feel more positive about their abilities as writers as well as help me to understand the difficulties they encounter as they place a pen to paper.

By working through each major paper in peer editing groups, students gain confidence as they revise and shape their writing. We use the following sequence for each assignment over a three-week period: prewriting discussions, peer editing groups, revision, an audio-taped response from the teacher, revision, peer editing groups, a conference with the teacher, editing, and publishing.

Our short compositions are frequently written in class on days when we need time to let our thoughts incubate for the major paper. These are some of our "Reflecting Day" activities:

1. *Word Bank.* My students draw on their reading of *Time* magazine and record at least four unfamiliar words. These words are pronounced aloud and discussed.
2. *Dear Abby.* I read a letter addressed to Abby and students answer. They are encouraged to be witty and sincere. The ESL students listen and respond to a situation that makes connections with the real world in America.
3. *Phone Conversation.* I play a tape of someone talking on the telephone. Students hear one end of the conversation. The tape is played again and the students fill in the other end of the conversation as I stop the tape after each utterance. This can be an excellent diagnostic instrument to find out how much the ESL student understands of our spoken language.
4. *How To.* I videotape and replay a demonstration show from television, then ask students to summarize the steps of the process.
5. *Applications.* I have students fill out forms such as a job application, an order blank, a passport application, a driver's license application, and a credit card application. These forms are often of immediate concern for ESL students.
6. *Interviews.* Students interview one another, incorporating exact quotations into a "people watching" piece. This provides a logical step toward the more academic research paper. It also helps students to accept one another in the beginning of the year.
7. *Games.* I use "add on" games for listening and for including details. In a small group of five or six students, one student begins

by saying, "I went to Sears, and I bought some pajamas." The next student repeats the statement and adds one more item. Each in turn must repeat from memory all preceding items and add one more. Insist on colorful descriptions of the items.

8. *Popular Songs.* I have found that playing Ray Conniff, Mitch Miller, and folk singers works well with ESL students. I ask students to write the words to the songs they hear. After students complete the exercise, I sometimes ask them to change all the verbs to past tense or to change all singular persons to plural persons. And I ask what other changes must be made when numbers are changed?

9. *Conversions.* The students make statements from questions, questions from statements, or change direct discourse into indirect discourse.

10. *More Conversions.* Students write a narrative paragraph from a dialogue or a dialogue from a narrative paragraph.

11. *Combinations.* Students combine a group of sentences using connectors such as *and, but, although,* and *because.*

12. *Mapping.* I divide the class into pairs, giving one student map A and the other map B. Each map is of the same area, with different places labeled. Following instructions, students take turns asking directions to places unmarked on their maps, but marked on their partners' maps. I remind students to avoid giving any "body language" directions—only spoken directions are permitted.

13. *News Stories.* As a news assignment, I ask students to clip all stories from the newspaper which they think may be historically important in 100 years. In small groups, students explain their choices and then share their final choices with the entire class.

14. *Want Ads.* In pairs, students read the want ad sections of the newspaper. Then, they determine the courses one should study in college in order to qualify for an advertised job opening.

15. *Browsing.* Using a collection of magazines, newspapers, junk mail, and catalogs, I have students prepare personal guidebooks which include:
   a. pictures for a particular room in the house;
   b. modes of transportation;
   c. foods we eat for breakfast, lunch, or dinner;
   d. words that signal sequence;
   e. synonyms, antonyms, homonyms, acronyms; and,
   f. words that classify.

My students write daily. In fact, I write with them. Together, we talk about our writing problems and respond honestly as readers who want to see and hear. We expose our insecurities and weaknesses, but we also discover meaning and craft for our writing.

The ESL students do not become fluent and cogent writers of English in this one course. They do, however, learn to write with some sophisticated sentences that embed several related thoughts. Though Chieko, Safia, Mara, and the others still become frustrated with their abilities to function in our English-speaking society, they now have a process which enables them to write their thoughts in English.

# Whole-Language Approach in Native Education

PHILIP D. PEDERSEN
*(Canada)*

Unless a child learns about the forces which shape him: the history of his people, their values and customs, their language, he will never really know himself or his potential as a human being.

*National Indian Brotherhood*

To try to teach language as something divorced from human purposes, meanings and perception is to try to teach nonsense.

*Fillion, Smith, and Swain*

The Cree Community of Mistassini Lake is located in the south-central region of James Bay, in northern Quebec. With a population of little more than 2,200, it is one of the larger of the James Bay Cree villages. Historically, the Cree have had little contact with the outside world; except for trading furs with the Hudson's Bay Company, they mainly hunted.

Incredible changes have taken place in the last three decades: there are 250 prefabricated houses and buildings in the village, most built in the 1970s, where formerly tents and cabins were. In the late 1960s, the Quebec government developed the hydroelectric power of this area, which led to the 1976 James Bay Agreement with the Cree and Inuit of northern Quebec. The Cree, granted control over their education subject to Quebec's budgetary approval, formed the Cree School Board to replace the Indian Affairs Department as the judicial body of Cree education.

Built in 1971 by the Department of Indian Affairs, Voyageur Memorial School serves the Mistassini Lake area. Aside from the community providing seven trailers to accommodate the doubled student enrollment and adding Cree culture (handicrafts) and Cree language courses to the curriculum, little has changed from an organizational viewpoint.

During 1983–1984, I was one of four new teachers (out of a staff of six) who came to Mistassini. I was assigned one of the three Grade 6 classes, a middle stream "B" class of 11- to 16-year-olds. My initial optimism was somewhat muted as I became aware of: (1) the lack of appropriate curriculum materials, supplies, and generally poor school facilities; (2) the community's negative and/or ambivalent attitude towards the school; (3) the reflection of these attitudes in the students' rebellious behavior (i.e., absenteeism, tardiness, vandalism, violence). I also increasingly felt that streaming these students deprived them of social interaction with better achieving students, who might help or inspire them to further education.

While teaching at Mistassini, many of us worked long hours trying to make up for the inadequacies inherent in the curriculum. Parents perceived the school as something outside the community; the school was "white," not native. Native teachers were seen as having chosen the "white path." This community attitude was reflected by many students asserting their cultural identity by actively rebelling against the school norms. The primary function of the school was to occupy the children's time during the day, as a baby-sitting service, instead of helping them attain their goals in life. All this was because our school and its curriculum were designed to meet the needs of a Euro-Canadian rather than a native culture.

In Canada each province and territory has control of its own education, developing its own curricula and deciding how to use and distribute federal and/or provincial funding. In 1983, the Quebec Ministry of Education published a new curriculum for the teaching of English as a first language in schools serving the English speaking communities. This programme advocated a whole language approach. Although my school was oriented toward a skills mastery approach, I received permission to operate a whole language classroom.

I chose to follow a whole language approach because:

1. Skills activities are not relevant to the lives of the children I teach.
2. Children learn more about using language by journal writing and reading real texts than by filling out phonic stencils or completing workbook pages on grammar and spelling.
3. The skills mastery approach, although superficially appealing, does not guarantee that students will, for example, be able to adapt such paper-pencil skills to real writing and real situations.
4. Children assimilate language structure at an early age by being exposed to it and using language.

At the start of the school year, the teachers submitted their teaching schedules to the Cree School Board. We were encouraged to allocate one half hour to spelling and another half hour to grammar and phonics. Since other subjects, such as Cree language, Cree culture, French, gym, and math had to be slotted into our schedules, I foresaw that there would be little time left for writing and reading. However, since we were allowed to use the whole language approach, we were saved from the skills and drills.

On the first day, I introduced my students to daily journal writing. At the beginning, none of the students was able to write more than a short paragraph; by June, most of my Grade 6 children were writing at least two full loose-leaf pages with ease. One child, who on the first day wrote a total of nine words interspersed with three periods placed at random, was regularly writing at least a page and a half of coherent and cohesive text. Although his grammar and spelling were not yet conventional, he was creative and expressive in his writing. I gained confidence in my students and an enthusiasm for their work. By recognizing and working with their strengths, I helped them become even more expressive, more communicative, and more positive about themselves as learners.

The children enjoyed writing in a number of ways. Each journal received positive response; each morning they would eagerly read the comments in their journals. We shared each other's journals and frequently talked about the importance of writing. Eventually, the children's writing became their major forum of expression. Thus, in my classroom, writing was a safe, socially allowed means of creating new ideas and expressing feelings without drawing attention to oneself. This was especially important because the children were of an age where they needed to be expressive, yet were at their quietest. Writing also became indispensable in the other subjects we learned together. For example, in social studies, we wrote our autobiographies, and in science, we kept careful records of our experiments.

In Mistassini, there are no book stores. The school library (the only library) has a few thousand books. The books aren't catalogued and there is no librarian. The book most likely to be owned by a Cree family is the *Bible.*

Reading in our classroom was important and included a broad and varied experience. On the average, each child read over eight novels during the school year. Some of the favorites were novels by Farley Mowat, Judy Blume, Jean Craighead George, Katherine Paterson, and Paul Zindel. The children appreciated such novels as Farley Mowat's *Lost in the Barrens,* set in a northern scene, and Mark Twain's *Tom Sawyer.* They also liked novels that had been made into movies they had seen; a favorite was *Rumble Fish* by S. E. Hinton. I showed the children that reading was something to savor and enjoy rather than to be analyzed, questioned, checked, or completed. One method which I found successful with children who do not enjoy reading or who are having difficulty reading was to start a story with them. For example, I would read them the first 20 or so pages; as they became engaged in a particular story, they would then finish it by themselves.

Having a well-stocked classroom library or frequent access to a good school library was of utmost importance, particularly in my situation. However, inexpensive literature was also to be found in magazines and newspapers. Whenever I was able to obtain newspapers, my children would devour them, especially if they contained entertainment articles about such personalities as Boy George or Michael Jackson. Magazine articles on fashion, snowmobiles, and cars were also popular. Reference books or popular knowledge books such as those published by Time-Life were great resources.

Discussions on subjects that interested the children were also an important part of what we learned in our classroom. One simple question, "What are you planning to do when you are finished with your education?" led to inquiries into professions. This culminated in "Career Week"; each child worked in the village for a couple of days within a chosen profession. The children worked as bankers, store clerks, nurses, disc jockeys, etc. This was then incorporated into other activities in the classroom requiring written and oral participation. This experience became important in maintaining the native language of the children and helping them to form goals for the future.

I believe that none of these gains would have come about if I had to spend large amounts of time teaching grammar, spelling, phonics, or punctuation rather than fostering a positive attitude towards and enjoyment of writing. My experience has reinforced my belief about the inadequacy of the skills approach to teaching writing as well as the other language arts.

I would like to share one experience which I had not anticipated would work so well. I had heard that some Cree students had quit the high school they had been attending in Montreal because they had not learned to take proper notes and had not acquired effective study skills. I taught a course entitled "The History of North American Indians" for approximately two hours every second week; the students were enrolled and took notes. Besides learning the art of note-taking as well as the skill of concentrated listening, there were a couple of bonuses to this course that I had not expected: the students' pride and self-confidence in their heritage increased.

For too long, those responsible for the education policy of natives in most parts of Canada have ignored the culture of the students and that of the communities served. Indians are becoming increasingly concerned about the loss of their native languages. Three distinct groups can be identified: first, the elders, fluent and literate in the Cree language as well as knowledgeable and skilled in Cree culture, crafts, and customs; second, younger adults whose attendance at boarding schools away from Mistassini deprives them of full participation in their culture; third, children, many of them the offspring of the second group, now in attendance at the school in their own community. According to the native teachers on our staff, many of our children speak Cree at a rudimentary level. I believe that language and culture are strongly interrelated, and that a loss of language may eventually lead to a loss of culture as well.

If the Cree culture is to survive in Quebec, the school and its curriculum must contribute to rather than undermine its viability. To achieve this, instead of having English or French as the dominant language of instruction, Cree must prevail, at least in the primary grades. However, many of the people (native and nonnative) who are connected with education in the area, believe that the best way to educate the children is to expose them to a second language as soon as they enter school. Certainly, much research in bilingual education supports this viewpoint. Teachers of native children are faced with contradictory claims from the literature on bilingual and multicultural education.

I believe that using Cree as the initial language of instruction is valuable for the following reasons: first, it enables the preservation of the Cree cultural heritage; second, students can utilize their cultural background and experience from the first day of school; and third, it is easier for the parents to relate to and support the education of their children in the school.

Native language and culture instruction is being used in other parts of Canada. One instance is in northern Quebec, where the Kativik School Board, comprised of Inuits, has recently implemented native language instruction in the lower grades in many of the communities it serves.

In summary, this approach should be considered for Canada's native communities for two reasons: it is a means of ensuring the viability of native cultural heritage, and it is probably more successful than immersing the children in the second language at the start of their schooling as long as natives are employed, involved, and can culturally identify with the educational system.

Since I drafted this essay, I have been transferred, due to a surplus of staff, by the Cree School Board to the village of Eastmain on the James Bay Coast. Eastmain, a small village of 340 people, has only 123 students attending the Wabannutoo Eyou School. The school has eleven levels but in two languages (French and English) divided between nine homeroom teachers. Therefore, there is only one teacher (myself) who does not have a multilevel classroom. This year, although unqualified, I am teaching Secondary III, which is the Quebec equivalent of Grade 9. I teach language arts, mathematics, biology, goegraphy, moral instruction, and computer science combined with a course entitled "Introduction to Technology." I have my own Apple computer.

In our school, we share many of the same problems with the school in Mistassini, such as a severe shortage of materials. As this is the first year that Secondary III is being taught in Eastmain, there were no textbooks or any other materials for this level when I arrived. I would be lost had I not brought my own personal library.

We are also faced with a shortage of teachers. Certainly, nine home-room teachers would seem sufficient, given our student clientele, but our problem is that there are too few teachers, given the number of levels and subjects that must be taught. As in Mistassini, our teachers are attempting to rectify these problems by working long hours.

Similar to Voyageur Memorial School, ours is spread throughout the village; trailers are used as classrooms. Many of these problems would be eased if more money were spent to hire additional teachers (preferably Cree), to develop relevant curricula, and to build suitable educational facilities. Although the people of Eastmain have been promised adequate facilities for over a decade, the Quebec government is only now considering building an extension to the main school despite the fact that the building's foundation has sustained fire damage and is therefore unsound.

The people are angry at being offered an extension because they need and want a new, modern, well-equipped school. This anger has rallied the people of Eastmain to create a document that demonstrates their need. Resolutions demanding a new school have been passed by virtually every organization in the community including The Band Council, The Students' Council, the parents of the students, and the teachers.

Even though the federal government finances 75 percent of the Cree School Board as opposed to the 25 percent that comes from the Quebec Ministry of Education, the province decides the Board's annual budget. Unfortunately, Quebec has shown itself to be ambivalent about Cree education: it is likely that our problems will continue.

However, one aspect of Eastmain that is completely different from Mistassini is community involvement. The parents see the school as an important part of the community, and are very concerned about their children's education, holding meetings each month together with their children about it. A recent meeting lasted over three hours, with parents making impassioned speeches urging their children to do well and to work hard in school. They made it clear that many of them were sorry that they were not offered the same opportunity. In this way, Eastmain is almost unique within Quebec's Cree communities and perhaps among schools in general.

Within the English sector of our school, three out of four home-room teachers are Cree. I am the exception. Although none has finished an undergraduate degree, I believe that they are more qualified to teach in Eastmain than is a "qualified" southern teacher. These native teachers know the culture of the children and have no difficulty in establishing a rapport with them. I find that my children are hard working, cooperative, and helpful to each other to an extent I had not witnessed in Mistassini. The benefits my students have accrued from such teachers has made what I can do for them that much easier as well as more enjoyable. Although neither teachers nor our Cree principal, Dorothy Gilpin, are fully versed in the trends of education, they nevertheless could be characterized as whole language teachers. They work with developing the child's experience within the classroom and cultural setting. Dorothy is a strong believer in getting the children to read a number of different materials. This year, she plans to open a community library. If she succeeds, Eastmain will be the first Cree community with a library serving more than just students.

# 7.
# Classroom Management

This part opens with a description of teaching conditions that can only be described as "grim." Jean Blunt (ironically of the *Summerhill* Middle School, U.K.) describes the problems she faces as a teacher without her own classroom. Her essay strikes a theme of "resources and constraints," of making do under difficult situations, of finding ways to manage instruction in keeping with the kinds of principles that have been articulated in the earlier segments of this book. Other writers touch on this same theme, a balancing of opportunity—say, the availability of video equipment—with constraints and problems—scheduling such equipment, learning how to run it, having enough supplies to make video education a reality. The writers describe such classroom management problems as large classes, individualizing reading, mass approaches to writing as process, explaining what one does to parents, structuring interdisciplinary studies, organizing for media instruction, and managing that old devil, time. This part is nuts-and-bolts, with explanations of how to set things up and get them done in a less-than-ideal world. It is here we most clearly gain a sense of good, thoughtful, practical, even *ingenious* English teachers at work.

# Resources and Constraints

JEAN BLUNT
*(England)*

I work in a school which has basically good resources. There are adequate numbers of lively, well-chosen texts; we have a new video recorder and working cassette players; the school is well run and there is a basic and genuine fund of good will existing between headmaster, staff, and pupils; mixed ability groups work happily. All would seem to be well.

However, the school is limited by its modern, cheaply-built structures. Teachers become itinerants, laden with bags and searching for a comfortable room. I find I do not have a base to operate from because I have to take rooms which happen to be free, and if there aren't any, then I am in the Form 5 common room! I suspect this situation arises for most teachers new to a school and all part-time teachers.

This makes my work as an English teacher much harder. For example, on one day of the week, I teach in five different rooms. So what? There are several disadvantages. I have to carry all the books I need around with me. If I am teaching English in a math room, then you can bet there won't even be a dictionary if I need it. There will be chalk if I am lucky. I also have to carry all the stationery I need. I must not poach from other departments. There is no available display area.

I cannot move other teachers' furniture to suit my groupings. I sometimes find myself in the modern languages block where communicating
doors are used to the full. Colleagues never expect me to be where I am,
and they are constantly looking for the person who "should be" in the
room I am teaching in. No one every visits me. Finally, since I am a
teacher of English, then the groups I take are large. Sometimes the
rooms we are in are just not big enough.

All these constraints make the business of teaching and learning,
writing and talking, listening and laughing (the dividing walls are paper
thin) more difficult. I have my best English lessons in a dilapidated
mobile classroom raised from the ground so that the cold and damp
of winter rise from beneath. In summer, we moan quietly and regularly
about the oppressive heat. It is mostly used by a math teacher who
cheerily moves out with her marking for me to have my double lesson
a week there. There are holes in the strange-looking lining of the walls.
The filling seems to puff out and grow week by week. I don't think the
walls would harbour drawing pins if there were a suitable display area.
Yet we are away from the main building and we can group the tables
to suit us and no one knows. Pity this is a luxury. Yet, within these
constraints, we do our best, knowing that we are not the only English
teachers by far to teach under such circumstances.

# Questions and Curriculum

RICHARD E. COLES
*(Canada)*

Teachers often return from conferences full of enthusiasm about
the new theories and their implication for the classroom. After a few
days back at school, however, the reality of their classroom situation
dampens their eagerness to try the new ideas. Staffroom conversations
reveal many difficult questions about classroom management. In this
essay, I will discuss four questions often asked by teachers.

1. *How can I get my students to do more reading?*

Students enjoy reading books that are interesting and meaningful.
In many classrooms, the availability of a variety of materials—novels,
collections of poems, jokes, riddles, tongue twisters and magazines—is
an important factor that determines whether the students decide to
read when they have some free time. Children enjoy browsing through
book displays, selecting new books, reading the covers, or searching for
a favorite author. Although the curriculum is overloaded with content

in many subject areas, the students need the opportunity to read on a daily basis.

The teacher plays an important role in facilitating classroom reading. Each day I read aloud to my class. When a new collection of books arrives from the school library, I introduce them to the class, and usually these books do not remain on the shelf for long. I also realize that students need to discuss their novels, jokes, or short stories with each other, and so I provide frequent opportunities for informal discussion. In a classroom where everyone reads, selecting a book, participating in a discussion, or reading quietly in a comfortable chair, becomes a natural part of a school day.

### 2. Why do my students not want to write in class?

Many students at the beginning of the school year appear to be fearful or hesitant about expressing themselves in writing. An announcement of a writing lesson is usually greeted with groans in multiple-part harmony, with polysemous voices enhancing the tune.

In the first few weeks of school it is important that students experience success in writing and that they enjoy the experience. I find that simple class activities—such as a team story or interviewing a classmate and presenting the student to the class—help to develop an atmosphere of acceptance and a feeling of success. Journals provide opportunities for students to write about topics of personal interest; many students do not realize how much they know about certain topics. I find an interest inventory helps me learn about the students' interests. When I interview a student concerning his or her interest inventory, the student and I discuss some possible topics to write about. The interview also helps to establish the conference as a regular part of the writing program. For many children, the opportunity to discuss their written pieces with a concerned adult, a committed audience, become a motivating force for writing.

### 3. How can I teach writing as a process with large classes?

When many teachers are exposed to a new theory about reading or writing, their initial response is easy to predict. They seem to believe that such a theory cannot be successfully implemented because of the school population or the class size.

I believe that teaching writing as a process is possible in large classroom management. It requires having the necessary materials, such as paper, pens, and markers readily available, and in making the best use of school time. Although a large class begins a writing program at the same time, individual writers require different amounts of time to draft, revise, and illustrate a selection. Some children have already decided on a topic and are anxious to begin writing. Others require more time to consider different possible story ideas. Since stories and writers vary, some selections need more revision or illustrations than others. Within a few days of the beginning of a project, my entire class appears to be at different stages of the writing process. By circulating around the classroom, I can easily help many writers with their specific needs. Not every student will require a long conference on the same day. One or two groups of students can be working on pieces in the library while I help other writers.

Students assist each other by reading and discussing one another's stories. Children with artistic interests act as illustrators for friends' selections. Students in older grades are useful editors when a primary class wants to publish its writing. Teaching writing as a process in a large class requires organization, enthusiasm, and energy. It is not always easy, but it *can* be done.

4. *How do I discuss my students' progress with parents in a multi-cultural community?*

In many multicultural communities, the parents seem reluctant to visit the school. Often, they do not feel comfortable expressing themselves in a second language. The school's curriculum and procedures are very different from their own educational experience. It is, however, necessary to discuss with parents the school's curriculum and the individual student's progress.

The school needs to be seen as part of the community. Fall fairs, concerts, and informal meetings with teachers afford parents an opportunity to visit the school and meet the staff. Students can help bridge the gap between the school and parents. On parents' night, I have my students act as guides, explaining displays and showing how they work at various centres. The students also have a feeling of pride, as they acquaint their parents with reading and writing folders and other resources.

I use the translators from the community to assist me in the parent-teacher interviews. I believe that a teacher's warmth and caring about a child is easily discerned by a parent despite a language barrier. After one successful visit, parents are not as reluctant to come to the school again.

Teachers constantly raise important questions about students and the curriculum. I have given brief answers here, but more important, I feel that by discussing possible solutions with their colleagues, teachers can provide a better learning experience for students.

# Organising for Television Study and Use

JO-ANNE EVERINGHAM
*(Australia)*

Some new demands and challenges are being presented to English teachers with the advent of analytical media studies courses and practical video work. Tasmanian secondary schools are fortunate in having at least the basic equipment for such courses, including video cassette recorders, 35-mm cameras, projectors, audio cassette recorders, and even video and film cameras. However, access to these items within the competing demands of a school can be a problem. Another problem is learning how to *use* the hardware in the classroom without having the class wait five minutes while the teacher mutters, twiddles dials, curses, and tries to work out how the machine operates. In this essay, I will focus on my work with just one of these media: television.

The single greatest asset in easing a teacher's burden of preparation and organisation for television study is the home or portable recorder and playback unit. Still there are considerable problems that we have to contend with, including:

1. *The ephemerality and topicality of television.* Programs often appear only once, and it is difficult to obtain detailed knowledge of them in advance to aid planning. The television networks and the Association of Teachers of Media in Australia are starting to provide some materials related to current screenings, which teachers can tailor to their needs. But problems still arise. A group of Tasmanian teachers put a lot of work into developing a unit of study related to the Australian police series *Cop Shop,* only to learn it had been taken off the schedules.

2. *The demands on teacher preparation time.* The teacher must gather, preview, and organise material within a day or two. At least I find I can utilise many of my daily media experiences and the parallel and overlapping ones of my students to produce an unusually high level of interest.

3. *The shortage of readily available support materials.* Australian materials are not being produced for media studies curricula in most states. Still, those long-standing teacher attributes—scrounging and hoarding—have to be heavily relied upon for resources such as local viewing figures, network ratings, advertising revenue, production house ownership, scripts, and program budgets.

4. *The difficulty of finding time in an already crowded curriculum for media study.* There is a real demand for time and organisation, but the solution is to teach media as an integral part of most English topics. For instance, I would be ignoring the most common experience of narrative that my students have had if I didn't examine it as one of television's main techniques for shaping the events it handles. News, documentaries, and sports programs, as well as dramas, comedy shows, and soap operas, create stories with heroes, villains, conflicts, and resolutions.

5. *The need for individualised learning and small group resources.* Newspapers, videos, and worksheets are required in quantity. Secondary English classrooms have been revolutionised recently by a classroom management technique we've learned from the primary school—the writing process—with its provision for individual and peer group work and conferencing. I find I can extend this idea and take more leaves from my primary colleagues' book in the physical organisation of my classroom to include specific activity or learning centres including a media-focused current events centre. This is possible for secondary teachers lucky enough to have a classroom of their own. I've also found it invaluable to appoint monitors who can save me setup time and preoccupation with the media equipment.

Of course, there are still those hair-raising times which no amount of organisation can forestall: when the equipment breaks down or the tape that I have carefully prepared is chewed and shredded by the machine, effectively destroying my lesson plans for next week.

Despite the problems, video equipment is enthusiastically used in a number of ways in Tasmanian schools, and each has its characteristic style of resource and student management.

1. *Practical work in television studies courses.* One of the popular approaches to media studies is a three-strand approach encompassing observation activities, analysis, and production. This third strand often makes use of video cameras for whole classes or groups within a class to do their own interviewing, design and produce a television advertisement, produce a pair of programs on the one subject from different viewpoints; to produce their own TV news bulletins to experience the constraints and decisions involved; and to conduct experiments, such as dubbing new sound to existing pictures, recording new pictures for an existing soundtrack, or breaking some conventions of dress, shot, camera angle, or eyeline. I find this a very rewarding and worthwhile application of the technology, but it needs ready access to the portapak and a VCR during lessons and students' basic familiarity with the technology.

2. *Optional activities.* Many schools have electives on special days or on a regular basis, others have a video club during lunch hours. In my school, we find that the video club enables small groups to participate in a major production over an extended time. For such an activity, students may tend to specialise in one particular task (e.g., acting, operating the camera, or sound recording) for a whole project. Most teachers who've produced a school play are familiar with providing "jobs for all." The greatest challenge is in determining what the group wants to say and who they want to communicate with. Experience in class story and poetry writing will be applicable to such exercises.

3. *Recording of special school events.* I'm not overly enthusiastic about requests to video athletics, carnivals, and such irregular occasions. The sort of record usually required demands that individual students be selected for technical proficiency and often I fall into a great deal of teacher input. Frequently, creativity and critical selection are not expected and so the main educational value is in terms of technical skills and responsibility.

4. *A project within a particular school subject.* I've seen video used by a speech and drama class exploring a new medium of self-expression; art students experimenting with surrealism; a social sciences class documenting their learning about an aspect of our society; and a primary class demystifying some film special effects by producing an accident sequence to show how "realistic" stunts, breakable props, and fake blood can be made to look.

5. *Introduction to the technology.* All of the above approaches can start with an introduction which gives beginners a clearly defined exercise to practise the main video conventions. The equipment I gather for such an exercise includes a portable video tape recorder, a battery, a camera, an AC/DC power adaptor, a double adaptor, an extension cord, video tape, a tripod, a TV monitor, cardboard sheets, and texts.

Each student practises assembling the portapak, focusing, using the zoom, framing different shots, adjusting for different camera angles, and making smooth panning movements. They are next told to plan in advance a six-part documentary on a topic such as "School Life" or "Our Local Industry":

1. Title and credits.
2. Introduction by anchorperson.
3. Interview with an over-the-shoulder two-shot.
4. Panel discussion requiring camera movements.
5. Action insight by a hand-held shot of a key individual with voiceover dubbed later.
6. An acted group scene or drama with more complex camera angles and movements.

Students are then assigned roles: talent, camera-person, VTR/ operator, sound recordist, studio manager, props and costumes organ- iser, graphic artist. The story is shot in sequence to avoid the need for editing.

In the end, confidence in resources and organisation are critical factors which determine whether teachers will attempt media study and video-making in their school and the success such ventures will have. I have outlined some of the parameters I work within and some approaches I've seen followed successfully. There are also valuable sup- port services available to Tasmanian teachers starting practical film and video work from the Tasmania Media Centre and the Tasmanian Coun- cil for Children's Film and Television.

# A Context for Teaching

LORRAINE COCKLE
*(Canada)*

After 13 years as a junior high school language arts teacher, fol- lowed by a serendipitous sabbatical year (devoted to probing language and art processes in the spectator role), I found myself back in the work force as an itinerant teacher of gifted and talented students. My itinerant status leaves me with no classroom to call my own and I haven't "taught" anything that remotely resembles a traditional Eng- lish lesson in the past three years. On the occasions when I work di- rectly with gifted students, curricula, methodologies, and resources are frequently dictated by the intentions of the students themselves. What do they want to learn; how do they want to go about learning it; what form do they want the outcome of their learning to take? More often than not, I am engaged in undertakings that seem to have more to do with math or science or art than they do with language. However, my students do use language—perhaps in the interest of developing the most "basic skill" of all, that of making sense of themselves and vari- ous aspects of their world. What gifted children can accomplish when they are freed from the standard expectations and curriculum objec- tives of a teacher is, of course, quite impressive. More importantly, there are compelling reasons for considering that the strategies and learning contexts advocated for the gifted may have wider applicability and that when such strategies are employed in the regular classroom setting, the education and personal growth of *all* students may be facilitated. In this essay, I will present three contexts that represent my interests as a teacher of the gifted.

### Scenario One

*The Setting:*  A gymnasium in one of the newer suburban schools.
*The Students:*  Seventy-five Grade 1 students in regular classroom placements.
*The Situation:*  Parents and friends have been invited to a celebration entitled "The Garden Party" (a take-off on Judy Chicago's innovative artwork, "The Dinner Party"), which completes a month-long study of butterflies.

A mass of vibrant tissue-paper butterflies clusters on the leafless branches of a small tree which is the centrepiece for "The Garden Party." Surrounding the tree is a triangular arrangement of long tables upon which 75 colourful place settings have been arranged. Each place setting consists of a batiked placemat, a paper plate which has been decorated with a butterfly theme, and a folder containing the work which each student has selected to share with his or her guests. Additional displays of student work as well as background information for parents have been set up around the perimeters of the triangle. Three terrariums complete the display and these contain the dozens of painted butterflies which the children have eagerly watched emerge from the cocoon stage. Following the opening ceremonies (which consist of several songs and a slide-tape show of the unit in progress), each child provides his or her guests with a guided tour of "The Garden Party."

*Flashback:*  In the course of completing the butterfly unit, these children experienced individualized, small group, and whole-class instructional strategies, and proceeded blithely across subject boundaries in their exploration of an engaging theme. The success with which they mastered the principles of transformational geometry in the creation of their paper plates as well as the complexities of batik suggests that they are also capable of exceeding many of the parameters we normally place upon their learning. While we might be hard pressed to describe this as a language arts unit, there can be little doubt that these children were using language to learn as well as learning about language.

### Scenario Two

*The Setting:*  A "closed" (as opposed to "open area") classroom in a junior high school.
*The Students:*  Twenty-eight Grade 7 students in a regular classroom placement.
*The Situation:*  The students are working on projects which mark the completion of a novel study.

In one corner of the room, three girls are working on a board game they have designed. Two of them are discussing the directions for play while the third works on the playing board, which consists of a large map of Middle Earth superimposed with various playing routes, each of which includes an assortment of hazards to be overcome or fortunes to be won. Kai, a Vietnamese student, is putting the finishing touches on one of several drawings he has made to illustrate his favorite passages of the novel. In this drawing, a distinctly Oriental-looking dragon swoops over a village of terrified people. Using the Uncial alphabet—a style of lettering that is frequently associated with the Middle Earth books—Jill and Kendra are making front and back covers for their recipe book, *The Middle Earth Gourmet*, which contains directions for such imaginary treats as "Smaug Flambé" and "Gollum's Riddle Cake." Oy Ping is busy arranging tiny dough-crafted objects in an intricately detailed diorama of Mirkwood, home of the giant spiders, and, nearby, Kirk works out an answer key to one of several coded messages he has designed using Tolkien's runic alphabet. Jason, one of two identified gifted students in the class—and an ardent Tolkien fan—is using a role of shelf paper to lay out an annotated, biographical timeline of his favorite author while Sam, the other gifted student, slouches in his desk thumbing through a pile of well-worn "X-men" comic books, the resource materials for his comparison of Bilbo's personal transformations with the more visual metamorphoses of his comic book heroes. Elsewhere, students are creating riddles, designing "Wanted" posters, or rehearsing reader's theatre presentations.

*Flashback:*  All of these diverse student projects were inspired by J. R. R. Tolkien's fantasy novel, *The Hobbit*. Group interactions prompted discussions, comparisons, and personal reflections that were not as evident in the novel study's original context and the divergent forms assumed by the numerous personal responses to the book seemed to provide the sort of stimulation and mutual appreciation that is difficult for a teacher to engineer when there is only one student involved. Students of varying interests have much to learn about and from one another!

### Scenario Three

*The Setting:*  A room in a convention centre which is hosting a language arts conference.

*The "Students":*  Twenty-four language arts teachers whose classroom responsibilities range from Grade 1 to Grade 12.

*The Situation:*  A professional development workshop entitled, "Beyond Words: Visual Thinking in the Language Arts Classroom."

- People are sitting in rapt concentration, some with their eyes shut, others making peculiar gestures in the air as they struggle to solve the "Painted Cube" problem (McKim, 1972). The task involves imagining a painted cube which has been evenly divided into 27 smaller cubes and then determining how many of the smaller cubes have paint on three sides, on two sides, one one side—and how many cubes are unpainted.

- Small groups of people are brainstorming ideas for using such items as a box of Wheaties, a coat hanger or a lightbulb in order to remove a ping-pong ball from a short pipe embedded in concrete—without damaging either the ball or the pipe (Adams, 1976).
- Individuals are volunteering descriptions of what they "see" in a visual closure exercise.
- Teachers are grouped according to their respective grade-level responsibilities and are brainstorming ideas for thematic language arts units using the "webbing" strategy.

*Flashback:* Conducting workshops on various aspects of gifted education is an integral part of my present job. Sometimes teachers request presentations on specific enrichment strategies such as Synectics, Futures Problem Solving, or the CoRT Thinking Program; sometimes they want opportunities for first-hand experience in planning or differentiating units for individual student needs. The workshop described in the scenario combined both approaches with the first half of the session devoted to an exploration of visual thinking and the other half spent in incorporating visual approaches in thematic language arts units.

Differentiation of the sort described in the preceding scenarios is not an overnight accomplishment. Children who are accustomed to an external locus of control need to make the transition to self-directed learning gradually—and in a climate which facilitates trust and risk-taking. Open-ended questioning techniques and frequent opportunities to generate divergent ideas were important preparatory activities before embarking upon independent studies or the creation of divergent products. Diversity obviously requires a departure from standardized evaluation strategies, but many teachers are beginning to realize that the school term provides ample time to attend to individual needs as well as to the language conventions valued by our society. In any case, we might do well to remember that, by the prevailing educational "standards," Albert Einstein was declared a failure in mathematics and that Adolph Eichmann was proclaimed an honours student in ethics.

# Individualizing Approaches to Poetry

RUDI ENGBRECHT
*(Canada)*

November 1983, Grant Park High School, Grade 12. The students were abuzz with excitement. For 11 class periods, they would participate in a research experience where they would teach themselves and each other to read poetry, where I, the teacher, would merely construct the learning environment. This first class reflected unusual excitement, the second some frustration, the third, fourth, and fifth considerable frustration and anxiety. However, the realization that my help provided the possibility to learn and not the answers to copy or anticipate became clear by period 7. The students realized it was their task, not ours or mine. The excitement gradually returned for the last three classes, but it was an excitement rooted in the craft of the text rather than the euphoria of merely experiencing something different evident in the first class period. It was an excitement rooted in a new confidence that they could in fact "read" a poem.

This research was a variation of an earlier study on independent student reading of poetry (Dias, 1979). Coralie Bryant, division English consultant, and I adapted and implemented this earlier model. A teacher in another school taught the control class.

I pursued this research because several questions remained unanswered in my present teaching methods, questions which Dr. Dias addressed in part in his earlier study:

1. Would collaborative exploration of poetry prepare students adequately to write a coherent interpretation?
2. Would students acquire increased confidence to read poetry?
3. Would daily journal writing provide the writing practice usually provided by traditional essay writing?

I had always felt comfortable with the teacher-centred approach—lecture, large group discussion, the like. Was it possible that students would learn to read, think, and write as well or better on their own as they had with my carefully structured, teacher-centred model?

Dias' experimental model called for 11 class periods of instruction of 75 minutes each. We designed a model in which each period was divided into three parts: 35 minutes for small group discussion, 15 minutes for journal writing, and 25 minutes for large group discussion. We chose 11 poems appropriate for Grade 12 study, exploring one poem a day.

In the small groups, chairpersons changed each day. It was the task of the chair to do an initial reading of the poem, call for reactions and subsequent readings from other group members, encourage discussion, and later present to the large group the main points of the small group discussion. During the journal writing session, students recorded their initial responses to the poem. (I, too, kept a journal during this time, noting observations about group interaction and about my feelings toward my "new" role.)

During the 25-minute, large group discussion (what we called our "plenary" session), I moderated. After chairpersons presented their small group's observations, each subsequent chairperson could react to these statements; then other students were free to respond.

During small group discussions, my role was to observe and to listen. I encouraged groups only if I thought frustration levels had reached excessive degrees and then only to suggest students reread the poem. During the large group discussion, I tried to listen and guide discussion until the last five minutes, when I could bring together points students had made or make suggestions for further thought. I had always been dedicated to the idea of student-centred learning, but through the Socratic method I had so carefully refined, I was able to control and dominate the learning. Consequently, my role in this experiment was a radical departure from what I had believed was student-centred learning, and as such I had to break with a whole series of conditioned responses. Needless to say, I was in pain.

There was one further step to the procedure. Students were asked to write a one-page, or half-hour, second journal entry as homework. They were to write their more comprehensive observations emerging from the reflection of the plenary discussion and the intervening hours. Students highly involved in the plenary usually wrote much more about the structure and the devices and their effect on meaning than they had in their initial entry on this poem. Students less involved tended to parrot their first entry.

In the control classroom, the same poems were taught over the same period of time, using the lecture, large group discussion, and traditional writing assignment approach. It was, in other words, teacher-centred. The written assignments, both in and out of class, were controlled (as far as possible) to match the time the experimental group spent writing.

To measure student growth, we pretested both groups, asking students to write their interpretation of "My Papa's Waltz" by Theodore Roethke. Following the 11 periods, students wrote an interpretation of another poem, "Corner" by Ralph Pomeroy. Two independent markers evaluated both sets of responses according to criteria we had set for general impression marking. The results were analyzed with the help of Dr. Stan Straw of the University of Manitoba. I had hoped my students would perform at least as well as the control group; this would suggest that students learn as well without the teacher taking such a central role. As it turned out, the experimental class scored significantly better, which reinforced, I believe, the value of collaborative learning.

The informal evidence—student responses and my own reflections—was as encouraging as the formal results. We asked students to give written responses to three questions one week after the last experimental class:

1. What was your overall reaction?
2. Comment on the process (any or all of the three parts).
3. Was there any change in your attitude toward poetry?

Here are some representative responses:

> When this program was first started, I have very negative feelings and opinions about it. This was because until then I had received very structured teachings and classes. But now that I have experienced it first hand, I see it as a very positive way of learning. I think it is a very good program and I feel more confident in approaching poems now.

> I feel that the small groups assisted in getting people who normally would not suggest ideas in the classroom to voice their opinions more freely. The plenary session brought many new ideas into thought. This made my understanding of the poems more stronger. The journals put our ideas down on paper. This helped but I found it very difficult to write about it at home.

> I hated poetry before and never seemed to get the right meaning for the poems. Now, I look for key words and ones that link together. I look at spacing and who is speaking in the poem. And I look for devices. I may not find all of these things, but at least I have a lot more confidence than I did before.

Needless to say, I felt the test results and the students comments made the experiment a significant success.

Not only did the students experience poetry in a different way, I, too, found the experience very different. For twenty years, I had used a variety of teaching methods. However, they were always teacher-centred. For example, I would use groups to explore a theme in a novel. They would research a theme I had given them, with references I had provided, and with a report that followed my format and allowed me to emphasize the points I would otherwise have made in a lecture. With this research model, I had to surrender much of this control to students. My urge to direct students to key words in poems, interpret lines, and pontificate biases was strong when groups seemed stalemated and frustrated.

In one instance, a group sat quietly feeling increasing frustration. I could not direct them except to show sympathy and encourage them to try again. I had to wait until the plenary session in which classmates could help them. Gradually, I acquired the patience that comes with careful listening.

I has become clear to me that research can augment our search for new teaching strategies. Two final comments from students reinforce my belief. One rather verbose young man informed me several months later that he now felt so much more relaxed with groups of people because the research setting had forced him to listen, something he had seldom done before. A quiet and studious young woman said she couldn't understand how she had scored five out of five on the post-test when she received one out of five on her pretest. She said: "All we did was talk and write. I guess I actually did learn." These responses may have occurred without this research, but I believe they came sooner because of it.

I had believed that research in the classroom meant tedium and trivia. I now know that it can mean excitement and significant learning. I encourage others to try it, even without formal analysis of results.

# Cronus, the Timekeeper

### CANDY CARTER
#### (United States)

In the Greek myth, Cronus, representing time, devours his children; thus time devours all it creates. In the late '80s and '90s, we in the United States will probably see an increased preoccupation with time. School years have been lengthened in many states, as have school days. Increasingly, principals are looking at students' "time on task" when evaluating teacher and student performance.

The preoccupation with time has also brought about a renewed interest in classroom management methodology. One of the most notable of these has been Madeline Hunter's clinical instruction program. This program sets up a "five-step lesson plan," involving all stages of teaching from introduction of material to retesting and evaluation. This pattern of clinical instruction has been required in-service in many school districts in California and has been used as a strategy for helping teachers structure their materials in a way that students have greater opportunities to learn the subject matter being presented.

However, increased time in school, improved time-on-task scores, and better knowledge of effective presentation of material is unimportant if the subject matter is presented in an unstimulating or uninspired manner. Good classroom management must go hand in hand with—in fact, must complement—the desire to motivate and inspire students. The following precepts, some obvious, others perhaps not so, are guidelines I try to observe in planning my classes.

1. *The class period needs to be broken up into varied activities whenever possible.* The younger the student, the greater the need for variety. By the time a student is in junior high, my ideal class period of 50 minutes contains three different activities. One of these is a more routine activity; another involves discussion or interaction with other students in the class; the third involves an open-ended assignment. Sometimes, this variety is not possible to achieve; perhaps the students are working on a long-term group assignment that requires concentrated periods of time. Nevertheless, avoiding long stretches of sameness in class activities is a goal we should try to achieve whenever we can.

2. *Likewise, the content itself should be varied.* Some students are most successful with highly structured assignments; others blossom when projects are open ended. By varying the content of a class, teachers give as many students as possible a chance to be successful in class. For example, in a typical eighth-grade English class, a three-week unit on mapping and paragraph writing could be followed by a unit on the history of the English language containing activities on language play. Thus a skill-oriented content could be followed by one in which those same skills could be applied in activities that require imagination and creativity. A teacher who sticks to one text or one single plan is limiting the opportunities for learning for those students who, for various reasons, do not have a learning style that meshes with the book or the plan.

3. *Structure should not be confused with routine.* By structuring assignments carefully, by presenting projects and activities in a way that the guidelines and expectations are clear, teachers maximize student success. D. N. Perkins (1984) writes, "Creative thinking depends on working at the edge more than at the center of one's competence." Structure provides the "edge of competence" necessary for critical and creative thought.

4. *Try to reach for higher order thinking skills, but lead students through basic knowledge as a building block to critical thinking.* Sometimes, we stop at basic knowledge questions and do not move on to questions or assignments that require students to analyze, synthesize, and evaluate. Other times we ask students to make creative judgments without making sure that they have the knowledge base to make such decisions. By ensuring that students are familiar with basic material,

we can then logically progress to asking students to apply that knowledge to their own lives and the world as they see it. For example, if we were working with the play *The Crucible,* we would first help them discover the intricacies of the characters and their relationships in the play. From there, we could discuss the similarities between the Puritan society of 1692 and our own. However, to jump directly to the second discussion might leave many students behind, still trying to make the connections between the piece of literature and their own world.

   5. *Make it a mission to make as many students successful in class.* Helping students to be successful does not mean giving out "easy 'A's." It does involve stating expectations and goals clearly, so that students are aware that you are all working toward a common end. Activities should be designed, whenever possible, so that the completion of work is presented in a step-by-step process that leads to an end product of which students can feel proud. By keeping students self-esteem and sense of accomplishment as a constant goal in class, the teacher is giving his or her students a gift that is greater than subject matter and basic knowledge.

   The concern of U.S. school administrators with time need not lead to a Cronus-like state of affairs with children being devoured. For teachers, determining the quality of that time will be as important as increasing the quantity. By allowing variation in the presentation of material, but structuring assignments to allow for work in the "higher order thinking skills," and by providing many opportunities for student success, teachers find that quality time will coincide with increased time-on-task. Increased time with skills and drills will only serve to further deaden, rather than improve, American schools.

# 8.
# The English Curriculum

It is significant that no contributors to this part describe the physical object of a curriculum *guide* or *handbook*. To a person, they are concerned about the process of evolving good language arts programs, with a focus on the development of individual teaching units within a broad and contemporary language arts philosophy. The circumstances and programs they describe differ considerably: from two teachers working on the curriculum of an alternative school in Canada to a U.S. supervisor of English developing a program for a large city system. However, three common elements appear in these essays:

- Strong emphasis on teacher development of curriculum rather than imposition of curriculum by higher authorities.
- Creating ample room for student choice, for negotiation among students and teachers at all levels of schooling.
- Continuing concern for the politics of curriculum, of satisfying the felt needs of parents and administrators, while maintaining a coherent, sound philosophy of English.

Is it significant that of all the contributions to this volume, no elementary or primary school teacher chose to write about curriculum?

# An Alternative to English

SHARON GLADMAN and BILL MOWAT
*(Canada)*

The halls of our Alternative High School are filled with sound. Conversation spills out of classrooms and rhythms of the newest rock sensation echo from the lounge where students discuss the merits of their favourite groups. The real aural excitement, though, is taking place, not between the speakers of Jesse's stereo, but in Room 10 where an English discussion group is meeting.

The artist, outdrawing even "The Jam," is seventeenth century English poet, John Donne. "Valediction Forbidding Mourning" is a typical choice for a seminar these days.

"What's this dude, Donne?" quips Wade, twentieth century Blackfoot Indian.

The group laughs, secure in the expectation of another lively discussion.

It wasn't always like this.

There were the days of trouble enough with the independent students whom our school draws. Having rebelled against restrictive classrooms and imposed curricula, they had found in this school the informal and open environment they had sought, but which still too often

failed to challenge them. No matter how carefully we chose the literature, the vocal ones would respond with moans of boredom, "Why do
we have to read this, Sharon?" or, "What good is this going to do me,
Bill?" The quiet ones simply ignored us. Lectures, assigned reading,
and carefully thought-out discussions in whatever guise we could present them hadn't workd. It was frustrating.

The first step towards a necessary breakthrough came after Merron
Chorny of the University of Calgary visited the school to talk about
"The New Paradigm in Learning." He chatted of "the old model" and
the "new." The next class we had was faced with two large, chalked
circles on the blackboard.

"What are those for?" asked Nancy, always wary about potential
restrictions in her environment.

"Well, we thought we'd label this one the 'Old Model' and in it
try to list all the things you used to expect when you had to write
something in school. In that one we'll see whether we can come up
with the 'New Model'."

"How are *we* going to do that?"

In fifteen minutes they had. The circles held it all. These circles
have made the rounds and writers come in much sooner and more confidently as a result.

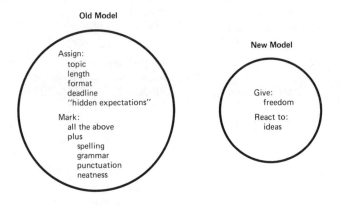

Our experience indicates that, with freedom, time, and confidence, some students can actually alter their consciousness to tap the subconscious in a fascinating phenomenon which Sharon, in researching it, has termed "compelled writing." In a relaxed, meditative state, such students become swept up and carried away on a wave of language which flows effortlessly from within them. This writing, surprisingly, is much richer in imagery, vocabulary, and syntax than their "normal" work; it surprises the students themselves who delight in reading, rereading, and deciphering their own creative insights. In enjoying what they do, in discovering value for themselves, and in finding in writing the expressive symbolism of art, our students are not alone: the "new model" has brought us teachers to the realization that many teenagers can write far better than we used to believe they could.

We weren't having the same success with talk. Oh, we knew its value, because consciously or otherwise all of us use talk as a tool in our own learning. But, we found class discussions disappointing. We had given reading assignments, but faced with what to us were gripping universal themes, the students had merely played the old game of acting out without personal commitment. Rather than fight, we switched to "relevant" issues, but given relevance, they kept things cool. We could have taken their superficial interest as acceptable: in our old schools, we would probably have done so. Here, the students' signals were evident enough for us to know that they were meeting with us more to spend required time together than because of intrinsic value in the discussions. We shifted to, "What should we talk about today?" but asked for input; they didn't often put much out.

We tried convincing outselves that the discussions were alright, but despite a good evaluation from a visiting supervisor, we were becoming more and more discouraged. Finally, boredom hit us. That we couldn't take.

We canceled classes. We set up a table in the corridor outside the discussion room, and on the wall above the table we pinned a notice. It listed times and reading material for a week's "discussion sessions," and announced: "Over the semester, you will be required to attend a minimum of 20 sessions; which ones you choose are up to you. For whichever of this week's sessions you choose to attend, select from the table the relevant reading: you will need to have read it in order to join the discussion."

For the first session, no one turned up; for the second, two appeared; for the third, five. Within three weeks, we had more students than we wanted at some of the sessions, and we gladly added an extra session.

Along the way we learned. Discussions go better when the material to be read has had time to incubate: those last-minute readers are anathema. A warm-up period of relevant chatter, which includes feeling responses and pulls in everyone, is twice as important as a lesson plan. The move from chatter to discussion cannot be predetermined: it depends upon individual responses to the material and the chatter. The most fruitful discussions flow naturally among personal interests and insights, going where they will: a course to be steered or an objective to be reached became constraining.

To our delight, the more complex reading, the more lively the discussion. John Donne intrigued; T.S. Eliot enthralled; Chief Dan George and Alan Paton challenged our complacency. The first and only session we tried to record was our discussion of Flannery O'Connor's "A Good Man Is Hard to Find." With our recording equipment, the tape proves impossible to transcribe. After a warm-up period, during which James talks about another story he's reminded of, the move from chatter to discussion comes suddenly, and even so early in the discussion, engagement with the selection is strong. The talkers draw upon relevant experience, search for understanding, and, through their role playing and spectator responses, deepen their appreciation of the characters. With frequent references to the text, the talk escalates until everyone is sharing interpretations.

Konrad Lorenz, George Kelly, James Britton, and Michael Polanyi have all said in their ways that just as we were organisms who needed to know our territory in order to survive, we have become scientists intent on mastering the universe. The more we know, the better we can survive. When slices of talking and writing challenge and enrich us as manna, when through them we personally discover more of ourselves and our world, that's when they are exciting.

The discovery that surprises the two of us is that all the theory we've read, the talking we've done, and the experimenting we've tried distills down to so simple a pattern. It is the "new model": "Give us freedom to choose and then respond to our ideas." It reappears in group discussions and in the major-genre reading conferences we hold with individual students: in both the discussions and the major-genre reading, choice from as wide a selection as possible is followed by talk about ideas. Its simplicity makes sense, though, because we are evolving as independent organisms with an increasing ability to control our own survival, and as intelligent beings for whom understanding our world and ourselves is vital.

The model is further extended in our school by the students' involvement in decision making at a community level. A weekly group meeting of all staff and students, in which everyone's vote is equal and everyone's opinion respected, results in a wealth of additional talking and personal involvement, particularly as rather than teacher-imposed rules, group-formulated agreements are voted upon. These agreements, arrived at by the whole community, promote in students a far-reaching involvement, a sense of responsibility for their own actions, and an awareness of the rights of others. The meetings and their discussions and agreements beautifully supplement and strengthen our attempt in English to encourage students to act upon their desire to be active participants in their own learning.

As a result of the positive learning we see occurring wherever students use language for their own purposes in our school, we realize that as adults we have for too long underestimated what Lev Vygotsky calls the "zone of proximal development," the expanding circle of development a learner can handle. Teenagers who write and talk freely, spontaneously bringing in their own wide-ranging experiences, can move out masterfully to make sophisticated sense of life. Curiosity and learning skills operating free of constraints and anxiety serve them well. They need to. If we are to survive in the new era, we need active learners who make their own sense of life and know their own minds.

# An Australian Planning Model

PETER FORRESTAL
*(Australia)*

The development in our English teaching that seems most significant and exciting in its possibilities is our search for structure and sequence in the development of our school's English courses from Year 8 to 12.

Our search for structure is prompted by a felt need to ensure that our teaching practice is in line with our learning theory. Because we believe that learning involves students moving from information towards understanding, we believe that learning must be seen as a process involving several stages.

As teachers, our initial responsibility is to structure the learning situation so that students will become engaged, moving from an initial tentative exploration of new information towards an understanding of that information which they will be able to articulate.

The Geraldton Model provides a programming structure which places a strong emphasis on what students must do if they are to move from information towards understanding. (The Geraldton Model was developed by teachers exploring the role of talk in learning as part of a Schools Commission Innovations Project in 1978. The Model owes much to the work of Douglas Barnes and discussions at the Curriculum Branch of the Western Australian Education Department in 1979 and 1980.)

*Input:* This is the stage of the learning process, during which students acquire information and engage in an experience that provides the basis, or content, of their ensuing learning. There are many ways of providing input in the classroom (or outside), including:

- Teacher talk.
- Films, pictures, or other visual means.
- Reading—textbooks, reference books, stories, etc.
- Tape recordings, records.
- Blackboard explanations.
- Demonstrations—experiments, skills, etc.
- Excursions, trips, visits, etc.

The input should become a shared experience for the learners.

*Exploration:* At this stage, the learner is given the opportunity to make an initial exploration of the information, to make some tentative judgments, and to bring past experience and understanding to bear as he or she endeavours to come to terms with new information.

- Exploration can be either through small group exploratory talk, or through individual exploratory writing followed by small group talk.

*Reshaping:* During the reshaping stage, the learner is required to work with the new information in some way, either individually or with the small group, to enable him or her to move closer to understanding. Reshaping activities are determined by the aims of the teacher and what the students are expected to learn from the lesson or unit of work. The learner is actively involved with the information. This can involve clarifying, ordering, reorganizing, elaborating, practising, and using the information in a purposeful way.

*Presentation:* Here the learner is placed in a situation where he or she is required to present what has been learned to an interested and critical audience in order to help the learning process further. In other words, the learner is required to *show* what has been learned. The importance of providing a *real* purpose and audience for the learners needs to be stressed. Students who are aware that they are required to present their knowledge to a real audience, whether their small group, another group, the whole class, the teacher, other teachers, other classes, or people from outside the school, will work towards a quality end product *because* it is for real.

*Reflection:* Asking students to reflect upon what they have learned helps them to understand its content. Asking students to reflect on how they have learned helps them to understand how they can continue to learn, and increases their sense of involvement in the learning process. Asking students to reflect upon what and how they have learned helps the teacher to evaluate the learning and the learning programme, and to base further activities on the information gained.

Although most of our programming uses the Geraldton Model, there is a need for other structures—particularly to give *cohesion* to units of work. Any model which takes students from lower towards higher levels of thinking seems appropriate to us. We have, however, used Graham Little's Model.

Thinking Levels

| High levels | Imagining |
| --- | --- |
| | Speculating, hypothesising, theorising |
| ↕ | Generalising |
| | Reporting |
| Low levels | Recording |

An example of how this model informs our programming can be seen by looking at Forrestal and Reid (1984).

The students study two or three short stories using the Geraldton Model. The focus, at this stage, is on understanding each of the stories independently of the others.

Once the stories have been studied, the concept of the ironic twist is explained to the students using new examples. The students are then asked to look at the short stories in order to see how the concept of the ironic twist operates there. They are then asked to make a *generalised* statement about how the concept applies to the stories they've studied.

After this, they are given the opportunity to move into the imaginative realm and produce their own story with an ironic twist. But this only occurs after the students have had a thorough exploration of the concept and the ways in which other writers have handled it.

Another issue we see as significant in English curriculum development at present is the question of sequence.

Taking the unit in Forrestal and Reid (1984) as an example may serve to suggest some possibilities. First, such a unit really needs to be preceded by one in which students look at plot structure. They will best understand the irregular plot structure of stories which rely on anticlimax for their impact if they have a sound understanding of regular plot structure.

There are many possibilities for follow-up work to the unit either in the same year or as part of the following year's programme. One unit that we have written focuses on "Crime Stories." One of the stories in the unit has an ironic twist in its ending, and has an ironic title. Another involves a thief caught in an ironic situation. (The stories are "The Accomplice" and "It Takes a Thief," both by Arthur Miller.) The programme is designed so that the words "ironic twist" or "irony" are not used by the teacher. However, students have the opportunity to recognize and comment on the ironic title, the ironic twist, and the ironic situation where these arise. We have been delighted by the number of students, of all ability levels, who have shown an understanding of these concepts without being prompted.

Another successful programme which we have developed for a later year, looks at three stories of Roald Dahl from *Tales of the Unexpected.* The focus of this unit has been on Dahl as a writer and on his use of point of view. Although we have not used the terms "ironic twist" or "irony" in discussion of the stories, students freely referred to these concepts, thus linking their current work with units they had previously studied.

# Real World Curriculum Development

BETTY SWIGGETT
*(United States)*

Ideally, the curriculum development process begins in a wholesome atmosphere growing out of a mutual sense of need on the part of all those involved to improve the teaching/learning processes. If the process is to be productive, it entails skillful leadership, an understanding of the curriculum development process, an openness to new ideas, and a genuine interest and willingness to work on the part of the participants. It requires, moreover, a reasonable amount of funding and time to ensure the completion of the total process: curriculum development, implementation, evaluation, and refinement.

In the real world of curriculum development, however, circumstances are seldom ideal. This essay is an account of real-world English curriculum development in the '80s, where the rules for leadership behavior are sophisticated and highly political, and where the fundamental development processes are not always clearly understood by educators. It is an account of an attempt to apply the best of current knowledge on the nature of the learner, the language processes, and English language programs in the midst of powerful, explicit demands to revive old methods and adopt a "back-to-basics" approach. The setting is one school system of medium size in Hampton, Virginia; the problems, constraints, and challenges are similar, however, to those experienced by other local English curriculum developers.

## The Existing Curriculum

From the perspective of current theory and practice, the existing English curriculum, once considered innovative, was aging. It was a phase-elective program that had undergone considerable revision and refinement over a 10-year period. The program had worn well because of the flexibility with which courses could be added, deleted, or changed in response to new interests and new knowledge in the field. Criticism was leveled at only one aspect of the program, its elective nature.

The program had a more serious flaw not usually recognized by the local critics: it needed a consistent theoretical basis for structuring learning experiences. It contained courses based on an old-fashioned sense of the basics alongside those that focused on the language processes as basic. Curriculum change was clearly needed, but funds were lacking, teacher morale was low, and the conservative spirit of the times offered little encouragement for making major innovative curriculum change.

Curriculum change came, however, and came abruptly. The impetus for change was a new superintendent, a young man schooled in finance, management, and power tactics. Intent on establishing his reputation as a top administrator able to effect major change quickly, he defined his decision-making processes as politically based and targeted the English program as an area to demonstrate his skill. G. G. Unruh (1983) advises that "political astuteness is an indispensable qualification for curriculum leaders and developers. Naiveté about the politics of education or willful disregard of formal and informal power centers are out of place today" (p. 99). This new local political milieu was supercharged, however. Strategies were highly calculated, public, and blunt. As English curriculum specialist for the school system, I would soon learn new skills in the uses of power.

The superintendent established a two-tiered, curriculum development model composed of a Coordinating Review Council and a Curriculum Development Task Force. The first, a group of 15, was heavily weighted with top school officials, including the superintendent. Its task was to determine the philosophy and the external design of the new English program. The second, containing 25 members of varied backgrounds, was assigned to develop curriculum. English teachers were a minority on each committee, constituting about one-third of the membership. An English teacher chaired both committees. The curriculum specialist served as consultant to both groups. The thinking behind this structure was that any program that passed the scrutiny of these two committees would have credibility in the community.

The superintendent's charge to the committees was to develop a core program that would concentrate on "basic skills," lend itself to accountability through standardized testing, and please all—the public, the administration, and classroom teachers alike. The program was to be ready for full implementation, Grades 7-12, at the beginning of the next school year.

The situation appeared bleak for the development of a solidly grounded, new English program. Three characteristics of the curriculum-building climate dominant on the national level were emerging locally: a suspicion of expertise, a lack of understanding of the process skills needed for curriculum development, and a willingness to use curriculum as barter in the search for increased financial support of schools. English teachers responded by becoming strongly defensive of the elective program.

The new environment was one of curriculum control rather than curriculum building. On the positive side, however, the new committee structure had now established a framework for dialogue and curriculum change. With English curriculum development chosen as a major division goal, the superintendent allotted funding for teachers to be released from classes to do curriculum planning as needed. He also approved full funding for new textbooks, with additional monies for in-service and consultant services. Teachers who had committed themselves to working only during the contract day could now participate in curriculum development. Provisions for two important factors had thus been made.

The new chair of the curriculum committees, drawn from the ranks of English teachers because of her understanding of group dynamics and her steadfastness in completing major tasks, concluded that the best safeguard for sound curriculum development would be improved communications, both upward and down. All reports, minutes, and numerous articles on English instruction were distributed not only to committee members but also to all 100 English teachers. She took on, in addition, the education of the assistant superintendent of instruction with regard to quality English programs. This approach helped to crystalize issues, but it also led to sharp confrontation between those who thought that the choice was between only two curriculum models: the current elective one and a "back-to-basics" one.

In a political setting, one learns quickly to take advantage of special power bases. As consultant to the committees, I turned to the the use of expertise power. There was a need for the 40 members of the committees to gain perspective on current trends in secondary English education. One week prior to the first joint session of the committees, the Virginia Association of Teachers of English held its annual conference in our city. The keynote speaker was Stephen Tchudi, at that time president-elect of the National Council of Teachers of English. The assistant superintendent approved funding for all committee members to attend the conference. The good fortune was that Professor

Tchudi's topic was "Synthesis in English." He presented to conference participants a developmental, integrated model of English instruction that synthesized the philosophical and practical concerns of the '80s. Committee members attending the conference recognized in Tchudi's model a workable structure for the local English curriculum. Before the conference was over, Tchudi was invited to be the outside consultant ot the local English curriculum committee.

As consultant, Tchudi set a positive tone in the joint session of the committees by placing the elective program in its historical context. It had helped teachers, he said, to break away from the domination of the textbook and to think seriously about students' needs. Drawing in part on the curriculum models of Creber (1965) and Moffett (1973), he recommended a curriculum model that was developmental, integrated, and thematic in structure (Judy, 1980). He explained to the committees, moreover, that English teachers should write their own curriculum. Other committee members could participate in a variety of related tasks, including (1) assessing student growth in writing, (2) preparing statements about developmental expectations, and (3) determining the broad organizational pattern of the new curriculum. The committees accepted, in principle, the direction outlined. Now, two other important factors—the committee's understanding of the curriculum development process and its sense of purpose—were emerging.

Progress in curriculum building did not follow automatically. The translation of theory and models of curriculum into local programs requires informed, day-to-day consultation at the local level. It soon became clear that without assertive leadership on the part of the local curriculum specialist, the program would bog down or even take a direction inimical to an organic curriculum.

The coordination of the entire program was thus placed on the chair, a classroom teacher, who turned to the curriculum specialist for direction. The specialist, in turn, arranged for Tchudi to serve as a continuing consultant. The result was a three-person leadership team in the area of expertise. It should be kept in mind also that from a committee organization perspective there was a four-member leadership team, which included the chair, two administrators, and the specialist. Early committee discussions were sometimes fraught with debate and polarization of positions, but by June 1 all major decisions had been made by committees concerning philosophy, curriculum design, core content, and primary resources.

Although the broad organizational pattern of the program was determined and course syllabi drafted by June 1, the full writing of curriculum units occurred during a two-week summer workshop conducted by Tchudi for curriculum writers. Teachers learned the meaning of an integrated, holistic approach to English by reading and responding to literature, examining their writing processes, dramatizing literature, and observing the instructor, who modeled an integrated, process approach to instruction. The outcome was that teachers not only wrote curriculum units, but also discovered that language is learned by using it for one's own purposes of learning.

### The New Curriculum

The new program has an integrated, thematic organization, Grades 7–12, with an overarching theme of "a search for self." On each grade level, there are four to six units appropriate for the developmental level of students. Each unit of study has a small core of common readings and activities, after which students branch out individually and in small groups for related activities. The entire program contains 32 units with all themes focusing on what it means to be human. The sequence of units progresses from the study of heroes—mythological, folk, popular, and family—at Grade 7 to more sophisticated exploration of self and society—"Choice and Consequence," "Foibles," and "Critics of Society"—at Grade 12.

Evaluation is broadly based with a division-wide use of composition folders, reading record cards, and notes on the achievement of state-mandated objectives. Although a literature anthology serves as the common source for core readings, approximately 40 percent of the textbook budget was used for paperbook books. The program lends itself to either heterogeneous or homogeneous groupings.

Reflecting back on this highly politicized but productive year, I find it encouraging that good English curriculum can be developed even in the midst of powerful public/administrative pressures for conventional strategies and quick change.

# An Australian Senior Secondary Programme

BARNEY DEVLIN and JANET RICKWOOD
(Australia)

Stirling College is one of the senior colleges set up in 1976 for students in Years 11 and 12, the final two years of secondary schooling. The college system removed a number of constraints on both teachers and students, but of particular interest to this essay is the replacement of externally set, final exams with teacher assessment and the development of school-based curriculum.

The English courses in all colleges consist of a smorgasbord of units. These cover a variety of aspects of English and include traditional classical literature units as well as more innovative units, such as creative drama and children's literature. This choice allows for the interests of the varied student population. To complete a course in English, students must do a minimum of five, 12-week term units of four hours a week. They may do as many as 12 such units. Here, we will describe two of the units we teach.

### Teaching a Favourite Literary Work (by Barney Devlin)

While the concept of negotiation is a fundamental tenet of our approach to teaching English at Stirling College, there are occasions when I exercise my teacher's prerogative and insist that a whole class study a particular text. The fact that students are usually fully involved in selecting the material to be studied in our English classes makes me feel less uncertain about insisting upon a nonnegotiable component, and, of course, they are made aware that they can significantly influence how the text is studied and assessed. It is probably a sign of the changed climate of English teaching today that I feel it is necessary to justify such a course of action.

First, and most obviously, English teachers have had a much greater experience of literature than their students and have a responsibility to ensure that works of quality are studied. While this may be best achieved by making a wide choice of good literature available, the shared experience of a class text remains a valuable activity, especially in promoting a cooperative learning environment. Further, in a newly formed class, I find that beginning the unit with a class text helps to overcome initial hesitancy to open up with relative strangers and also assists in developing a sense of cohesion.

While any literary genre may be used, I find that the novel is less suitable because of great variations in reading abilities in any class, even allegedly homogeneous classes. I also find poetry less successful early in the term when it is difficult to establish the confidence in each other that allows the delicacy and intimacy of so much verse to be fully explored in classroom discussions. Short stories can be very good as class texts, but in my experience for best results "the play's the thing."

Peter Kenna's *A Hard God*, which I use in second term with Year 11 classes, works well for this purpose. I first saw the play shortly after I emigrated to Australia from Ireland in 1972, and was deeply moved by the poetic way in which it seemed to capture the migrant experience —and hence the Australian experience. The play deals with the Cassidy family, who are Irish Catholics, a group which has contributed much to what is distinctively Australian. My classes are mixed-ability groups of about 25 students, aged 16–17 years, and contain students from a

variety of ethnic communities, each of which is also making a distinctive contribution. The play examines in detail the question of belief in
God and also explores such issues as family relationships and homo-
sexuality, all issues of considerable interest to students at this age.

Before engaging with the text, I introduce students to the dramatic situation via creative improvisations. One such method is to give
full details of the setting and the eight characters, and have students
improvise various situations from the play. In addition, two students
are assigned to watch the behaviour of each character and to comment
on her or his reactions to the situations. My aim here is to have students devise their own dramatic resolutions to the problems and issues
explored by Kenna in the play. By giving the students' solutions a place
alongside those of the playwright, I hope to overcome the artificial barriers often erected in the minds of students by the mystique and power
of the printed word. In addition, their appreciation of the play is enhanced when they see the author addressing the same problems and
issues for which they themselves have attempted dramatic resolutions.
This seems to apply even where their own predictions of likely outcomes are very wide of the mark.

Next, the students read the text fairly quickly, while at the same
time deriving some sense of the play as performance. (In the best of all
possible worlds, they see a stage production.) The class divides into
three groups, thus allowing each student to read a part, and each group
workshops the play. My role is simply to participate in each group,
intervening only when difficulties are insuperable or in response to
questions.

At the end of the first workshop lesson, I bring the class together
to compare notes briefly before I issue a sheet of paper to each student,
with the instruction to make "a comment" on the play within 30 sec-
onds. If the class is keeping a journal for the unit, then the students
use it to record their comments. These comments are collected and
typed on a sheet and this process is repeated when the workshopping
is finished. It is remarkable how perceptive and all-embracing these
tentative first responses are, and they form a sound basis for much
discussion. One very useful exercise is to have each group select
two comments: one they support most and one least. I find that ob-
taining and using the students' comments on literary works in this
way goes a long way towards giving them a sense of ownership of the
responses. Furthermore, the quality of the responses satisfies me that
students do not need teacher or expert interpretations, and, indeed,
that such interpretations are a bypass around learning rather than an
easy access to it.

Finally, there are written responses. For convenience, these can
be divided into three categories: *creative, personal,* and *literary critical.*
I do not believe that there is any fundamental difference between the

three nor that they are mutually exclusive. For each, a variety of topics can be devised and in each the emphasis must be on honest and individual responses.

Creative responses can range from writing in ways close to the original text, such as rewriting part(s) of the play or adding a scene(s), to writing a completely original piece(s) related to the play. Similarly, personal responses can involve close reference to the text, such as writing as a character(s) or examining how the student might contribute to a production of the play, to such distant responses as writing about ways in which the students have learned about themselves or their world as a result of reading the play. Students can be helped to devise topics for both types of response by referring back to the improvisations and by further discussion on the sheet of comments.

The range of responses using the literary critical format tends to be more restricted. The form is usually the essay, with its many conventions, and the emphasis in these is much more upon demonstrating an understanding of the text. Nonetheless, it is possible to have students use this form to respond honestly and individually, especially if they devise their own topics. Again, the sheet of comments is very useful, in particular to provide a record of which comments the students supported most and least.

I always allow plenty of class time for students to work on their written responses and they are strongly encouraged to share, rehearse, draft, conference, edit, etc. The quality of the written responses, together with the seriousness and the fun which characterise the various class activities, convince me that I am justified in imposing this favourite literary work on my classes each year.

### The Power of Writing in the English Course (by Janet Rickwood)

In 1977, we decided that we needed at least one unit of "expressive" writing in our programme because:

- Most of the other units were strongly literature oriented.
- Expressive writing was not developed in any of the other units.
- Many staff felt that writing was a good way to improve students' language competence.
- Many student writers asked for such a unit.
- At least two teachers were committed to developing the unit.

One of these two teachers "scribbled" herself and mixed with other writers, some professional. She discussed with these writers how best to teach writing. Because of this research, it is not surprising that our first units were so close in strategies to those proposed by Moffett, Graves, and Murray. But their direct influence did not come until later.

We decided to develop two units. The first was open to any students who wanted it, either because they enjoyed writing or because they wanted to improve their writing. The second was for the committed writers who wanted more writing. Students had to demonstrate a good control of language to enroll in this unit—a prerequisite we were to drop later.

The following two units were those initially developed and they deserve a close study.

### Writing I

This unit consisted of three components.

1. *The Journal.* The journal was included because of the influence of Daniel Fader (1966) and Peter Elbow (1975). Students wrote in the journals at every lesson and at other times if they wished. The aim was to have students write freely without concern for surface features, simply to have their thoughts flow and to remove the teacher with the red pen from their shoulders.

2. *Class Exercises.* These were teacher organised exercises arising from lessons of a "stimulus" nature. A variety of responses was encouraged and not all exercises had to be attempted. The writing was handed in to teachers for comment, the beginning of "conferencing," and students redrafted in the light of these suggestions. Four pieces, selected by the student at the end of the term, were to be graded.

3. *Majors.* Students wrote two sustained pieces of writing, such as autobiographies, children's stories, short stories, personal essays, and plays. The majors were easily the most successful component of this unit as they allowed for all the "right" things to take place. Students discussed their topics with their teachers and their writing group, they discussed their drafts with teachers and peers, and they had time to develop ideas, draft, reflect, and polish.

### Writing II

This unit originally catered for the committed writer and was chosen by some of the most able students of English in the college. It consisted of four components and allowed for more student control than Writing I.

1. *The Journal.* The nature of the journal differed in this unit, where it was used to jot down or explore ideas that could be developed into finished pieces. Many students also used it in a reflective way to examine experiences they were undergoing. The journals were collected every two weeks for comment by the teachers. A dialogue between teacher and student often developed within the journal.

2. *Folio.* In this unit, students were encouraged to find their own topics and "stimulus" lessons were very few. Literature was discussed and writers from the community came in to discuss their writing experiences with the class. All writing was presented at the end of the term and was graded for both quantity and quality.

3. *Major.* Only one sustained piece of writing was expected in this unit, as the students attempted quite sophisticated pieces; some even wrote the opening chapters of novels. The quality and quantity were quite remarkable and often magical. I had, in this unit, the best writing from students I had experienced in 25 years of teaching.

4. *Workshops.* The idea of the workshop came from discussions with adult writers who said they grew as writers when they discussed their writing with other writers. Classes divided into groups of five or six early in the term. Each group met with the teacher once a week. During the first few weeks, students developed their abilities to criticize writing in a helpful, supportive way. The pieces used for these early lessons were teacher writings (of the brave ones), literature, and student writings (if they wished). In the last six weeks of term, each student ran a half-hour workshop. The students selected two or three pieces of work, photocopied so each group member had a copy, for group criticism. The student also prepared questions to elicit help to improve the writing. Students were assessed both on their own workshops and as participants in the group. To assist in this assessment, an evaluation sheet was completed at the end of each workshop by each student in which they commented on the workshop leader and their own involvement.

Discussions with students at the end of this unit revealed that most of them believed that the workshops had been the most valuable part of the unit for them as writers.

The units were very successful and popular with students and were unchanged until 1980 when a number of influences brought about modifications. These forces of change were the International Conference for the Teaching of English that a number of the staff attended, the research of Moffett (1981a, 1981b), Graves (1981, 1983), and Murray (1982), and a weekend writing workshop run by Garth Boomer that some of us experienced.

There are now three units of writing and no prerequisites for any of them. Both our experience and our reading has convinced us that all students, regardless of their so-called ability, both enjoy and benefit from writing. Students are encouraged to stagger the units throughout their two years because their language experiences in other units are valuable in their development as writers.

The formal workshop has been replaced with conferences in all units. Students are encouraged and helped to find their own writing topics and their folios, with a set minimum number of polished pieces, are the major part of the assessment for each unit. The journal has been retained, but is now completely student controlled, shared only at the student's wish. Discussions of literature, each others' writings, and the writing process form the basis of class work.

The success of the writing units is an achievement in itself, but the theory underlying these units has permeated the rest of the English courses and affected the practice of all the teachers. Whereas in 1977 only two teachers felt competent or confident enough to teach writing, now all members of staff take writing units. To do this, they read and discuss the teacher references to become informed of the philosophy on which the practice in the units is founded. There is much ongoing interchange of ideas as student folios are marked by groups of teachers to ensure comparability of grades.

So teachers have examined their practice in other units and this has resulted in the theory underlying the writing units, causing dramatic changes in the other units.

# The Evolution of a Global Studies Program

JONATHAN SWIFT
*(United States)*

The biggest hurdle for curriculum leaders is jumping from the printed page to the classroom. In 1977, when the staff of Livonia's School of Global Education began to formulate ideas on curriculum, there was no real awareness that the hurdles would be less theoretical than practical: teacher insecurity, lack of administrative support, personal backbiting, rumor and myth became daily problems. Progress through the years—at least in terms of teacher acceptance in the building—is now evidenced by the fact that the general school staff has moved from hostility to apathy. This represents something positive, however, because it means that coupled with an enthusiastic global education team, there is a real chance of continued success.

Thanks to some federal and state funding from 1977 to 1980, teachers at Stevenson High School in Livonia (a senior high school with a student population of 1800) were able to develop a three-year curriculum in English, social studies, foreign language (Spanish), science, and mathematics. These courses were taught with a global perspective, sequentially, by a team of teachers who constantly worked together. What was created was, in fact, a school within a school which was interdisciplinary and team taught. Within three years, however, science, mathematics and Spanish were dropped because the teachers who had been trained were laid off due to decreasing school enrollment. The result was that English and social studies were left even more closely woven together. For four years, recruiting for the program had been done by the director and the student enrollment stayed at about 70–75. The decision was made, however, to send the *students* out to the middle schools to do the recruiting. The following year, and since then, enrollment rose to 150.

Several of the goals of global education are related to language arts, cultures, and the humanities:

1. To increase students' awareness of the nature and development of world literature, languages, the arts, and their interrelationship with national behavior.
2. To foster awareness of scientific and technological achievements and their relation to society.
3. To foster self-awareness.

The global education curriculum is an experiential one which requires the participation of students, often their families, in field trips, simulations, and classroom study. It is divided into three year-long sequences. The first deals with the beginnings of humankind, creativity, the development of language and art, myth and epic, archaeology, anthropology, and the first societies. The main geographical areas studied are Europe, Asia, and Africa. The second year focuses on modern humankind, particularly Americans. This means that American history, literature, immigration are studied in relation to the rest of the world. Other forms of literature—the novel, the short story, the play, and poetry are continued. The writing program reaches over the years developmentally so that students begin by writing paragraphs and letters and end with the formal essay and research paper.

The third year, called "futuristics," deals with the period deemed "current" into the 21st century. This allows students to look at developmental trends in literature, writing, art, society, technology and science, and encourages them to make choices among the most to the least desirable alternatives.

Recently added to these three years are two further courses, each only one semester long: the first is an independent research opportunity, the second a course in debate using national and international topics.

Field trips include visits to career-oriented locations, world religious institutions, theaters, and concert halls. The main stimulation beyond the school, however, is one in which participation has grown rapidly. In 1978, the school sent 20 delegates to the 600-member Great-Lakes-Model United Nations. In 1985, this number had swelled to 110. The social studies aspects of such role playing are obvious. Less obvious, perhaps, are the language arts advantages. A recent survey highlights these:

1. Letter writing: 96 percent of the students wrote letters (most received replies) to the Unites States Department of State, foreign embassies, and other sources.
2. Note taking: 95 percent took notes on their own from reading and conferences.
3. Writing revision: 18 percent rewrote their work *once,* 18 percent *twice,* 20 percent more than twice; that is, a total of 56 percent *voluntarily* rewrote some of their work.
4. Types of learning: 68 percent thought group work was effective for them, 65 percent rated individual research significant, and 43 percent believed that listening to lectures or advice from older students or teachers was important.
5. Parliamentary procedure: 78 percent believed that the lessons in procedure before the model UN were helpful.
6. Research: The experienced group of students tended to do more research—55 percent doing more than 16 hours of research as opposed to the beginners' 13 percent. Eighty-three percent said that most of their information on current groups and topics came from magazines.
7. Public speaking: 30 percent of the students spoke publicly at general sessions more than three times in the five days, 35 percent at least once.
8. Skills: To accomplish their role-playing tasks, the students agreed that they had to use skills of persuasion (43 percent), diplomacy/tact (45 percent), bargaining (35 percent), compromise (73 percent), and even threat (10 percent) throughout the simulation.

In summary, these students did use reading, writing, listening and talking with practical purpose, with various intended audiences.

Without minimizing the effect of the enthusiasm and hard work of both students and staff in increasing the strength of the global education curriculum, I want to say a few words about parental involvement. When the program began in 1978, there was an understanding that parents and other members of the community would be involved. The staff groaned. Surely parents involved in high school academics would become too demanding. The first activity for the Parents Association was to write out their objectives, which stated very clearly their advisory as well as supportive role. They have lived up to this. They have been responsible for public relations, for fund raising, for field trips to theaters, to the model UN, and to countries overseas. They have participated in assignments with the students that involved the entire family, thus spreading skills and knowledge to the community.

It is probable that there would be no global education curriculum in Livonia were it not for the synergistic strength of the students, parents, staff and administration. It is a microcosm of global cooperation.

# 9.
# Evaluation and Assessment in English

"Assessment is the bane of the schoolteacher's day," writes Debbie Myhill of England; "private time is infringed by it, reports are dominated by it, and children and parents are obsessed with it." Like most educators, Debbie is not opposed to assessing her pupil's growth as a part of her teaching process, but she resents demands for evaluation imposed by nonteachers that are destructive to student risk taking and exploration with language. Classroom assessment—of the productive sort—has become quite sophisticated in the five IFTE countries, and one reads of the skillful use of process and product evaluation, of language profiles and portfolios, of a blending of paper-and-pencil evaluation with observation and conferences.

As a profession, we do indeed know how to assess growth in that illusive field called "English." Yet the standardized tests and certificate examinations cast a pall over the proceedings in virtually all the five countries. The writers here are polite in suggesting that politically imposed examinations sometimes lead teachers to assess and reassess their values and their patterns of instruction; yet, it takes little skill to read the message between the lines: external examinations are poor measures of pupil performance, regressive in their view of English, and counterproductive to the evolution of sound English curricula.

In this respect, *English Teachers at Work* ends on a negative note. But in another way, our conclusion is quite positive. Bernard Gadd of New Zealand is the final essayist in this collection. He and his colleagues at Hillary College secondary school, Otaua, were deeply worried that the state certificate examinations doomed their Maori children to failure even before the beginning of the school year. So they devised their own internally evaluated certificate of achievement. One would suppose that this Hillary certificate might not carry great weight in the "real world," where state credentials are the coin of the realm, but Bernard reports that the certificate matters deeply to the people who are most important, giving the students themselves "a sense of an achievable and worthwhile objective for the year." Bernard's independence of spirit, his concern for students, and his knowledge of both good theory and practice in English teaching sum up the spirit of *English Teachers at Work*.

# Classroom Assessment

MIKE MARSHALL
*(England)*

A distinction needs to be made between grading and assessment. In grading a piece of written work, the teacher is making either (a) a judgment about its worth in relation to all other similar pieces of work, or (b) relating it to criteria which he (or an examination board) has defined. In either case, the estimate of its "worth" is likely to be based almost entirely on the "performance features" it demonstrates. Whatever the "value" ascribed to it through the grade given, this is unlikely to reflect either its more elusive qualities or the teacher's impressions of the individual pupil's personal qualities as discerned in the broader contexts of the subject. It is within these "broader contexts"—covering the full range of the pupil's activities and personal qualities—that assessment (as I understand it) occurs; grading is a discrete activity relating to a single piece of work or to a series which shares the same criteria (as in C.S.E. Mode 1 coursework).

Most English teachers probably sense a tension between grading—by nature, "objective" and comparative—and the writing of comments which amplify their response and highlight the positive features of the work. Where a grade is given (or required), the comment will often serve to temper its stark message. The comment is the teacher's dialogue with the pupil, transforming assessment into a more personal, positive, and humane experience. Assessment can then become a "language of encouragement" in which the pupil can recognise his successes, but also consider where further improvements can be made, both here and in the future. Such comments are important in defining the relationship between teacher and pupil; their character and quality will affect the pupil's attitudes and thus his progress.

What forms can this personal dialogue take? A few examples from second and third year pupils' exercise books will, I think, help to answer this question. Each, in a different way, communicates (a) some helpful and specific advice, (b) a great deal of encouragement, and (c) a sense of the teacher's personal interest in both the work and the pupil:

1. "I think you need some final comment at the end of this piece—some sense of relief that everything passed off peacefully."
2. "I don't think I find this final part convincing, Nicola. But it starts well and much of the writing is pleasingly accurate."
3. "You need to develop the key parts of your story in much greater detail. The part where you befriend the dolphin is obviously very

important—but you rather gloss over it. Think about where the concentration needs to be."

4. "You like sad endings, don't you?! A good story, Justina, and you tell it quite well—but it becomes rather confusing because you don't make clear who is who and who is talking. You need to add more storytelling and description to your dialogue. Dialogue cannot really tell the story for you."

5. "You have presented the facts and the information very well, although occasionally a little too fully! What attitude would a 'white press' have to all this?"

As English teachers, we see a great deal of written work, perhaps more than many of our colleagues in other subject areas. This often brings unsolicited insights into the private worlds of our pupils and obligations which it would be insensitive to ignore. The personal and creative work of our pupils has to be treated with sensitivity and respect. We must show that we are interested in what has been produced and have found something of value in it. This "message" is conveyed through our comments which should seek both to appraise and encourage: after all, the teacher's professional *advice,* as well as his personal enthusiasm, is important.

What results can this combination of advice and encouragement have? I can best illustrate this by recalling an experience I had some 10 years ago when I was teaching a fourth-year group containing pupils who were considered to be below average in ability. The group was always unpredictable and potentially difficult, although our relationship and their work improved quite a lot over the two years we spent together.

One boy—Ian—I particularly remember. He wasn't very articulate and was rather shy, despite his attempts to be part of the more boisterous and sometimes disruptive element in the group. Over a period of time, it became evident that he was actually interested in writing, although he found it laborious and frustrating—he often gave up and failed to complete a piece of work, or rushed through and handed it in despite its clearly inadequate quality.

My persistence, and his eventual realisation that I was genuinely interested in his work, gradually produced results. He began to work harder on improving a piece of work before handing it in, and was even willing to make several attempts at it despite the dogged effort required. This, I felt, was a measure of his faith in my interest and encouragement, and, more importantly, of his determination to try again in the light of my comments and advice.

During our time together, he produced one particular piece of writing which I considered exceptional for someone who experienced his difficulties. It was painstakingly written and initially full of mechanical errors, but it revealed a vivid imagination and language used to astonishing effect:

## The Bend

The car moves on without a driver, its direction-finder and master, for he is in a deep sleep. The car hits a lump and the unconscious body falls upon the steering-wheel. There's a sudden swerve; an ashtray falls to the car floor; a pillow flies from one seat to another; a door swings open and objects fall from the metal coffin.

The driver is bruised and awakes in a daze; inhuman horror, the reality of remembered stories from newspapers comes alive. There's confusion; a test of nerves. He comes to his senses and pulls on the steering-wheel. There's no reaction. His foot clumsily wanders towards the brake-pedal; an error is made and in place of a sudden stop there is rapid acceleration.

No longer is there a clear path round the corner but instead a black-green hedge which seems to converge with the car. The driver has a heart attack and is no longer in fear of a car crash: he is dead. As the hedge swallows up the sealed carton, the screen collapses like a cracked egg and the car caves in, mutilating its soft centre; there is no longer any movement.

*Ian (Fourth Year)*

Its inclusion in the school magazine later that year was an accolade which he had never expected to receive and which few like him had experienced.

My belief is that the quality of the teacher's comments—judged in terms of the interest, encouragement, and advice it conveys—is important in both eliciting and assessing progress. However, I would be the first to admit that there is often pressure to emphasise grade rather than personal comment. Pressure often comes from the school system, as well as from the pupils themselves, for all work to be formally assessed and graded. Pupils who expect to be successful, and who therefore seek confirmation of their success in the teacher's grades, are often a source of considerable pressure. There is also a carry-over effect from other subject areas where grading (in course work and periodic tests) is the norm. Progress in subjects such as math and French is often related to regular exercises and periodic tests. These all exert pressure on the English teacher to grade every aspect of his pupils' work. Most, fortunately, are able to resist these pressures and concern themselves with a broader view of assessment.

This, of course, still leaves an important question: What tangible measures do the eager pupils find in their English lessons to assure them that they are making progress—doing as well as they appear to be in other subjects?

It has to be admitted that "progress" in English is easier to recognise than it is to quantify, especially in terms of what the pupils can do now which they couldn't do in the recent past. I think the English teacher, of necessity, takes a longer-term view of progress than may be the case in those subject areas where short-term objectives can be set and their achievement objectively measured. These kinds of objectives are difficult to define or set in English, although the latest H.M.I. statement, "English 5-16," has made some attempt to define specific objectives at the crucial times in a pupil's school career. Most English teachers are probably happier talking about aims rather than prespecifiable objectives. These aims, of course, will imply some sense of timing in the setting of priorities, but few English teachers (in my experience) could say precisely how far these aims have been achieved for any group or individual at any moment in time—or, perhaps, would wish to. The net result is that many pupils are unable to find the assurance they seek through the periodic "measurement" of their progress.

What then can be done to allay the genuine anxiety felt by some pupils and the scepticism expressed by others?

A partial but important answer may well be found in the quality and frequency of the teacher's responses and—to an extent through these—the quality of his relationship with group and individual. This relationship, in turn, will affect the directness and quality of the dialogue between teachers and pupils. The teacher's work-specific comments will, over a period of time, define the key attitudes and criteria from which these responses arise. Pupils will sense the teacher's predilections and priorities, internalise them, and use them as a guide to their success and progress. Put more simply and baldly: pupils will soon learn what teachers regard as important and what count as successes in their eyes and, by extension, in the subject.

The teachers' assessments of their pupils' progress will tend to be made through qualitative—rather than quantitative—judgments. These qualitative judgments will first and foremost be made through their contacts with, and insights into, their pupils' work. The record of appraisals—irrespective of the coding system used—will trace patterns which can later be translated into descriptive evaluations of the pupils' level of response in the work they have done. This data will be cumulative and over an extended period (a term or a year) will present and assist the recall of significant responses by and about the individual pupil.

This method of assessment may appear at first sight rather nebulous and imprecise, but experienced English teachers can use these cues to retrieve from their memories substantial impressions of the individual pupil's pattern of work so that progress can be confirmed, if not quantified in any precise way.

Unease about this unscientific system of assessment has led some teachers to guide observation and formalise record keeping through some form of skills-related profile which is completed during the course of a term or a year. Such profiles can provide a circumscribed record of achievement (and progress) which can satisfy external demands for accountability as well as aiding the move to a new teacher at the beginning of the academic year. Skills profiles (most are of this kind) are of value; they can provide both a useful diagnostic tool and a series of talking points between teachers and pupils. They can also intimate some further understanding of what the teachers see to be important and how their judgments are made. An inherent danger, of course, is that the profile itself defines a set of priorities which may only partially accord with the teachers' real perceptions of value in this subject; it may present only an incomplete and superficial set of criteria or performance objectives.

"Profiling" has much to recommend it if it enhances the quality of the teacher's relationship with the pupil and creates a better mutual understanding of goals, aims, objectives, and standards; it can also provide a useful, transferable record of particular (discrete) achievement. What it cannot be a substitute for are those more elusive insights gained in the daily encounters between the teacher, his pupils, and their work. It is these insights which often provide a more profound awareness of motivation and performance and therefore a keener appreciation of present and future progress.

# The Other Side of the Coin

DEBBIE MYHILL
*(England)*

Assessment is the bane of a teacher's day—private time is infringed by it, reports are dominated by it, and children and parents alike are obsessed with it. Our educational system is becoming increasingly dependent upon assessment of all kinds, be it everyday grading and marking, public examinations, pupil profiling, or possibly, in the future, the reciprocal assessment of teachers themselves. Much has already been written about methods and theories of assessment in the classroom, but somewhat less attention paid to the role of the child's self-evaluations. It is perhaps obvious to state that the aim of all assessment should be towards developing a critical and perceptive ability to judge one's own work—less obvious is the significant part played by the unrefined evaluation of many children.

It is an unfortunate truth that children are taught to expect evaluation from a very early age, either in terms of an authoritative comment or a given grade. Furthermore, rigid, pedagogical teaching styles tend to foster such expectations, and cripple the child's ability to consider his own work critically. The majority of marking in schools concentrates heavily upon technical, syntactical, and visual aspects of the work, and a recent survey suggests that a very small proportion of marking contains constructive comments (Barnes, 1982). The creative demands of the English curriculum are directly undermined by such an atmosphere. Spaulding (1963) and Torrance (1965), amongst others, have stressed the negative effect that fear of assessment may have upon the creative potential of a child. They note that a considerable proportion of a teacher's evaluative behaviour is used to control or coerce the class into conforming to desired norms and has little if anything to do with judging the quality of work. The threat of evaluation is closely allied to the fear of failure in the individual, and it is crucial to remove this factor from the classroom. Writing is frequently about taking risks, experimenting and exploring language and ideas, and excessive anxiety about success or failure will prevent any real progress occurring. Jones (1972) emphasises the importance of this:

> The pupil must feel that he is not on trial as a person, and that activity, individuality and personality differences are valued. . . . Discrimination of the product is necessary, but the pupil must never be made to feel . . . rejected as a person.

Sadly, a large proportion of children today are so acutely conscious of social and educational dependence on assessment that they have absorbed the expectation of evaluation into their whole work pattern. In a study with a small group of thirteen- and fourteen-year-olds into writing and revision processes in poetry, I found that two pupils out of twelve were so crippled by this inner expectation of evaluation that they found it very hard to commit anything to paper and were highly critical of all their own work. They expected and anticipated failure. An additional three children in the group were highly dependent upon approval and agreement from the teacher at every stage in the writing process—to the point of being willing to accept any suggestion as "right" and superior to their own.

Such underlying self-evaluations are fundamentally counterproductive in all creative work, which is by its very nature dependent on drafting, revisions, rewriting, and editing. Revision bears all the pointers to the child of the system of assessment and evaluation in which he is placed. Revision is only the final step before the marking, the last hope of eradicating the glaring mistakes, and the last chance of attempting to synchronise one's efforts with the teacher's expectations. Too often teachers use the terminology of revision to indicate the tidying up of spelling, syntax, and grammar, and implying no reworking or reshaping of the content. Furthermore, the practice of handing back poor work to be rewritten reinforces the negative, even punitive, overtones of revision. In my own schooldays, RW (returned work) ringed enthusiastically in red signaled the ultimate failure. Rewriting and revision for the child are essentially unproductive and infinitely tedious processes, unmistakeably overshadowed by assessment.

However, the difficulties presented by developing a constructively critical perception in the child are not wholly dominated by the underlying strictures of external evaluation. Assessing one's own work demands many skills not often called upon elsewhere in the curriculum. Child or adult, it is always hard to see one's own mistakes. And the notion of "being finished," with its triumphal echoes, frequently implies a race to the finishing line which militates against balanced judgment and revision. There is much emphasis on completion in the classroom: homework deadlines, lesson bells, enticing baits for those who finish early and a subliminal hint that to finish is to succeed. Most children regard the first reasonably fair copy as a finished product, somehow inviolable and untouchable, and find it exceedingly difficult to apply themselves to this product with the same energy and enthusiasm that the creating of the piece earned.

How then can the shadows of assessment and hurried completion be demoted to their rightful perspective, and the child be encouraged to write and evaluate his own work with a balanced and unprejudiced judgment? Fundamental and perhaps obvious is the changing role of the teacher from authoritarian overseer to a more openly encouraging position, from "instructor and pedagogue to entrepreneur and consultant" (Doughty, 1974), and the creation of what Torrance (1965) calls the responsive environment. No child will develop critical abilities if his opinion and estimations are given no value. Similarly, the revision process must receive a new place in the work schedule to give it a more constructive tenor. Allowing more and more assessment to take place within the classroom by groups, pairs, or individuals, releases the teacher to spend time with individuals discussing work—time more highly regarded by pupils than marks in books (Dunsbee and Ford, 1980).

In my own research, the study group of third-year pupils found talking together about the poetry they had written positively helpful, and taped recordings of their talk reveal that they were discussing in detail the appropriateness of chosen words or images and the structures of the poems. One such discussion hinged upon the validity of using the word "booze" in a poem about a tramp—initially, several in the group felt that it wasn't "good English" and should be replaced by a more seeming word, perhaps "drink" or "alcohol." After discussion, the majority decided that the original word suggested more vividly the world of the tramp.

Interestingly, though I suspect not typically, they preferred to discuss their work in groups other than friendship groups, as they felt there was less self-consciousness in random groupings. Working in pairs, reading work aloud, taking each other's work home for comment later can all be valuable ways of fostering mature self-evaluation. One of the difficulties for most children is attaining a critical perspective on their work; this may be helped simply by allowing a time gap between initial effort and revision. Additionally, the use of tape recorders, typed copies, or any other technique which helps temporarily to divorce the writer from the writing may assist this critical perspective.

Counteracting the negative overtones of assessment which inhibit the creative work in the classroom may also be achieved by indicating that each piece of work is intrinsically meritable, regardless of its place in any course or examination syllabus. Using written work in ways other than in exercise books is an obvious way of doing this. The possibilities are many: classroom displays, school magazines, special anthologies, the local newspaper, exchanges with other schools; the imagination of the teacher will create its own possibilities. Above all, it is the prime responsibility of the teacher to be aware of the individual problems and difficulties that children encounter constantly in our overtly assessment-dominated classrooms: to appreciate that assessment both constructive and destructive occurs in more shades than red ink, that not all children will be miraculously stimulated by seeing their work in print, that not all children will find group work easy, that children already evaluate their efforts, with sometimes alarming consequences, but that nevertheless children can be guided and encouraged to the point where they respect themselves, their teacher, and their work sufficiently to make constructive comment.

# Evaluation and Assessment in Queensland

SHAUNA O'CONNOR
(Australia)

In Queensland in 1976, a committee was set up by the Board of Secondary School Studies to review evaluation and assessment. The report of this committee was published in 1978.

With any new system being implemented across an entire education system, there are bound to be some problems. Review of School Based Assessment (ROSBA) has meant continual, school-based assessment. The major difference between the former system and the new one is that evaluation has shifted from being norm based to criterion based. Each school is responsible for writing a work programme for each subject which it offers and for having such work programmes accredited by the Board of Secondary Studies. Students are awarded exit levels of achievement which reflect their success in meeting criteria laid out in these work programmes. Because writing sets of criteria was a new experience for many teachers, it was inevitable that considerable uncertainty would prevail; however, this problem is gradually being confronted.

In 1983, the Queensland Curriculum Services Branch responded to the number of problems associated with assessment and evaluation under ROSBA. John Carr and Wayne Murphy of the Branch produced a document which suggested an approach involving the specification of objectives and evaluation criteria in English in Years 8 to 10. They worked with a number of teachers in designing this document as a discussion paper in schools and as a basis for in-service activities. The document was intended to help teachers of English to implement some of the recommendations of ROSBA, especially those relating to the evaluation of student performance.

I was one of the teachers working on the preparation of this document, working with two other English teachers in the writing of a unit on "Leisure in Our Community." We specifically looked at the objectives of the unit and the types of criteria needed for the formative and summative assessment of the unit. It was through developing in detail one specific unit of work that my fellow teachers and I gained an understanding of how to apply generalized sets of criteria to any English tasks.

This has provided an invaluable means of assessing students' work, whether it be for grading or for monitoring the extent of student growth through and in English. Both teacher and student know what is expected from each piece of work; and, therefore, after an item has been viewed by the teacher, it is clearly evident where student strengths and weaknesses lie.

The unit involved students in a wide range of activities, especially ones relating to the investigation of various aspects of the topic. These included the forms of language associated with leisure pursuits and the provisions of leisure practices in the local communities. All of the student tasks in this unit were activity based, so that in the course of the unit, the students used the full range of language modes. In addition, all activities provided opportunities for the explicit study of language in context.

Only the introductory activities were obligatory and the many exploratory and action activities suggested were optional. This particular unit, therefore, was a catalogue of varied but related activities from which the teacher and students could construct sufficient logical sequences of activities to suit every student in the class.

The diagram on page 271, entitled "Leisure in Our Community," is an overview of the unit. The evaluation criteria for item C3, "Preparation of Brochure," follows.

### Evaluation

*Formative Evaluation.* All activities in the unit are open to formative evaluation, that is, the means can be found of providing feedback to the teacher and students. These means can be subjective or objective, incidental or planned. In any case, account should be taken of the objectives of the activity, the learning process, and the products arising from the activity, whether tangible or intangible.

With respect to products, due regard should be paid to:

- The language mode(s) and genre(s) used.
- The purposes of the language used.
- The context within which the language was used (the subject matter dealt with, the roles and relationships of the participants, and the setting).
- The appropriateness and effectiveness of the language used in the light of purpose and context.
- The knowledge gained.

*Summative Evaluation.* Summative evaluation of students' performance in the unit, whether or not it involves the assessment of students' level of achievement, will be most directly based on the "Action" activities, C1 to C5. Students' learnings in earlier activities should be evident here. The evaluation criteria for each of the five activities will follow the guidelines outlined above. Only one representative set is provided here.

### C3 Preparation of Brochure

Overall, effectiveness of the students' brochure in providing information on local leisure facilities for newcomers to the district, as revealed by:

- Apparent awareness of the purpose and nature of information brochures.
- Apparent awareness of the background and information needs of newcomers to the district, both children and adults.
- Apparent knowledge of existing local leisure facilities.
- Appropriate selection of information on local leisure facilities for inclusion in the brochure.

**LEISURE IN OUR COMMUNITY**

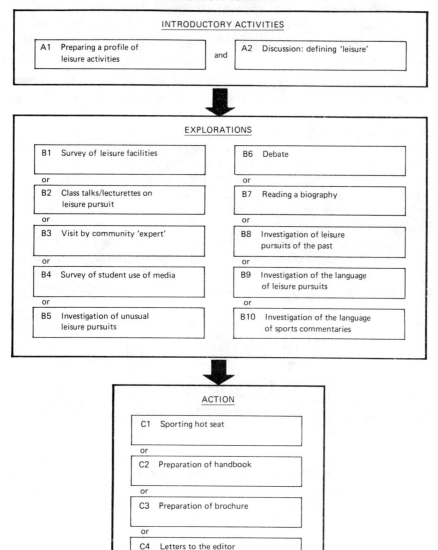

INTRODUCTORY ACTIVITIES

A1 Preparing a profile of
   leisure activities

and

A2 Discussion: defining 'leisure'

EXPLORATIONS

B1 Survey of leisure facilities

or

B2 Class talks/lecturettes on
   leisure pursuit

or

B3 Visit by community 'expert'

or

B4 Survey of student use of media

or

B5 Investigation of unusual
   leisure pursuits

B6 Debate

or

B7 Reading a biography

or

B8 Investigation of leisure
   pursuits of the past

or

B9 Investigation of the language
   of leisure pursuits

or

B10 Investigation of the language
    of sports commentaries

ACTION

C1 Sporting hot seat

or

C2 Preparation of handbook

or

C3 Preparation of brochure

or

C4 Letters to the editor

or

C5 Starting a club

- Logical ordering of this information.
- Choice of appropriate words and idioms.
- Coherence of text and appropriateness of paragraphing.
- Appropriate division of text into sections and use of headings.
- Clear, expressive, correct sentences.
- Correct spelling.

The criteria were based on Carr and Murphy. Once one has written a few of these criterion lists, the writing of subsequent ones becomes relatively easy. This, in turn, promotes consistency and brings some degree of unity to the English department.

Marks in English, based on the criteria, are arrived at holistically. The criteria inform the evaluators' judgment and clarify issues in discussion. As well as using criterion sheets for evaluation purposes, the English department and individual teachers retain folios of student work and sample student profiles to assist in determining students' exit achievement levels.

I personally feel that this is the best method of assessment that I have used, and that it does foster student growth through and in English by defining for students the criteria on which they are being assessed and indicating specifically where their strengths and weaknesses lie.

# The Evaluation of Fifth-Grade Writers

### CORA FIVE
#### (United States)

Writing evaluation in my fifth-grade classroom takes many forms. Continual assessment throughout the year, some holistic grading of writing pieces, folders containing samples of student writing from previous years, and a state-administered standardized test help me determine the growth my students have made in writing.

Classroom assessment is the most important and most realistic way of measuring student progress. My students and I evaluate their writing together. Our emphasis is on certain criteria, the qualities of good writing and the processes involved in writing, and growth over time. We embark on writing the first week of school as we go through the stages of the writing process together, brainstorming, drafting, revising, editing, and finally publishing. The students are involved in peer group and teacher conferences at each stage in the process.

Sharing sessions are one form of evaluation. Early in the school year, I establish a sharing time that occurs during each writing period. Students may share completed pieces or drafted pieces needing revision. It is here that they receive response from the whole class and from me. Here, also, we begin to discuss and establish the qualities of good writing. The class listens and points out positive qualities in the shared pieces. They also try to help the writer revise drafts for clarity, supportive details, and voice.

I like his ending because it's connected to his lead.

I liked all the good words she used.

I could smell the spaghetti and I could see it falling off the fork and landing on the floor.

I don't understand the part about how you fell off the horse. Were you in the saddle and then let go of the reins? How did you feel when you knew you were going to fall and the horse started going faster up the hill?

The writers are encouraged to tell what they liked about their piece and how it compares to some of their other writing pieces. The feedback students receive does much to promote their ability to evaluate their own pieces and their growth in writing. As the year progresses, my class views this sharing time as an increasingly vital part of the writing process. Requests to share begin as soon as students enter my room, and, at the beginning of each writing period, I have a long list of students who want to read their pieces. If for any reason sharing time has to be eliminated, their disappointment is obvious.

A more formal type of assessment takes place at the end of each marking period when I have a writing evaluation conference with each student. A week before I begin my conferences, I ask each child to fill out a Writing Evaluation Conference Sheet. They respond to the following types of questions suggested by Nancie Atwell (1982):

1. What do you have to do to be a good writer?
2. What is the hardest part of writing for you?
3. What is the easiest?
4. Which is your best piece of writing this marking period? Why?
5. Which is your worst piece? Why?
6. What kinds of changes do you make when you revise?
7. What problems are you having?
8. What do you want to work on next?

They spend a week thinking about their answers and selecting their pieces.

My students bring their writing folders, which contain all completed pieces and attached drafts, and their writing evaluation forms to their conference. We discuss their responses together and examine their best piece. At the first conference, which occurs in November, the students and I may talk about the stages of the writing process with a concentration on their developing strategies for revision. By the second and third conferences, we compare previous evaluation sheets, discuss changes in the answers to the same questions, and look for growth in writing ability by examining their best pieces. During these later conferences, the students can use the qualities of good writing established during our sharing sessions to tell me how they have progressed as writers. Dana told me in November: "The hardest part for me is brainstorming. It's hard because I never really get any terrific interesting topics." In March she said: "Revising is hardest. I'm not good at creating a lead. My middle is usually okay but it takes so long for me to get a good ending. I need to put more details in."

The columns below show the responses of two students when asked about the kinds of changes they made when they revised:

|  | *Nathan* | *Jennifer* |
|---|---|---|
| *November* | "I focus on one topic." | "I add details and I take out words." |
| *March* | "I add better words and better sentences. I write clearer words, more describing paragraphs." | "I add details, change the lead and ending. I change the order a little." |
| *June* | "I make better leads and endings. I change words, sentences, and the sequence. I do more editing—add more precise words." | "I add details, change the order of my piece and change the lead and ending. I also try to make my piece as clear as I can and I try to make it flow from paragraph to paragraph. And last but not least, I try to show what I'm writing, not tell what I'm writing." |

In response to what you have to do to be a good writer, Lee wrote:

| *November* | "You have to have a good imagination." |
|---|---|
| *March* | "You have to be able to describe every little detail and be able to focus on one thing." |
| *June* | "You have to use vivid language. You have to be able to revise well. You need an interesting lead, and a strong ending." |

The writing evaluation sheets showed the growth the students felt they were making from simply focusing on a topic or a lead to developing more complex strategies for revision. More specifically, we see that in November the students wrote a vague generalization of the whole. By March, there was a specific evaluation of concrete parts. June's response reveals a more abstract understanding and evaluation of the writing process. The evaluation sheets also showed greater depth of self-evaluation. By June, not only are the students able to look at the process of writing, but they take the initiative to do so. The teacher ceases to function as the stimulus for evaluation. The students take pleasure in being their own evaluators.

At the end of the writing evaluation conference, the students and I agree on a grade for their report card. We also set goals for the next few months. The students will tell me how many pieces they will try to complete. (With some input from the class earlier in the year, I had already established a minimum of one piece per month.) They will also tell me where and how they want to improve; for example: "I have to work on my endings. I want to make them better because now they just drop off," or "I have to remember to do better on mechanics. I don't always remember where to put the quotation marks. I want to learn how to do it so I don't always have to go to Emily or come to you for help."

At the end of the year, another important type of assessment takes place. Students in my school district must select, with teacher guidance, two samples of their best writing to be placed in a blue folder that will be sent to the next year's teacher. At the end of ninth grade, students and their parents will have a folder representing growth in writing from kindergarten through the first year of high school. Writing pieces with attached drafts are labeled with the year or grade and arranged in chronological order.

On the inside of the blue permanent folder is a section used for comments by either the teacher, the student, or both. My students write a few sentences describing their progress during the year. In this way, the students have a record of their own assessment of their writing throughout elementary school.

In June, the following evaluations of the fifth-grade writing experience were copied carefully onto the blue folders:

> Before I came into fifth grade I was a writer with potential. But now I am a TRUE WRITER! In my opinion I have progressed beyond belief! Before this my teachers had praised me but I didn't feel like I had deserved it. Back then I had never heard of leads, endings, details, and vivid language. But now I don't consider writing a chore but a hobby.
>
> *Mindy*

I think I have improved in my writing, mostly in my organization of sentences and paragraphs, and most of all in the quality of my writing. I find it easier to write a piece of good writing this year than last.

*Neil*

I stunk at writing last year. Whenever we did reports we copied straight out of the book. Imagine that! When I came into fifth grade I had never heard of words like ending, leads, revising, editing or proofreading. Now they're everyday words to me. I think I improved tremendously over this year. I think my specialty is conferencing with others. I hope I can continue writing for the rest of my life. I guess I have to face facts—I LOVE WRITING!

*Jennifer*

I think I've improved in writing a lot because Miss Five taught me to put in details, to use vivid language and make good leads that would make the reader want to keep on reading my story. I think a good writer needs to focus on a topic. If I have an exciting story writing is fun. If not, its not fun at all. I like doing leads the best because I can make them exciting. I dislike endings because its hard to stop.

*Jen*

I'm not bragging but I think I did very well this year. Last year I was terrible. Now I've really improved. Fiction, I think, is my best. Personal writing is all right but fiction tends to be more creative for me. Leads and endings are my specialties. Writing the body and keeping it short are hard for me. Revising, editing, and proof-reading are things I'm good at, too. Sixth grade looks promising for a good writing year.

*Heather*

The manner in which these permanent folders are maintained coincides with the philosophy underlying the writing process—that of student ownership. The students select their best pieces and evaluate their own growth.

The last form of evaluation is a state standardized writing test. In May of 1983, New York State began focusing on writing in the elementary schools by developing a test for all fifth graders. Its purpose is twofold: to identify the writing problems of students and to encourage school systems to focus on writing.

The test has two parts which involve writing on assigned topics. Part one assigns a topic related to personal experience; part two is a more imaginative topic. The students are asked to write a piece of about 150 words. They are encouraged to write a first draft which can be revised and edited before writing the copy in pen.

Criteria for Rating Student Responses

| Level 4 | Level 3 | Level 2 | Level 1 |
|---|---|---|---|
| Develops the assigned topic in an interesting and imaginative way. | Develops the assigned topic in an acceptable but unimaginative way. | Attempts to develop the assigned topic but includes digressions. | Minimally addresses the assigned topic. |
| Demonstrates a logical plan of organization and coherence in the development of ideas. | Has a plan of organization and a satisfactory development of ideas. | Demonstrates weakness in organization and the development of ideas. | Shows lack of organization and development of ideas. |
| Uses support material that is relevant and appropriate for the purpose and audience. | Uses adequate support material. | Uses little support material. | Uses no support material. or uses irrelevant material. |
| Shows skillful use of sentence variety. | Uses some sentence variety. | Demonstrates sentence sense but has little sentence variety. | Demonstrates a lack of sentence sense. |
| Uses specific, vivid language. | Uses appropriate language. | Uses trite and/or imprecise language. | Uses immature and/or inappropriate language. |
| Makes few or no mechanical errors. | Makes mechanical errors which do not interfere with communication. | Makes mechanical errors which interfere with communication. | Makes mechanical errors which seriously interfere with communication. |

*Zero Paper:* Is totally unrelated to the topic; *or* Is illegible; i.e., includes so many indecipherable words that no sense can be made of the response; *or* Is incoherent; i.e., words are legible but syntax is so garbled that the response makes no sense; *or* Is a blank paper.

The test is scored holistically by teachers in the school district who have been trained to score according to the state's criteria. Holistic scoring involves making a single judgment about the overall quality of a writing sample instead of giving separate scores for content, organization, and mechanics. The rater basically looks at the whole message as an indication of how well the writer has communicated.

My school district encouraged preparation for this test through a series of practice tests on assigned topics. To help my class learn how to score these practice tests holistically, I introduced them to the criteria for scoring established by the New York State Department of Education and shown on the table on page 277.

I gave my students a checklist of the level 4 criteria so they could evaluate their practice tests individually. After each practice test, they would check off the criteria on the checklist, and then in a conference we would score the test. Sometimes the whole class would discuss a test for its qualities and then we would give it a 4, 3, 2, or 1.

As the students became aware of the criteria for a high scoring paper, they were again learning the qualities of good writing that we established during our sharing sessions earlier in the year. My students began to internalize these criteria to guide their own revisions and editing.

The practice tests proved to be a helpful teaching tool and added variety of form and audience to my regular writing program.

When I compared the writing on the test with the work my students had done throughout the year, I noticed that their class work was superior to their writing for the test. A writing test fails to reflect accurately every student's work during the year.

After considering the various forms of assessment I've used, I believe periodic writing evaluation conferences are most valuable to me and to my students. The conference allows me to observe not only the students' continuing development as writers, but their increased involvement in the writing process itself. By the second and third conferences, they can tell me their strengths and weaknesses. They can establish their own goals. I see them as independent writers taking initiative and responsibility for self-evaluation.

# The Language Profile

TREVOR WILLIAMS

*(New Zealand)*

I thought I'd describe just one method of assessment which we operate as part of our Form 6 English programme. This method involves work presented by students through a language profile. The language profile runs parallel to but underneath classroom work. It is an attempt to record lines of growth during the Form 6 year (16-year-olds); consequently, sufficient time and status has to be given to it. It is presented in the final term of the year and counts for one-third of the pupil's overall grade for the year.

The best way to justify the rationale behind the language profile is to reproduce the format which is presented to the pupils at the beginning of their Form 6 year. I should add, though, that Form 6 teachers set aside at least one lesson per month to see what the students are doing, and every week they nominate one or two students to report some aspect of their profile data to the class. In this way stimulation and supervision are maintained.

The language profile is evolving all the time. Here is the Mark III version.

### The Language Profile

The key to English studies is *growth*—growth in the ability to use language accurately and effectively, growth in an increasing perceptiveness into your own thoughts and feelings and those of others.

Inside the classroom, you will be challenged by some ideas that you meet and discuss in literature; outside the classroom, you are arguing, reading, viewing, thinking, and feeling. This year, we want to bring those two spheres closer together. Your task in a language profile is to trace your development in language over the year. To do this, you will need to record what you think and feel about a variety of influences going on in your language environment.

#### First Exercise

Your first exercise (due at the end of the first two weeks) is to assess in at least 400–500 words where you consider yourself to be at the moment.

- What do you value?
- Do you know why you think that's important to you?
- What do you believe?
- What ideals do you have?

- What disturbs you?
- How do you regard yourself?
- How do others regard you?
- What do you consider to be man's most important ideas?
- What trends do you see going on today?
- Do these worry you? Why?
- What sticks in your mind about your life so far?
- Have you read anything that's really meant something to you?
- What was it?
- What was meaningful about it?
- What would you like to say about yourself if only you could?

*These questions are meant only to stimulate your thinking about you, to help you formulate some autobiographical statement. They are not conclusive or definitive.*

If this exercise is to be worthwhile, it is important that you approach it with honesty and the determination to identify yourself to yourself. Since your thoughts are private, no one else will read them. The exercise will be sealed in an envelope and returned to you at the end of the year. At that time, you will then conclude your language profile with a reassessment of yourself (suitable for others to read), outlining the "distance" you think you have traveled this year, the growth you are aware of.

### The Rest of the Profile

All entries in the profile should record the date on which the item took place.

*What can you include? Some or all of these, and anything else you can think of.*

- *Reading* is a must. Your profile must include comment and discussion on literature you have read outside the classroom. If you are not a reader, then learn to become one. If you don't know what to read, or what might be suitable to include, then present your teacher with the challenge of finding something interesting and worthwhile.

  To this end, you are required to read *at least three books* other than the ones studied in class. (Of course, you can read a lot more. The record is 52.) These three books should be commented on as follows:

  *Title and Author*
  > *Summary:* 200–300 words.
  > *Value:* About 200–300 words. Here, you should attempt to identify some of the ideas in the book and explain why you

think these ideas are important. Or you should attempt to equate this book's themes with ones you have studied in class. Or you should try to pinpoint the effect the book had on you.

Obviously you will have to choose your books wisely. Some books are entertaining and lightweight; some are entertaining and profound; some are difficult and profound.

Here is a scheme with some suggested titles arranged under possible themes. The list is not exhaustive, but it may give you some titles to start following up. Most of the titles will be available in the library.

Another approach, of course, is to follow an author, or a sequence of books, e.g., *Dune* and sequels, *The Wounder Land* and sequels, *The Crystal Cave* and sequels, John Le Carré's novels about the master-spy, George Smiley.

Relationships:
*Dibs, The Godboy, Tangi, Sons and Lovers, Death of a Salesman, Look Back in Anger, Catcher in the Rye. L-Shaped Room, Sons for the Return Home*

Women:
*Dibs, A Doll's House, One Flew Over the Cuckoo's Nest, To the Is-Land, L-Shaped Room, Frances*

Psychology:
*Dibs, Frances, Sybil, Catch-22, The Bell Jar, Faces in the Water, The Crucible, I Never Promised You a Rose Garden*

War:
*Schindler's Ark, Catch-22, The Red Badge of Courage, Royal Hunt of the Sun, Heavy Sand, Blind Eye to Murder, Anus Mundi, Slaughterhouse-Five*

"Systems":
*1984, One Day in the Life of Ivan Denisovich, Brave New World, A Clockwork Orange, One Flew Over the Cuckoo's Nest, Darkness at Noon, Catch-22, Fahrenheit 451, Schindler's Ark, The Autobiography of Malcolm X, The Spy Who Came in from the Cold, Gorky Park, The Trial, Smith's Dream, Glide Time, The Crucible, Ragtime*

Parent/Child:
*Dibs, Bless the Beasts and Children, To Kill a Mockingbird, Tangi, Death of a Salesman, Sons and Lovers, To the Is-Land, The Godboy*

Love:

*Dibs, Look Back in Anger, Tangi, Sons for the Return Home, L-Shaped Room, Sons and Lovers, The Spy Who Came in from the Cold*

Culture Clashes:

*Savages, The Royal Hunt of the Sun, Sons for the Return Home, Cry, the Beloved Country, Tomorrow Will Be a Lovely Day, The Autobiography of Malcolm X*

- It would be a good idea to check first with your teacher the three titles you are presenting in this format.
- Some pupils think that a profile has to be full of private thoughts and feelings. That is not so. If a teacher asked you to write an exposition on a given topic, you would have to do it. If he or she asked you to compose a description, you would have to comply, and similarly with any other language exercise. All the profile does is to allow you to set your own topics, to follow your own interests and justify them. Perhaps this exercise might make you aware that your interests are not wide enough, and that your exposure to ideas needs broadening. In that case, you will have grown.
- Your thoughts about the ideas you meet in literature studies in class. Your reaction does not and should not stop with your compulsory essays. *Teachers may require you to write an exercise in a class period especially for your profile.* This may take place, for instance, after a class trip to a performance or film.
- Your thoughts on other books, etc., you read outside of class. Do any of the ideas tie in? Are any common themes emerging?
- What films have you seen this year? What TV shows? What plays, performances, shows, exhibitions, viewings? How did they impress you? How did they depress you?
- Had an argument lately? What about?
- Did something on the news disturb you deeply?
- You were listening to others talking, to the radio, but you thought. . . .
- You overheard a conversation the other day and it stuck in your mind because. . . .
- You watch people. Record your impressions.
- Write a poem, a letter, a story.
- Present a taped talk.
- Keep a diary or journal.
- You want to get this off your chest. . . .
- You collect articles/headlines. Arrange them in a dossier. Discuss what interested you in this collection.

- Illustrate an idea you have had; use photographs or make a collage to represent a theme from your class.
- Research an idea you have with other people. Compile a questionnaire.
- Consult your English teacher.
- Do a little, often.

READ • VIEW • TALK • LISTEN • WRITE • SHAPE

Give thought to presenting your language profile in an attractive format. Include:

1. A bibliography at the end of the profile.
2. A final statement of self-assessment.
3. A final statement identifying lines of development obvious in the work included in the profile. That means you review the material you have composed and compiled and try to see what have been major preoccupations, themes, and interests.
4. Your compulsory class essays.

The profile is judged under four main criteria:

1. The variety of material presented.
2. Perceptiveness—the quality of insight into the material; the ability to identify themes and comment upon them.
3. Sincerity—the impression that is gained of your genuine concern to trace your development and the pressure of thought and feeling behind your items.
4. Quality of presentation—the profile has been set out with an eye for format; that it is clean, arranged thematically or chronologically, attractive, and perhaps even original.

# Bloom's Taxonomy and Assessment

### JAMES LALLEY
*(United States)*

Much of the research into levels of cognition by Benjamin Bloom has given new insights and urged new ways of looking at evaluation and assessment in education. This new sophistication in assessment has not only given me a vocabulary for clarifying what I want to assess but has also led me to more efficient and effective ways of assessment.

Bloom has reminded us of the obvious. Assessment is only part of the instructional process; assessment and evaluation methods flow naturally from the objectives set for the course. Usually, objectives set for a course aim at all levels of cognition, from the lowest, knowledge, to the highest, evaluation. Yet often times, our assessment is limited to the lower levels, such as recall. Since there is a variety of levels of cognition, and the objectives of the course are to have students operate at all levels, then instruction as well as testing methods must be aimed at the various levels.

I will illustrate how the ideas and the vocabulary of Bloom's taxonomy have clarified objectives and established more precise assessment in classroom questioning and on objective and essay test questions for the teaching of Shakespeare's play *Macbeth.*

Bloom identifies six cognitive operations in his taxonomy. The levels of cognition move from the lower to the higher levels, and Bloom emphasizes that our goals and our assessment should aim at all levels of cognition.

### 1. *Knowledge is the remembering of previously learned material.*

This operation is signaled by the use of such words as *know, recall, define, repeat, list, record, relate, name.* Thus, some of the objectives that would stress this lower level of cognition for the instruction unit on *Macbeth* would be:

*Objectives:*

- The student will be able to recall the names of major characters.
- The student will be able to define the term "the tragic hero."
- The student will be able to list the witches' statements.

*Questions:*

- What is the name of the King of Scotland at the beginning of the play?
- Repeat Aristotle's definition of "tragedy."
- Recite the lines that the witches spoke to Macbeth and Banquo.

Knowledge is considered the "lowest" level of cognition, but knowledge of the material is a prerequisite for the higher levels.

### 2. *Comprehension is the ability to grasp the meaning of the material.*

This operation is signaled in objectives by such words as *restate, discuss, describe, express, identify, report, review, explain, locate, tell, recognize.*

*Objectives:*

- The student will be able to paraphrase lines from the play.
- The student will be able to explain Aristotle's definition of tragedy.
- The student will be able to express in his own words Macbeth's hesitation about killing the king.

*Questions:*

- Paraphrase Lady Macbeth's reflections on Macbeth's letter.
- In your own words, explain Aristotle's definition of tragedy.
- Express in your own words Macbeth's reasons for not wanting to kill Duncan.

**3. *Application is the ability to use learned materials in new and concrete situations.***

This operation is assessed using such words as *apply, schedule, operate, dramatize, illustrate, interpret, sketch, translate, use, practice.*

*Objectives:*

- The student will be able to apply Aristotle's definition of tragedy and the characteristics of the tragic hero to this play and its main character.
- The student will be able to illustrate the definition by illustrative quotes from the text.

*Questions:*

- Apply Aristotle's definition of tragedy to the play *Macbeth.* Does it apply? Would Macbeth be a tragic hero?
- List three examples of Macbeth's dialogue which illustrate his reluctance to kill.

**4. *Analysis is the ability to break down material into its component parts so that its organizational structures may be understood.***

This is assessed using such words as *distinguish, differentiate, calculate, solve, diagram, compare, question, analyze, appraise, test, debate, experiment, inventory, relate (show relationship).*

*Objectives:*

- The students will be able to see the relationship between actions, scenes, and acts within the play.
- The students will be able to compare and contrast characters in the play.

*Questions:*

- Diagram the main plot actions in *Macbeth* showing how the events lead to Macbeth's downfall.
- Using examples of dialogue and actions from the play, compare and contrast Macbeth and Banquo.

**5. *Synthesis is the ability to put parts together to form a new whole.***

This is assessed using such words as *categorize, combine, devise, compose, plan, reconstruct, reorganize, rewrite, design, explain, modify, generate, rearrange, revise, summarize.*

*Objectives:*

- The student will be able to construct new material based on the information gleaned from the play.
- The student will be able to sum up the theme of the play.

*Questions or Activities:*

- Rewrite the ending of *Macbeth* so that Macbeth lives. What would he say, what would he do?
- Compose a soliloquy for Lady Macbeth just before she commits suicide. (The soliloquy may not begin, "To be or not to be. . . .")
- Explain what are Shakespeare's thoughts on human nature, power, and evil based on your reading of this play.

**6. *Evaluation is the ability to judge the value of material for a given purpose.***

This is assessed using such words as *judge, rate, score, assess, appraise, value, select, estimate, evaluate, choose, measure.*

*Objectives:*

- The student should be able to make informed judgments about the play, the techniques used, diction employed, themes presented.

*Questions:*

- Which of Macbeth's soliloquies best captures him as a tragic figure? Explain.
- Does *Macbeth* or *Hamlet* best fit Aristotle's definition of tragedy?

Bloom's identification of levels of cognition and the key words which signal the levels has helped me focus student objectives and sharpen assessment procedures.

# Evaluating a Whole-Language Secondary-English Curriculum: A First Year Study

BETTY SWIGGETT
*(United States)*

In the fall of 1983, our school division began the implementation of a new English curriculum, Grades 7-12. The program, created through intensive efforts during the previous 12 months, was a topic of considerable interest among English teachers, other staff members, the school board, and several influential members of the community. Thus, in response to this interest, planning for formal evaluation began with the placement of the last cover on the curriculum guides.

The new curriculum uses a whole-language approach to language learning. With units organized around topics of importance to adolescents, such as "Family Courage" and "The American Dream," activities are organized to create a natural integration of reading, writing, listening, and speaking activities. The focus is on experiencing language in its many different forms, with students using language and learning language simultaneously as they make sense of "what are essentially meaningful situations" (Smith, 1983, p. 9). Some beliefs about learning, which guided curricular decisions and which influenced the modes of inquiry chosen, are as follows:

- Students are curious, active learners.
- Learning how to learn is of primary value.
- Skills development is more fostered than taught.
- Learning involves the whole person—mentally, socially, emotionally.
- The English classroom can be a pleasurable, stimulating learning experience.

In reflecting on personal perspectives and curricular decisions, Wolfson (1985) asserts:

When we think about designing curriculum, it *does* make a difference whether we assume that people learn because they are rewarded or because it is a natural part of life. It *does* make a difference whether we assume that what people think and feel are essential aspects of learning, or that the "right" responses are our only concern. (p. 58)

The modes of inquiry suited to a whole-language curriculum need then to include ones which examine learning in the contexts of whole experiences occurring in the classroom. Observers, moreover, must be sufficiently knowledgeable to recognize how the whole encompasses the parts—how paragraphing, for example, is a part of revision, how usage and vocabulary may blend into one when discussing wording, how dramatic activities serve to make links between written texts and personal experience.

The modes of inquiry best suited to a whole-language curriculum tend to be qualitative ones—observation, interview, surveys of perceptions and attitudes—rather than the conventional ones associated with standardized tests scores and a skills approach. Fortunately, for a first-year study, the weight can shift to the more qualitative, descriptive data because formal test data are not immediately available. In our case, we were able to use for our first-year study the qualitative modes of inquiry—modes that are congruent with the humanistic insights that influenced the development of the program.

The evaluation was conducted by an 11-member committee containing a cross section of individuals—teachers, administrators, central office specialists, and a parent—who had worked at one or more stages of the curriculum development process. Serving also on the committee was Stephen Tchudi, who had been the ongoing external consultant during curriculum development. The Director of Program Evaluation served on this committee as well. The nature of the membership greatly facilitated the evaluation planning process, eliminating the need for extensive orientation. The committee could turn immediately to its task.

Three major questions were addressed in the study:

1. Was the curriculum being implemented in accordance with its aims, contents, and recommended teaching strategies?
2. Were the groups most involved with the curriculum satisfied with its implementation?
3. Was there evidence of increased learning?

These questions led to the selection of the following modes of inquiry:

- School visitation to observe classroom/department activities, including informal interviewing of principals, teachers, and students, and the examination of student products and record keeping procedures.
- Survey questionnaires of the in-school groups most concerned with the curriculum—teachers, students, principals, and guidance counselors.
- Analysis of test data.

These three major approaches would provide ample insights into the effectiveness of the program. The committee divided itself into five subgroups to plan the procedures and instruments for the evaluation. Committee work began in February and continued through April, except for the test data subcommittee, which carried its study through the following year.

The chair of the classroom/department observations subgroup was Stephen Tchudi. All committee members participated in classroom observation, making a total of approximately 150 observations. Some used a checklist as an informal guide to aid observation. Tchudi made trips to the school system in February and April to participate in committee work and to make school observations. He visited approximately 50 classrooms, conducted informal interviews with students, teachers, and administrators, and examined student writing portfolios, reading record cards, project-related materials, and other departmental records. He could perceive the extent to which instruction was in accordance with the principles and practices of the new program.

In his final report, Tchudi (1984) wrote:

> It is evident from all sources that the new program is going extremely well. In my classroom observations, I saw numerous instances of: posted course syllabi, daily objectives on the board, writing growing from reading selections, grammar and vocabulary taught incidentally as part of the writing/reading processes, oral and dramatic presentation of literature, writing taught as process, small-group work, individualized reading, careful record keeping (including writing folders, reading record cards, and notes on SOL objectives), and bulletin boards filled with examples of student work. I was, in fact, surprised that the new program seems to have taken hold in a vast majority of classes in the city. (p. 8)

Observations made by local committee members were similar to those of Tchudi.

In addition, questionnaires were prepared for four groups: teachers, students, administrators, and guidance counselors. Each questionnaire contained two parts, the first part asking specific questions, the second part soliciting additional comments. The surveys were administered anonymously to all English teachers, principals, assistant principals of instruction, counselors, and a representative sampling of students.

### Survey of Teachers

Part I of the teacher questionnaire contained 15 questions to which teachers made one of the following responses: (a) strongly agree, (b) agree, (c) disagree, and (d) strongly disagree. In Part II, teachers were asked to make written comments under three headings: (a) implementation of the new curriculum, (b) textbooks and other resources, and (c) staff development. Each topic in Part II matched one or more items in Part I and thus provided teachers an opportunity to clarify their forced-choice responses. Ninety-seven percent of the teachers answered the questionnaire.

The makers of the teacher questionnaire did not avoid tough questions. The very first question went to the heart of the inquiry, asking for a response to the statement, "I am personally satisfied with the new curriculum." Seventy-six percent of the teachers gave positive responses to this question. Other questions were similarly direct. Several questions tapped the teachers' perceptions of the ease with which they could implement the curriculum. Teachers responded that the suggested strategies were successful in actual classroom situations (73 percent), the curriculum provided for integrated, sequential instruction (73 percent), and lesson plans evolved naturally from the course of study (83 percent). Only 50 percent of the teachers believed that they made effective use of small-group work, an important component of recommended strategies. In contrast, 82 percent of the students stated that small-group work helped them to learn. This difference in self-reports suggested that even though many of the teachers were not satisfied with their skills in conducting group work, students were learning, and perhaps more than they would have otherwise.

### Survey of Students

The questionnaire designed to determine student satisfaction with the new English curriculum was distributed to 605 students, approximately six percent of the student population, but using a random sampling procedure by grade and ability. Response categories for Part I of the student questionnaire were (a) frequent, (b) sometimes, (c) seldom, and (d) never. In addition to the statement regarding small-group work, the questionnaire included 17 other questions dealing with reading, writing, dramatic activities, and self-reliance as learners.

Students reported that they had frequent writing assignments (69 percent), writing in English helped with writing in other subjects (87 percent), small-group work helped them to recognize and correct grammar usage and punctuation errors (82 percent), and they enjoyed participating in oral reading (68 percent). Overall, students appeared to be pleased with the new English curriculum. The average of the ratings for all 18 questions was 76 percent favorable.

In Part II of the student questionnaire, the students were asked to list activities (1) that helped them to learn the most and (2) that helped them the least. Since this part included no promptings, the responses can be considered genuine reflections of instructional strategies

of greatest importance to students. The activities that students considered most helpful were small-group work, writing, oral reading, reading in general, and class discussion. The activities cited most often as
least helpful were written book reports, career awareness activities
(Grade 7), and journal writing (Grades 9–10).

## Survey of Administrators

The subgroup that developed the questionnaire for administrators
drew their inspiration, but not the bulk of their questions, from Squire
and Applebee's (1968) 12 hypotheses regarding English programs. They
selected 12 general indicators of quality English programs and prepared
a five-point rating scale for respondents with "strongly agree" the highest rating (5) and "strongly disagree" the lowest (1). All 18 secondary
principals and assistant principals for instruction were polled. Eleven
responses were submitted.

Administrators gave the program the highest rating (strongly agree)
on the frequency of writing activities and language in use and on the
use of multiple textbooks and other materials. They rated the program
as good (agree) in teacher preparation, interpersonal skills of teachers,
quality of curriculum guides, departmental intellectual climate, and
other general qualities. Their responses differed sharply on the questions of the equal strength of the program for all ability and interest
groups (40 percent agreed, 40 percent disagreed, 20 percent unsure),
creating a neutral rating.

In Part II, the most frequent comment dealt with the need to
strengthen the skills of basic students. The phraseology of several comments indicated that several administrators had expectations for the
program which were contrary to its stated philosophy and purposes.

## Survey of Guidance Counselors

The questionnaire on English curriculum implementation distributed to guidance counselors contained four questions and a section
for additional comments. Answers were in short essay form. Topics
explored were their perceptions with regard to (1) individualization of
instruction for students with special needs, (2) the strength of the program for all ability groups, and (3) the availability of elective courses
for students. They were also asked to comment on their satisfaction
with the total English curriculum.

The rate of return for this questionnaire was low (30 percent),
stemming possibly from the essay format, or insufficient knowledge of
the program to answer the questions with confidence, or a combination
of these two elements. Those who responded stated that individualization varied with the teachers, "some more, some less," believed that
the program was equally strong for average and above-average ability

groups but not for below-average groups, and recommended more teacher efforts toward recruitment for elective courses. Although the majority (65 percent) was satisfied with the program, some cited a need for more vocabulary study as preparation for the SAT and the infusion of more grammar. A few counselors commented on a need for in-service with regard to the new English program.

The responses of counselors suggested that some needed a fuller understanding of the new English program. The following year, in-service was provided to counselors on the philosophy, purposes, and design of the English program.

The final aspect of program evaluation was examination of test data. During the first-year evaluation, the work and report of the test data subcommittee were not completed. This committee, chaired by the Director of Program Evaluation, has tended to focus on external test data, reports, and analyses: SAT scores, norm-referenced, standardized tests given at Grades 8 and 11, advanced placement standing, and the ratings given by graduates of the adequacy of their English preparation for advanced studies or the world of work. This committee's work has now burgeoned into a full-scale study and has been absorbed into a larger evaluation plan containing curriculum analysis for test-related content, analytical scoring of student compositions written six months apart, and more recently a survey of parents regarding their perceptions of the new English program. The first-year and second-year studies have been combined to form what the division describes as a comprehensive plan and a model for evaluating other academic programs.

After one year of implementation of the new program, standardized test data show no great gains; nor do they show losses. Had they shown either, we would have been surprised. Language growth is a complex, slowly developing process, many aspects of which are not tapped by a single standardized test. Students were performing well under the previous English programs, but we believe that they will do even better with the new program.

English teachers in Hampton have worked this year to act on the evaluation presented by the first-year study. Action has entailed both changes in the program and efforts to change certain perspectives with regard to the program. Because the program has a solid theoretical and practical foundation, the changes in the program have turned out to be minor—some curricular revision, some additional resources. When the need has been for changing certain perspectives, the department has taken the initiative to provide in-service. The area of greatest misunderstanding, and, thus, of concern with our program, was grammar instruction in an integrated program. The English department has taken the initiative to provide in-service through workshops, newsletters, and videotaped programs for teachers, support staff, and the general public on grammar instruction in the program.

As the public learns more about our program, we anticipate that they will be able to make observations similar to that of one parent published in the local newspaper:

> In May, I evaluated one of my son's themes and found great improvement in the development of his thoughts, the organization and flow of his work, and his use of more complex sentence structures. I also observed my son reading and choosing to read more mature literature. At times his comments about his reading helped me realize that he was beginning to respond critically. Generally, I have been pleased with my son's growth in his English class, particularly in a skill I could observe easily, his writing. (Tinder, 1984)

# External Examinations
# in New York

### ROBERT SQUIRES
*(United States)*

The growing trend by state governments in the United States to establish minimum competency examinations in writing has been greeted by teachers with reactions ranging from enthusiasm to alarm. Whatever the reaction, however, the examinations are a fact of our educational life and must be dealt with. New York State's Comprehensive Examination in English is one of the oldest of standardized examinations, and students must pass it to receive the highly valued state Regents' diploma. Until recently, however, students who did not pass the comprehensive examination could receive a local Board of Education diploma. New York now has a minimum competency examination in writing intended primarily for students who cannot pass or who choose not to take the comprehensive examination. Students must now pass one or the other to receive any diploma at all. (There are parallel competency examinations in reading and in mathematics.) The examination is given three times a year, January, June, and August. Students take the examination in the eleventh grade so that each student has five chances before graduation.

Because of great differences in demographic patterns in the state, percentages of student bodies who must take and pass the competency test vary widely. In my district, the percentage taking the minimal examination is never higher than 15 percent, and we have not yet had a student not graduate because of failure to pass it. However, I have heard of one school in one of our larger cities in which as many as 85 percent take the minimum competency exam, and many of those have difficulty passing. Inevitably, some students in such schools become discouraged early and terminate their education before they have received any of the benefits the school can give them.

It is not my purpose here to debate the pros and cons of the examination, but to discuss one of the outgrowths of the examination. When the state established the examination, it also mandated that each school would provide students scheduled to take it with remedial instruction beyond what they receive in their English courses. Since the state does not provide additional funds for this remedial instruction, it is something of a problem for very small schools with only one or two English teachers; at the same time, most of those schools should have very few qualifying students. In large and medium-sized schools with seven or more English teachers, the provision of remedial instruction is considerably easier to manage. Most schools simply remove the supervision of study halls from the English teachers' loads and reassign them to writing labs, writing clinics, or writing centers. In this way, every period in the day can be covered by at least one English teacher. In my school (eight English teachers) in the 1983–1984 year, only one of the seven periods did not have a writing lab; for 1984–1985, writing labs were scheduled for all seven periods.

In my school, determination of which students are assigned to a writing lab is made in one of three ways. Some students are assigned on the basis of their performance on a preliminary competency examination which all students take in eighth grade. Some students are assigned by recommendation of a teacher (not necessarily an English teacher). And some students assign themselves for differing reasons and for varying lengths of time. For example, twelfth graders are likely to drop in for help with the mechanical aspects of research papers, and in 1983–1984, I had two honors-level tenth graders who simply wanted a quiet place to work.

The physical facilities allocated to writing labs and the management of them also vary widely across the state. Declining enrollments in some schools have permitted the assignment of a classroom or a suite of rooms to this function. In my school, most teachers can find an empty classroom; one teacher was able to use one of the library's conference rooms, and one was forced to use a corner of a study hall, but he never had more than three students at a time.

In some schools, the management of the lab is highly organized. Writing weaknesses are diagnosed and then students work through sequenced series of exercises designed to correct those weaknesses. Although our school's program started that way five years ago, we have found it more beneficial to the students to work with them individually on whatever writing tasks they have been given in any of their courses. With eleventh and twelfth graders, we give intensive practice in the three writing tasks on the competency examination (business letter, writing a report from data provided, and persuasion). But for ninth and tenth grade students, the competency examination is too remote, and for some the writing tasks too sophisticated. The immediate writing assignments they have been given in English, social studies, science, home economics, and industrial arts are far more pressing and necessary to their survival in school.

All in all the writing labs are a good thing. They provide many students with the discipline and security they need to improve their skills. We should have had them long ago; it is unfortunate that it took the competency examination to get them started.

# Certificate Examinations in New Zealand

BERNARD GADD
*(New Zealand)*

The most important way of assessing New Zealand secondary students to most New Zealanders is that done by the School Certificate Examination which is sat by Form 5 (Grade 10) students. This examination is the major determinant of whether a student can continue on into Form 6 (Grade 11), and in Form 6 the only nonexamination form of assessment is the Form 6 Certificate. This certificate itself is like a shadow thrown by the previous year's School Certificate results for each school, since the grades awarded must be related to the school's attainments in that earlier examination.

The School Certificate Examinations are administered by the education department and are therefore under political control. Raw marks from the School Certificate Examinations are ranked, then processed statistically, so that every examination subject is given a pass rate which the bureaucrats in charge believe reflects the academic ability of the students. Raw marks are scaled to bring them into accord with the selected medians.

These School Certificate Examinations are highly verbal, pen-and-paper examinations even when they examine second languages, such as Maori, in which the oral component is merely some 15 percent of the total mark. As a consequence, ethnic and social-economic maldistribution of passes can be predicted long before the students sit the papers. New Zealand has two main sets of normed group tests of language. The Progressive Achievement Tests (PAT) and Tests of Scholastic Ability (TOSCA) evaluate (deliberately) very similar kinds of reading and vocabulary competencies to those examined in School Certificate. The results are predictable: ethnic minorities, who are also mainly working class, and Pakeha (European/Caucasian) working-class schools get the lowest pass rates, and schools with students from the most affluent and privileged communities get 80 percent and better pass rates in both the tests and the public examinations.

The upshot is that in predominantly Maori and working-class areas, 90 to nearly 100 percent of school leavers have no formal qualifications. This has most serious implications during this era of high youth unemployment. At the other end of the social continuum, the socially and economically privileged managed to pass their more favourable opportunities for employment and further education on to almost all their children.

What can a teacher do when faced by a class he knows at the year's start will produce 90 to 100 percent failure in these public examinations? What can a teacher do especially since so many parents accept the state's propaganda that these are fair examinations, and wish their children to "have a go"? This is an attitude especially prevalent among the immigrant Polynesians who see these examinations as a kind of certificate of citizenship or of social acceptance.

I try to plan the curriculum so that the students cover matters that will help them as adult citizens, while also giving them a course that will enable them to try the School Certificate Examinations in English. I want to help them not to be duped by advertising or political propaganda. I want to stimulate their creativity, I want to give them some experience of facing employers and other decision-making middle-class people, e.g., in role play job interviews. I want to give them experience of making their own videos, newspapers and books to show them how control of these can be in their hands. I want to give them some idea of how social change can come about, so that they can try, if they wish, to promote social change. I want to build up their confidence in themselves and their respect for their own and others' cultural identity.

But we go further at our school. We have devised our own entirely internally evaluated certificate of language development. Every student may receive one of these. The certificate gives some sense of an achievable and worthwhile objective for the year. Similar, though less formalised evaluation systems operate in the junior classes.

Yet the most basic education objectives even in Form 5 English classes are to have the students attend regularly, to stay on for the year, and to go on to the next form. In the fluctuating success and failure in achieving these simple aims, we see the success or failure of our school to adapt to the changing needs of the students and of the community and of the stresses upon each. The stresses upon the community are very great, as they are upon working-class and ethnic minority communities everywhere, when a capitalistic society is failing to provide for the needs and expectations even of some of those who manage it.

There is unanimity among our Form 5 and 6 teachers of English that the public examination system and the normed tests are failing to serve minority students in any way at all. Indeed the psychometricians in them have given the privileged yet another set of instruments with which to maintain their dominance and to exact a price of cultural and linguistic assimilation upon others who wish to join them in their privilege and relative prosperity, in their social status, and in their breadth of life opportunities.

The context within which these tests and examinations operate is changing swiftly. New Zealand schools are in the exciting position where recently hundreds of Maori parents have served notice upon the education system that if it cannot adapt to offer genuine equality of education and of opportunity to their children, then they will withdraw their children and build up alternative education systems or expect the state to offer alternative education systems within the state system. The threat is serious. At the time of writing, we await the response of those who control the education system and the principals who control the individual schools. In short, the schools in the system have been assessed by the Maori parents—and been found to fail.

# References

The reader will appreciate the difficulty of providing a uniform reference list for a book which originated in five countries with different academic traditions. The references which follow were supplied by the authors. The material is not always complete, but in virtually every instance enough information has been supplied so that a reader can track down the original source if he or she would find it useful. Readers may also want to write directly to an author, whose current affiliation is found in the list of contributors in the front of this book. The **bold** headings that follow are the article titles.

## United States
Fader, D. (1966). *Hooked on books.* New York: Berkley Medallion.
Hillocks, G. (1972). *Alternatives in English: A critical appraisal.* Urbana, IL, United States: National Council of Teachers of English.

## Conscience and Teaching
Barnes, D. (1969). *Language, the learner and the school.* London: Penguin.
Britton, J. (1970). *Language and learning.* London: Penguin.
Creber, J. W. P. (1972). *Lost for words: Language and educational failure.* London: Penguin.
Holt, J. (1969). *How children fail.* London: Penguin.

## Helping Children Make Sense of Their World
Creber, J. W. P. (1972). *Lost for words: Language and educational failure.* London: Penguin.
Donaldson, M. (1978). *Children's minds.* Fontana.
Graves, D. (1982). *Writing: Teachers and children at work.* Portsmouth, New Hampshire, United States: Heinemann.
Harlen, W., Oliver, & Boyd. (1977). *Miss and mismatch.* London: Schools Council.
Martin, N. et al. (1976). *Writing and learning across the curriculum.* London: Ward Lock/Schools Council.
Oxford Pre-school Research Project. *Working with under-fives.* London: Grant McIntyre.
Rosen, C. & Rosen, H. (1973). *The language of primary school children.* London: Penguin.
Smith, F. (1979). *Reading without nonsense.* New York: Holt.
Smith, F. (1982). *Writing and the writer.* New York: Holt.

Tough, J. (1973). *Focus on meaning.* London: Unwin.
University of Waikato, Science Education Research Unit. (1984). *Making sense of our world: An interactive teaching approach.* New Zealand: Author.

## How Many Trees Does It Take to Educate an American?
Goodlad, J. & Scherer, M. (1984, January). A place called school. *Instructor, 92*(5), 56–58.
Naisbitt, J. (1982). *Megatrends.* New York: Warner.

## Megatrends in English Teaching
Naisbitt, J. (1982). *Megatrends.* New York: Warner.

## Restoring the Imagination in Secondary Education
Roberts, M. & Tamburrini, J. (1981). *Child development 0–5.* London.
Sartre, J. P. (1940). *The psychology of imagination.* (Philosophical Library of New York, Trans.). London.
Smith, F. (1982). *Writing and the writer.* New York: Holt.

## New Directions for the Eighties and Nineties
Postman, N. & Weingartner, C. (1969). *Teaching as a subversive activity.* New York: Delta.
Walshe, R. (1982). *"Children want to write . . ." Donald Graves in Australia.* Portsmouth, New Hampshire, United States: Heinemann.

## My English Teaching in the Eighties
Boyer, E. L. (1983). *High school: A report on secondary education in America.* New York: Harper and Row.
Holdaway, D. (1979). *The foundations of literacy.* Portsmouth, New Hampshire, United States: Heinemann.
Langer, J. A. (1982, April). Reading, thinking, writing . . . teaching. *Language Arts, 59*(4), 336–341.

## The Uses of Literature
Frye, N. (1985). Keynote address given at the Springboards '85 Language Arts Conference, Montreal, Quebec, Canada.
Huck, C. S. (1976). *Children's literature in the elementary school.* (3rd ed.). New York: Holt.
Jennings, F. G. (1965). *This is reading.* New York: Teachers College Press.
Lukens, R. J. (1976). *A critical handbook of children's literature.* Glenview, Illinois, United States: Scott.
Richler, M. (1977). *Jacob two-two meets the hooded fang.* New York: Bantam.

Sebasta, S. & Iverson, W. (1975). *Literature for Thursday's child.* Chicago: Science Research Associates.

Sendak, M. (1974). *Where the wild things are.* New York: Scholastic.

Sloan, G. D. (1975). *The child as critic: Teaching literature in elementary and middle schools.* New York: Teachers College Press.

## One Teacher's Approach in a New Zealand Primary School

Biddulph, L. J. (1983). *A group programme to train parents of children with reading difficulties to tutor their children at home* (Research Report). Christchurch, New Zealand: University of Canterbury.

Clay, M. M. (1979). *The early detection of reading difficulties: A diagnostic survey with recovery procedures.* Auckland, New Zealand: Heinemann.

Clay, M. M. (1979). *The patterning of complex behaviour.* Auckland, New Zealand: Heinemann.

Nicholson, T. (1982). *An anatomy of reading.* Sydney: Martin.

Nicholson, T. (1984). *The process of reading.* Sydney: Martin.

Wittrock, M. C. (1981). *Generative reading comprehension.* Unpublished manuscript, University of California, Los Angeles.

## Letting Fantasy Go Free

Bauer, C. F. (1983). *This way to books.* New York: Wilson.

Cullinan, B. E. (1977). Books in the life of the young child. In B. E. Cullinan & C. Carmichael (Eds.), *Literature and young children.* Urbana, Illinois, United States: National Council of Teachers of English.

Forsythe, S. S. (1981). *The effect of vocabulary-related cultural difference on inferential comprehension between British and American students.* Unpublished doctoral dissertation, University of Arkansas, United States.

Goodman, Y. & Burke, C. (1980) *Reading strategies: Focus on comprehension.* New York: Holt.

Lehr, F. (1982, November/December). Teacher effectiveness research and reading instruction. *Language Arts, 59,* 883–887.

Otto, J. (1982, October). The new debate in reading. *Reading Teacher, 36,* 14–18.

Pearson, D. P. & Johnson, D. D. (1978). *Teaching reading comprehension.* New York: Holt.

## Personalized Reading Programs

Barnes, C. P. (1979). *Questioning strategies to develop critical thinking skills.* Paper presented at the forty-sixth annual meeting of the Claremont Reading Conference, Claremont, California, United States.

Christenbury, L. & Kelly, P. P. (1983). *Questioning: A path to critical thinking.* Urbana, Illinois, United States: ERIC, Clearinghouse on Reading and Communication Skills.

Coles, R. E. (1981). *The reading strategies of selected junior high school students in the content areas.* Unpublished doctoral dissertation, University of Arizona, Tucson, Arizona, United States.

Coody, B. & Nelson, D. (1982). *Teaching elementary language arts: A literature approach.* Belmont, California, United States: Wadsworth.

Goodman, K. S. (1973). Miscues: Windows on the reading process. In K. S. Goodman (Ed.), *Miscue analysis: Applications to reading instruction.* Urbana, Illinois, United States: ERIC, Clearinghouse on Reading and Communication Skills, National Council of Teachers of English.

Goodman, K. S. (1975). Do you have to be smart to read? Do you have to read to be smart? *Reading Teacher.*

Goodman, K. S. & Goodman, Y. (1977). Learning about psycholinguistic processes by analyzing oral reading. *Harvard Educational Review, 40*(3).

Goodman, K. S. & Goodman, Y. (1981). *A whole-language, comprehension-centered reading program.* A position paper. Program in Language and Literacy, University of Arizona, Tucson, Arizona, United States.

Goodman, K. S., Goodman, Y., & Burke, C. C. (1978). Reading for life: The psycholinguistic base. In E. Hunter-Grundin & H. U. Grundin (Eds.), *Reading: Implementing the Bullock report.* London: Ward Lock.

Goodman, Y. (1978, June). Kid-watching: An alternative to testing. *National Elementary Principal, 57*(4).

Goodman, Y. & Burke, C. (1973). *The reading miscue inventory.* New York: Macmillan.

Goodman, Y. & Burke, C. (1980). *Reading strategies: Focus on comprehension.* New York: Holt.

Lee, D. (1983). Language experience. In B. A. Busching and J. I. Schwartz (Eds.), *Integrating the language arts in the elementary school.* Urbana, Illinois, United States: National Council of Teachers of English.

**Engaging Students in Reading**
Polhemus, R. (1981, Autumn). *The Stanford English Department Newsletter, 111*(1).

**Reading in the Secondary English Classroom**
Lawton, D. (1973). *Social change, educational theory and curriculum planning.* London: Hodder and Stoughton.

## English and Reading the New Media

Fiske, J. & Hartley, J. (1978). *Reading television.* London: Methuen.

Munro, A. (1982). *Language activities using newspapers, radio and television.* London: Longman Cheshire.

Noble, G. *Television and oracy: A psychological viewpoint.* A paper presented at the Australian Association for the Teaching of English.

## Introducing Poetry

Harding, D. W. (1962). Psychological processes in the reading of fiction. *The British Journal of Aesthetics, 2.*

Harding, D. W. (1972). The role of the onlooker. In *Language in Education.* London: Routledge and Kegan Paul.

## Making Evaulative Responses to Literature Through Imaginative Writing

Brown, L. J. (1982, October). Do we teach the way we read? *English in Australia, 62,* 33–36.

Brown, L. J., et al. (1983). *A single impulse: Developing responses to literature.* Education Department of South Australia.

Jackson, D. (1980, Winter). First encounters: The importance of initial responses to literature. *Children's Literature in Education, 11* (4), 149–160.

Jones, A. & Buttrey, J. (1940). *Children and stories.* London: Blackwell.

## Literature and Vision

Garfield, L. & Blishen, E. (1970). *The god beneath the sea.* London: Longmans.

Graves, R. (1955). *The Greek myths. Volumes 1 and 2.* Harmondsworth, England: Penguin.

## Writing as Discovery

Britton, J. (1972). *Writing to learn and learning to write.* Urbana, Illinois, United States: National Council of Teachers of English.

Emig, J. (1977, May). Writing as a mode of learning. *College Composition and Communication, 28,* 122–128.

Emig, J. (1983). The uses of the unconscious in composing. In D. Goswami & M. Butler (Eds.), *The web of meaning: Essays on writing, teaching, learning and thinking.* Upper Montclair, New Jersey, United States: Boynton/Cook.

Mandel, B. (1978, December). Losing one's mind: Learning to write and edit. *College Composition and Communication, 29,* 362–368.

Stoehr, T. (1967, March). Writing as thinking. *College English, 28,* 411–421.

### Teaching Written Composition as Process

Graves, D. (1982). *Writing: Teachers and children at work.* Portsmouth, New Hampshire, United States: Heinemann.

Murray, D. M. (1972, Fall). Teaching writing as a process not product. *The Leaflet.* New England Association of Teachers of English.

### The Skeleton in the Cupboard

Baldwin, M. (1976). Flattering the muse. In T. Blackburn (Ed.), *Presenting poetry.* London.

Graves, D. (1983). *Writing: Teachers and children at work.* London: Heinemann.

Kubie, L. S. (1957). *Neurotic distortion of the creative process.* Lawrence, Kansas, United States: University of Kansas Press.

Powell, B. (1968). *English through poetry writing.* London.

Smith, F. (1982). *Writing and the writer.* London: Heinemann.

Torrance, E. P. (1970). *Creative learning and teaching.* New York.

Wade, B. (1975). Haiku: The great leveller. *English in Education, 9*(2), 16–23.

Witkin, R. (1974). *The intelligence of feeling.* London.

### Successful Strategies in Teaching Composition

Graves, D. (1983). *Writing: Teachers and children at work.* London: Heinemann.

Richardson, E. S. (1972). In the early world. New Zealand: NZCER.

Richardson, E. S. (1984). *The wonder of child reality.* Henderson, New Zealand: Richardson.

### History Through a Child's Voice

Tchudi, S. & Tchudi, S. J. (1983). *Teaching writing in the content areas: Elementary school.* Washington, DC: National Education Association.

### Beyond Writing: Extending Revision Strategies

Graves, D. (1982). *Writing: Teachers and children at work.* Portsmouth, New Hampshire, United States: Heinemann.

### Writing: From Motivation to Correction

Crump, B. *A good keen man.*

Grace, P. (1975). *Waiariki.* Longman Paul.

Grace, P. (1978). *Mutuwhenua.* Longman Paul.

Grace, P. (1980). *The dream sleepers.* Longman Paul.

Gee, M. (1978). *Plumb.* Wellington, New Zealand: Open University Press.

Gee, M. (1979). *Games of choice.* London: Faber.

Gee, M. (1979). *Meg.* London: Faber.

Gee, M. (1979). *My father's den.* London: Faber.

Gee, M. (1979). *Under the mountain.* New Zealand: Ashton Scholastic.

Swarthout. *Bless the beasts and children.*

Tuwhare, H. (1964). *No ordinary sun.* Auckland, New Zealand: Blackwood and Paul.

Tuwhare, H. (1970). *Come rain hail.* New Zealand: Caveman Press.

## Personal Involvement in Writing

White, R. W. (1952). *Lives in progress: A study of the natural growth of personality.* New York: Holt.

## Classroom Drama—Another Approach

Heathcote, D. (1980). In B. J. Wagner (Ed.), *Drama as a learning medium.* London: Hutchinson.

## Teaching Oral English and Drama

Barnes, D. (1973). *Language in the classroom.* Milton Keynes, England: Open University Press.

Barnes, D. (1975). *From communication to curriculum.* Harmondsworth, England: Penguin.

Dumont, R. V. (1972). Learning English and how to be silent: Studies in Sioux and Cherokee classrooms. In C. Cazden, V. Johns, & D. Hymes (Eds.), *Functions of language in the classroom.* New York: Columbia University Press.

Gibson, R. E. (1975). The strip story: A catalyst for communication. *TESOL Quarterly, 9*(2).

Gumperz, J. J. (1977). The conversational analysis of interethnic communication. In E. L. Ross (Ed.), *Interethnic Communication, Proceedings of the Southern Anthropological Society.* Athens, Georgia, United States: University of Georgia Press.

Labov, W. (1972). The logic of non-standard English. In P. Giglioli (Ed.), *Language and social change* (pp. 179–215). Harmondsworth, England: Penguin.

Labov, W. (1974). *Language in the inner city* (pp. 354–395). Philadelphia: University of Pennsylvania Press.

Nation, I. (1976). *Language teaching techniques* (2nd ed.). Wellington, New Zealand: English Language Institute, Victoria University.

Philips, S. U. (1972). Participant structures and communicative competence: Warm Springs children in community and classroom. In C. Cazden, V. Johns, & D. Hymes (Eds.), *Functions of language in the classroom* (pp. 370–394). New York: Columbia University Press.

Pride, J. (1978). *Communication needs in the use and learning of English.* Paper presented at the Hawaii Linguistic Conference. Wellington, New Zealand: Victoria University.

Stubbs, M. (1976). *Language, schools and classrooms* (pp. 113–114). London: Methuen.

**Writing in Role**
Britton, J. (1970). *Language and learning.* London: Penguin.

**Language and Learning**
Anonymous. (1972, January). School made him square and brown inside (a poem written by a UK pupil who later committed suicide). *National Education.*
Department of Education. (1972). *Forms 6–7 language prescriptions.* New Zealand: Author.
Department of Education. (1983). *Statement of aims, English: Forms 3–5.* New Zealand: Author.
Holmes, J. (1982). *Language for learning.* Wellington, New Zealand: Department of Education.

**Good Language**
Smith, E. B., Goodman, K., & Meredith, R. (1976). *Language and thinking in school* (2nd ed.). New York: Holt.

**Teaching the Language of Media**
Masterman, L. (1980). *Teaching about television.* London: Macmillan.
Pingree, S. & Hawkins, R. (1980). *Media and society.* Australian Film and Television School.

**From the Barricades**
Spender, Dale. (1982). *Invisible women: The schooling scandal.* New York: Writers and Readers.
Taylor, L. (1980). *Reading rights for girls.* New Zealand: Department of Education.
Women's Research and Resources Centre. (1981). *Gender and schooling: A study of sexual divisions in the classroom.* London: Author.

**International Perspectives on Language Learning**
Allport, G. W. (1979). *The nature of prejudice.* Reading, Massachusetts: Addison-Wesley.
Creber, J. W. P. (1965). *Sense and sensitivity.* London: University of London Press.
Illich, I. (1970). *Deschooling society.* New York: Harper.
Judy, S. (1980). *The ABC's of literacy: A guide for parents and educators.* New York: Oxford University Press.
Postman, N. & Weingartner, C. (1969). *Teaching as a subversive activity.* New York: Delta.

**English and Multicultural Education in New Zealand**
McCombs Report. (1976). *Towards partnership: Report of the committee on secondary education.* Wellington, New Zealand.

McKay, H. & Smart, P. R. (1972). *Use your imagination: An introduction through mythology to literature, creative writing and general studies* (pp. 132–159). London: Longman Paul.

Parker, P. & Gadd, B. (1980). *The philosophy of multicultural education and its implications for schools and school systems.* Paper presented at the International Conference of English Teachers, Sydney, Australia.

Parkinson, R. *ESL peer tutoring.* Auckland, New Zealand: Department of Education.

Rogers, M. (1971). Developing a language unit. In J. McNeal & M. Rogers (Eds.), *Multiracial school.* Harmondsworth, England: Penguin.

Scott, R. (1971). *A wedding man is better than cats, miss.* Newton Abbot, England: David and Charles.

### Sound and System

Bullock Report. (1974). *Children from families of overseas origin.*

Bullock Report. (1974). *Written language.*

### A Context for Teaching

Adams, J. (1976). *Conceptual blockbusting: A guide to better ideas.* San Francisco: San Francisco Book.

McKim, R. (1972). *Experience in visual thinking.* Monterey, California: Brooks/Cole.

### Individualizing Approaches to Poetry

Dias, P. (1979, Spring). *McGill Journal of Education.*

### Cronus, the Timekeeper

Perkins, D. N. (1984, September). Creativity by design. *Educational Leadership.*

### An Australian Curriculum Planning Model

Forrestal, P. & Reid, J. (1984). Stories with an ironic twist. In *Space to dream.* Australia: Thomas Nelson.

### Real World Curriculum Development

Creber, J. W. P. (1965). *Sense and sensitivity.* London: University of London Press.

Judy, S. (1980). *The ABC's of literacy: A guide for parents and educators.* New York: Oxford University Press.

Moffett, J. (1973). *A student-centered language arts curriculum, grades K–13: A handbook for teachers.* Boston: Houghton Mifflin.

Unruh, G. G. (1983). Curriculum politics. In F. W. English (Ed.), *Fundamental curriculum decisions* (ASCD 1983 Yearbook). Alexandria, Virginia: Association for Supervision and Curriculum Development.

**An Australian Senior Secondary Programme**

Elbow, P. (1975). *Writing without teachers.* New York: Oxford University Press.

Fader, D. (1966). *Hooked on books.* New York: Berkley Medallion.

Graves, D. (1981). *Children want to write.* Australia: Primary English Teaching Association of Australia.

Graves, D. (1982). *Writing: Teachers and children at work.* Portsmouth, New Hampshire, United States: Heinemann.

Moffett, J. (1981). *Active voice: A writing program across the curriculum.* Upper Montclair, New Jersey, United States: Boynton/Cook.

Moffett, J. (1981). *Coming on center: English education in evolution.* Upper Montclair, New Jersey, United States: Boynton/Cook.

Murray, D. M. (1982). *Learning by teaching: Selected articles on writing and teaching.* Upper Montclair, New Jersey, United States: Boynton/Cook.

**The Other Side of the Coin**

Barnes, D. & Sherrilt, D. (1982). Transmission and interpretation. In B. Wade (Ed.), *Language perspectives.* London.

Doughty, P. (1974). *Language, English and the curriculum.* London: Methuen.

Dunsbee, T. & Ford, T. (1980). *Mark my words.* London.

Jones, T. P. (1972). *Creative learning in perspective.* London.

Spaulding, R. (1963). *Achievement, creativity, and self-concept correlates of teacher-pupil transactions in the elementary school classrooms.* Urbana, Illinois, United States.

Torrance, E. P. (1965). *Rewarding creative behavior.* Englewood Cliffs, New Jersey, United States: Prentice-Hall.

**Evaluation and Assessment in Queensland**

*A review of school based assessment (ROSBA) in Queensland secondary schools.* (1978). Australia.

Carr, J. & Murphy, W. Specifying objectives and evaluation criteria in English years 8 to 10. In *Language with a purpose.* Australia.

**The Evaluation of Fifth-Grade Writers**

Atwell, N. (1982). Paper presented at the Martha's Vineyard Summer Institute on Writing, Martha's Vineyard, Massachusetts, United States.

**Evaluating a Whole-Language Secondary-English Curriculum: A First-Year Study**

Smith, F. (1983). *Essays into literacy.* London: Heinemann.

Squire, J. & Applebee, R. (1968). *High school English instruction today: The national study of high school English programs.* New York: Appleton-Century-Crofts.

Tchudi, S. (1984, May). Classroom/departmental observations. In English Curriculum Evaluation Committee, *Report of evaluation of English curriculum, grades 7–12.* Hampton, Virginia, United States: Hampton City Schools.

Tinder, M. B. (1984, September 18). Hampton's English curriculum showed good results in this family. *Daily Press,* p. 5.

Wolfson, B. J. (1985). Psychological theory and curricular thinking. In Association for Supervision and Curriculum Development, *Current thought on curriculum.* Alexandria, Virginia, United States: Association for Supervision and Curriculum Development.